SCOTTISH HISTORICAL DOCUMENTS

SCOTTISH HISTORICAL DOCUMENTS

GORDON DONALDSON
(1913-1993)

Former Professor of Scottish History and Palaeography
University of Edinburgh (1963–1979)

Neil Wilson Publishing • Glasgow • Scotland

First published by Scottish Academic Press Ltd, 1970
Reprinted with corrections, 1974

This edition published by Neil Wilson Publishing Ltd
303a The Pentagon Centre
36 Washington Street
GLASGOW
G3 8AZ
Tel: 0141-221-1117
Fax: 0141-221-5363
E-mail: nwp@cqm.co.uk
http://www.nwp.co.uk/

A catalogue record for this book is available from the British Library.

Front jacket illustration is a page from a Household Book of James V, dated 1534. It shows expenditure of the King's Household in Latin. Although the writing is ornate throughout, this folio is unusually elaborately decorated, including a drawing of a woman playing the bagpipes. (Scottish Records Office ref: E31/6f.97r)

ISBN 1-897784-41-4

Printed by WSOY, Finland

CONTENTS

PREFACE

The purpose of this volume is to make conveniently accessible those texts which are most important for the teaching and the study of Scottish History. One consideration determining the selection is that a document should be such that its phraseology, and not merely its substance, is significant, so that something would be lost by a mere abridgment. The other guiding consideration has been that the documents should be contemporary with the events to which they relate. There is, however, a period of some centuries for which hardly any contemporary written evidence exists, and the volume therefore begins with a number of extracts from a variety of sources, some of which were written much later than the events they narrate and nearly all of which were written outside Scotland. From the twelfth century, when contemporary documents become available, such documents alone appear in the volume. Documents not in Scots or English have been translated. A simple chronological order has been followed, partly for convenience of reference and partly because it demonstrates how political, ecclesiastical and social developments were taking place concurrently.

The volume concludes in 1707. For the period since that date, the bulk of relevant material is vast and individual documents of significance tend to become ever longer, with the result that a selection for the period since 1707 could not be contained in one volume with the material essential for the period during which Scotland was an independent kingdom.

I have to acknowledge with gratitude the consent of Mrs M.O. Anderson to my making use of passages from her late husband's *Scottish Annals from English Chroniclers* and his *Early Sources of Scottish History*, and the permission which Messrs. Thomas Nelson and Sons gave for the inclusion of extracts from Professor Dickinson's edition of Knox's *History of the Reformation*. I am grateful, too, to my colleagues in the Scottish History Department in the University of Edinburgh, all of whom have contributed to the preparation of the volume, and to others with whom I have discussed the work and from whom I have received valuable suggestions.

G.D.

ABBREVIATIONS

A.P.S.	*Acts of the Parliaments of Scotland*
B.U.K.	*Acts and Proceedings of the General Assemblies* (Bannatyne and Maitland Clubs)
E.S.	*Early Sources of Scottish History,* ed. A.O. Anderson.
E.S.C.	*Early Scottish Charters,* ed. Sir Archibald Lawrie.
Nat. MSS. Scot.	*The National Manuscripts of Scotland*
P.R.O.	Public Record Office, London.
Reg. Ho.	General Register House, Edinburgh.
R.P.C.	*Register of the Privy Council of Scotland*
S.A.	*Scottish Annals from English Chroniclers,* ed. A.O. Anderson
S.H.R.	*Scottish Historical Review.*

The sign x between dates indicates 'not earlier than . . . and not later than . . . ': e.g., 1128x1136 means 'not earlier than 1128 and not later than 1136'.

EXTRACTS FROM
BEDE'S *ECCLESIASTICAL HISTORY*

Bede, although he wrote early in the eighth century, had the qualities of an historian, and he is so obviously careful and critical that his account of events long before his own day is regarded as valuable.

(i) Ninian and Columba, c. 400 and c. 565

In the year of our Lord 565, when Justin the younger [*i.e.,* Justin II], the successor of Justinian, received the government of the Roman empire,[1] there came from Ireland into Britain a famous priest and abbot, a monk by habit and life, whose name was Columba, to preach the word of God to the provinces of the northern Picts, that is, those who are separated from their southern districts by ranges of steep and rugged mountains. The southern Picts, who have their seats to this side of the same mountains, had, as they relate, a long time before forsaken the error of idolatry and received the faith of truth, when the word was preached to them by Ninias, a most reverend bishop and very holy man of the race of the Britons, who had been regularly instructed at Rome in the faith and the mysteries of the truth. And even now [*i.e.,* c. 730], the English nation holds the seat of his bishopric, notable for the name and church of the bishop St. Martin; and there also he rests in the body, along with very many saints. And this place, pertaining to the province of the Bernicians, is commonly called *Ad Candidam Casam,* because he made there a church of stone, after a custom strange to the Britons.

Columba came into Britain in the ninth year of the reign of Bridius, son of Meilochon,[2] a very powerful king of the Picts, and he converted that nation to the faith of Christ by his preaching and example, whereupon he also received of them the foresaid island [*i.e.,* Iona] for a monastery.... His successors hold it to this day.... Before he came to Britain,

---

1 Justin II became emperor in 565, but the date usually given for Columba's arrival in Iona is 563.
2 Brude, son of Maelchu (d. 584).

he had founded a noble monastery in Ireland. . . . From those two monasteries many others, both in Britain and in Ireland, were multiplied by his disciples; and the island monastery where his body lies has the headship over them all. That island is always wont to have as its ruler a presbyter-abbot, to whose rule must be subject the whole province, and, by an unusual arrangement, even the very bishops, according to the example of its first teacher, who was not a bishop, but a presbyter and monk. . . .

III, iv.

(ii) The Synod of Whitby, c. 664

Meantime, on the death of Bishop Aidan,[3] Finan, who had been ordained and sent by the Scots, received the bishopric in his place. . . . In those days a violent and persistent controversy arose over the observance of Easter; those who had come from Kent or from Gaul maintained that the Scots celebrated Easter Sunday contrary to the custom of the universal church. . . . Queen Eanfled[4] and her followers kept the custom which she had seen practised in Kent. . . . Thus it is said sometimes to have happened in those days that Easter was celebrated twice in one year; and when the king had finished his Lenten fast and kept Easter, then the queen and her followers were still fasting and keeping Palm Sunday.[5] This disagreement over the observance of Easter was patiently borne by all as long as Aidan lived. . . . But after the death of Finan, who came after Aidan, when Colman, who likewise was sent from Scotland, succeeded to the bishopric, the controversy became greater, over the observance of Easter and also over other matters of ecclesiastical discipline (*de aliis ecclesiasticae vitae disciplinis*). . . . This came to the ears of the kings, namely Oswiu and his son Alchfrid[6] . . . Alchfrid, who had as a master in Christian instruction the most learned Wilfrid (who had formerly gone to Rome to learn church doctrine and had spent a long time at Lyons with Dalfin, archbishop of Gaul, from whom he received the ecclesiastical tonsure) knew that this doctrine was rightly to be preferred to all the traditions of the Scots. . . . Thus the controversy being there raised about

3 Bishop of the Angles, at Lindisfarne (d. 651).
4 Wife of Oswiu, king of Bernicia, 641-70, and of Northumbria, 654-70.
5 This would occur in 663.
6 Sub-king in Deira, c. 654-64.

2

Easter or the tonsure or other ecclesiastical matters, it was agreed that a synod be held in the monastery called Streaneshalch [*i.e.,* Whitby].

[*Colman spoke on the Celtic side, Wilfrid on the Roman, the latter winding up his argument by appealing to the unique position claimed for St. Peter, 'to whom our Lord said, "Thou art Peter, and upon this rock I will build my church, and the gates of hell shall not prevail against it, and to thee I will give the keys of the kingdom of heaven" '.*]

When Wilfrid had spoken thus, the king said, 'Is it true, Colman, that these words were spoken to Peter by our Lord?' He answered, 'It is true, O King.' Then says he, 'Can you show any such power given to your Columba?' Colman answered, 'None.' Then the king replied, 'Do you both agree fully that these words were principally spoken to Peter, and that the keys of heaven were given to him by our Lord?' They both answered, 'We do.' Then the king concluded, 'And I also say unto you, that he is the door-keeper, whom I will not contradict, but will, as far as I know and am able, in all things obey his decrees, lest, when I come to the gates of heaven, there should be none to unlock them, he being my adversary who is proved to have the keys.' The king having said this, all,who were present, both great and small, gave their assent, and, renouncing the less perfect order, resolved to conform to that which they found to be better.

III, xxv.

(iii) The defeat of the Angles at Nechtansmere, 685

For in the next year the same king [Egfrid], who had rashly led an army to ravage the province of the Picts, — although his friends greatly opposed it, and especially Cuthbert of blessed memory who had been recently ordained bishop — was led on by the enemy's feigning flight into the defiles of inaccessible mountains, and was killed along with the chief part of the troops which he had brought with him[7] . . .

And from this time the hope and valour of the kingdom of the Angles began to 'ebb, recede and sink.'[8] For both the Picts and the Scots who were in Britain recovered the land of their possession which the Angles held; of the Britons also

---

7 At Nechtansmere near Forfar.   8 Vergil, *Aeneid,* ii, 169.

3

considerable part recovered their liberty; and they have it even yet, after about forty-six years.

And there among very many of the English race who were slain by the sword, or given up to slavery, or who escaped by flight from the land of the Picts, the most reverend man of the Lord, Trumwin also, who had received the bishopric over them,[9] retreated with his followers who were in the monastery of Abercorn — placed, it is true, in the district of the Angles, but in the neighbourhood of the firth which separates the lands of Angles and of Picts. . . .

And Aldfrid succeeded Egfrid in the kingdom. . . . And he nobly restored, though within narrower bounds, the ruined state of the kingdom.

IV, xxvi (*S.A.*, 42-4).

(iv) Submission of the Pictish kingdom to Rome, ? 710

Nechtan, king of the Picts who inhabit the northern parts of Britain, warned by frequent study of the ecclesiastic writings, renounced the error by which he and his nation had been held hitherto in the observance of Easter, and persuaded himself and all his subjects to celebrate the catholic time of the Lord's resurrection.

And to accomplish this the more easily and with the greater authority he sought aid of the nation of the Angles, whom he knew to have long ago established their religion after the example of the holy Roman and apostolic church. For he sent messengers to the venerable man Ceolfrid, abbot of the monastery of the blessed apostles Peter and Paul, at the mouth of the river Wear and near the river Tyne in the place which is called Jarrow, . . . requesting him to send him exhortatory letters, with which the more effectively he might be able to confute those who presumed to observe Easter not at its time; as also concerning the manner or fashion of the tonsure with which it was fitting that clerics should be marked out. . . .

And he also asked that architects should be sent to him, to make a church of stone among his people after the manner of the Romans, promising to dedicate it in honour of the blessed prince of the apostles, and also that he himself and all his

9 In 681 Trumwin had been consecrated bishop for 'the Pictish province which at that time was subject to the empire of the Angles' (Bede, IV, xii).

subjects would always imitate the custom of the holy Roman and apostolic church; in so far at least as they had been able to learn it, being so far separated from the speech and race of the Romans.

And favouring his pious vows and prayers the most reverend abbot Ceolfrid sent the architects for whom he was asked, and sent to him also a letter. . . .

When this letter had been read in presence of king Nechtan and of many very learned men, and had been diligently interpreted into his own tongue by those who were able to understand it, he is said to have rejoiced greatly in its exhortation; insomuch that he rose up from the midst of the assembly of his nobles, and bowed his knees to the ground, giving thanks to God that he should be worthy to receive such a gift from the land of the Angles. . . .

'And I profess openly,' [he said] 'and protest to you present who sit here that I will ever observe, with my whole nation, this time of Easter; and decree that all clerics who are in my realm must receive this tonsure, which we have heard to be wholly reasonable.' And without delay he fulfilled by his royal authority what he had said. For immediately by public command the nineteen-year cycles of Easter were sent throughout all the provinces of the Picts to be transcribed, learned and observed; the faulty cycles of eighty-four years being everywhere suppressed. All servants of the altar and monks were tonsured in the manner of the crown; and the nation corrected rejoiced that it had been devoted as it were to a new discipleship of Peter, the most blessed prince of the apostles, and placed under the protection of his patronage.

V, xxi (*S.A.*, 47).

EXTRACTS FROM
ADAMNAN'S *LIFE OF COLUMBA*·

Adamnan[1] was one of Columba's successors as abbot of Iona, but, though writing only about a century after

---
1 Such is the conventional spelling, but the more correct version is Adomnán.

5

Columba's death, was concerned with miracles to demonstrate his hero's sanctity rather than with intrinsically significant facts. Yet from his rather naive narrative much can be inferred about the character of Columba and the way of life of his community, as well as about the nature of the Celtic church and the economy within which it operated.

(i) Bishop and Priest

A certain disciple . . . came to the Saint, and in humility he disguised himself as much as he could, so that no one might know that he was a bishop; but yet this could not be hidden from the Saint. For the next Lord's Day, being bidden by the Saint to consecrate the Body of Christ according to custom, he calls the Saint so that, as two priests, they might break the Lord's Bread together. The Saint thereupon, going up to the altar, suddenly looking on his face thus addresses him: 'Christ bless thee, Brother, break this bread alone with the episcopal rite, now we know that thou art a bishop. Why hast thou hitherto tried to disguise thyself that the veneration due to thee by us might not be rendered?'

I, xliv.

(ii) Sowing and Reaping

Twice three bushels of barley . . . being sent to the peasant, Findchan by name, according to the Saint's command, and set down before him, . . . he thankfully accepted them, saying: 'How can a crop mature if sown after midsummer, contrary to the nature of this land?' His wife, on the other hand, says: 'Do according to the Saint's command. . . .' The messengers also at the same time added this, saying, 'Saint Columba, who sent us to thee with this gift, gave also by us this command about thy crop, saying: "Let that man trust in the omnipotence of God; his crop, although sown fifteen days after the beginning of the month of June, shall be reaped in the beginning of the month of August." ' The peasant obeys, ploughing and sowing; and the crop, which he sowed against hope at the time above mentioned, he gathered in, ripe, in the beginning of the month of August, . . . to the wonder of all his neighbours.

II, iii.

(iii) Columba at the court of the Pictish king

At another time, that is, on the Saint's first laborious journey
to king Brude, it happened that the king, swollen by royal
pride, acted arrogantly, and did not open his castle gates upon
the blessed man's first arrival. As soon as the man of God
saw this he went with his comrades to the openings of the
gates, and, first imprinting on them the sign of the Lord's
cross, then laid his hand upon them, knocking against the
gates; and immediately, of their own accord, the bolts were
forcibly withdrawn, and the gates opened with all speed. And
immediately after they were opened, the Saint entered with
his companions. Learning this, the king and his council were
much afraid; and he left the house, and went to meet the
blessed man with reverence, and addressed him mildly with
peaceful words; and thenceforth from that day all the days
of his life the same ruler honoured the holy and venerable
man befittingly with very high esteem.

II, xxxv.

EXTRACT FROM
THE *SENCHUS FER NALBAN*

The Senchus Fer nAlban[1] *('History of the Men of Scotland')*
derives in its present form from the tenth century, but
internal evidence postulates a seventh-century original. The
genealogies of the ruling families of the three chief peoples
of Dalriada from c. 500 to c. 650 are recorded, together
with the number of houses belonging to each of
these peoples and the strength of their armed forces, military
and naval.

This is the Cenél nGabráin,[2] five hundred and sixty
houses, Kintyre and Crích Chomgaill[3] with its islands,
two seven-benchers every twenty houses in a sea expedition.

1 Ed. J. Bannerman, *Celtica*, vii, 142-62.
2 The kindred of Gabrán.
3 Present day Cowal.

Cenél nOengusa[4] has four hundred and thirty houses,
two seven-benchers every twenty houses in a sea expedition.
Cenél Loairnd[5] has four hundred and twenty houses,
two seven-benchers every twenty houses in a sea expedition.
It is thus throughout the three thirds of Dál Riata.

4 Probably in Islay.   5 In Lorne.

EXTRACTS FROM IRISH AND SCOTTISH ANNALS

The Annals of Ulster,[1] *from which all the extracts except
the second last are taken, are more or less contemporary
from the middle of the seventh century and many entries
relate to the Scots of Dalriada. Most, if not all, of the early
Scottish entries seem to derive from a chronicle compiled in
Iona before about 740.*

The Scottish Chronicle,[2] *from which the second last
extract comes, begins with the reign of Kenneth, son of
Alpin (d. 858) and concludes in the reign of Kenneth, son of
Malcolm (971-995). It may have been compiled in the latter
reign, in part at least from earlier written sources.*

*These entries illustrate the extremely meagre nature of the
evidence and the extent to which historians must rely on
inference. For example, the entry for 768 suggests that, if a
Dalriadic king was fighting in Pictland, the kingdom of the
Scots cannot have suffered the long subjection to the Picts
which other sources suggest. Again, the last five entries, taken
together, suggest that, when Iona became untenable owing
to Norse attacks, the relics of St. Columba were taken partly
to Ireland and partly to a church in Scotland which may be
identified with Dunkeld, so that both Kells and Dunkeld
were in a sense successors of Iona, and Dunkeld became the
ecclesiastical capital of the Scoto-Pictish kingdom.*

1 Ed. W.M. Hennessy, 1887. All quoted entries were checked by Dr.
Bannerman with photostat copies of MS A.
2 In Bib. Nat. (Paris) Latin 4126, 28v, a-29v, a; facsimile, W.F. Skene,
Chronicles of the Picts and Scots, 2x3. For the title, see M.O. Anderson,
'Scottish Materials in a Paris Manuscript', *S.H.R.*, xxviii, 38.

Some of the places mentioned under 719 and 736 are not identifiable.

719. The sea battle of Ard Esbi, between Dunchad Bec, with the Cenél nGabráin, and Selbach, with the Cenél Loairn; and Selbach was defeated. . . and certain *comites* fell in it.

736. Angus, son of Fergus, king of the Picts, wasted the regions of Dál Riata, and seized Dún At,[3] and burned Creic, and bound two sons of Selbach in chains, namely, Donngal and Feradach; and soon after Brude, son of Angus, son of Fergus, died. The battle of Cnoc Coirpri in Calathros[4] at Etarlinddu between the Dál Riata and the men of Fortriu[5] and Talorgan, son of Fergus, pursued the son[6] of Ainfcellach who fled with his army; in which encounter many nobles perished.

768. A battle in Fortriu, between Aed[7] and Kenneth.[8]

806. The community of Iona was slain by the gentiles, that is, (to the number of) sixty-eight.

807. The building of the new monastery of Colum Cille in Kells.

849. Indrechtach, abbot of Iona, came to Ireland with the relics of Colum Cille.

c. 849. Kenneth, son of Alpin, first of the Scots, ruled this Pictland prosperously. . . . . In the seventh year of his reign he transported the relics of Saint Columba to a church that he had built, and he invaded *Saxonia* six times; and he seized and burned Dunbar and Melrose.

865. Tuathal, son of Artgus, chief bishop of Fortriu and abbot of Dunkeld, died.

3 Dunadd.
4 Probably in Islay.
5 Picts.
6 Muredach of the Cenél Loairn and king of Dalriada.
7 Aed Find of the Cenél nGabráin and king of Dalriada (d. 778).
8 Kenneth, son of Feradach, king of the Picts (d. 775).

EXTRACTS FROM THE NORSE SAGAS

The Sagas of the Norse Kings were composed, in their existing form, only in the thirteenth century, by Snorre Sturlason, and the Orkneyinga Saga is very slightly earlier than Snorre's work. They certainly incorporate much older material, but it is uncertain how far Snorre's account of the earlier kings is historically sound, and even for periods nearer the points at which they were written the sagas contain information hard to reconcile with what we know from other sources.

(i) The Conquests of Harald the Fairhaired, c. 874-90

Many powerful men of Norway fled as outlaws before King Harold, and sailed into western piracy; they were in the Orkneys and the Hebrides in the winters, and in the summers they plundered in Norway, and did there great injury to the land. . . . Then he took out a levy every summer, and searched the islands and distant rocks; but as soon as the vikings were aware of his army, they all fled, and most of them out to sea. And when the king wearied of this, it happened one summer that King Harold sailed with his army to west beyond the sea. He came first to Shetland, and slew there all the vikings who did not flee thence. Then he sailed south to the Orkneys, and everywhere there cleaned out the vikings. After that, he sailed as far as the Hebrides, and plundered there; he slew there many vikings. . . . Then he plundered in Scotland, and fought a battle there. And when he came west to Man, they had learned already what warfare King Harold had been making before . . . ; so all the people had fled into Scotland. . . . King Harold when he sailed from the west gave to earl Ronald[1] the Orkneys and Shetland. But Ronald gave both lands immediately to his brother, Sigurd.[2]

Heimskringla, Harald Fairhair's Saga, in *E.S.* i, 324, 332-4.

1 Rognvald, earl of Möre in Norway, who is usually said to have been the father of Rolf the Ganger, first duke of Normandy and ancestor of William the Conqueror.

2 It seems possible that Harald set up the Orkney earldom in the course of an early expedition, c. 874, but his more extensive operations, as far as Man, must have been later in the century.

(ii) The Conversion of Orkney to Christianity, c. 995-1000

Then Olaf [Tryggvi's son, King of Norway][3] sailed from the west with five ships, [coming] first to the Hebrides. . . . Then he sailed to the Orkneys.

Earl Sigurd, Hlodve's son, lay then in [South] Ronaldshay, in Asmundarvagr,[4] with one long-ship, and he was intending to sail over to Caithness. Then Olaf sailed to the islands with his army from the west and put into harbour there, because the Pentland Firth was not passable. And when the king knew that the earl lay there already, he had the earl called to speak with him.

But when the earl came to speak with the king, they had spoken but little before the king said that the earl must have himself baptized, and all the people of his land, or as alternative he should die on the spot, immediately; and the king said that he would go with fire and burning through the islands, and devastate the land, unless the people were baptized. And since the earl was thus pressed he chose to take baptism; so he was baptized, and all the people who were there with the earl.

Heimskringla, Olaf Tryggvisson's Saga, in E.S., i, 509.

(iii) Earl Thorfinn of Orkney

When Earl Thorfinn heard of the death of King Magnus,[5] he sent men to Norway to King Harald[6] with a friendly message, saying that he wished to become his friend. When the messengers reached the king he received them well and promised the earl his friendship. When the earl received this message from the king he made himself ready, taking from the west two ships of twenty benches, with more than a hundred men, all fine troops, and went east to Norway. . . .

From thence the earl went southwards along the coast to Denmark. He went through the country, and found King Svein in Aalborg; he invited him to stay, and made a splendid feast for him. Then the earl made it known that he was going to Rome; but when he came to Germany he called on the Emperor Henry, who received him exceedingly well and gave

3 King 995-1000.
4 Osmundswall, which is actually in South Walls, on the west side of Scapa Flow, and not in South Ronaldsay, on the east side.
5 Magnus the Good, king of Norway, 1035-47.
6 Harald Sigurdson or 'Hardrada', king of Norway, 1047-66.

11

him many valuable presents. He also gave him many horses, and the earl rode south to Rome, and saw the pope, from whom he obtained absolution for all his sins. . . .

Earl Thorfinn retained all his dominions to his dying day, and it is truly said that he was the most powerful of all the earls of the Orkneys. He obtained possession of eleven[7] earldoms in Scotland, all the Sudreys and a large territory in Ireland. . . . Earl Thorfinn was five winters old when Malcolm, the king of Scots,[8] his mother's father, gave him the title of earl, and after that he was earl for seventy winters.[9] He died towards the end of Harald Sigurdson's reign. He is buried at Christ's Kirk in Birsay, which he had built.

Orkneyinga Saga, ed. Joseph Anderson, pp. 42-4.

(iv) The expedition of Magnus Barelegs, 1098

He took possession of Anglesey, the most southerly place where former kings of Norway had owned dominion. . . . King Magnus turned back with his army [and] proceeded first to Scotland. Then men went between him and Malcolm,[10] king of the Scots; and [the kings] made peace between them, to the effect that king Magnus should possess all the islands that lie to the west of Scotland, all between which and the mainland he could go, in a ship with the rudder in place. But when king Magnus came north to Kintyre, he caused [his men] to draw a skiff across the isthmus[11] of Kintyre, and to set the rudder in place: the king himself sat in the afterdeck, and held the helm. And thus he took possession of the land that then lay to the larboard.[12] Kintyre is a great land, and better than the best island in the Hebrides, excepting Man. A narrow isthmus is between it and the mainland of Scotland; there long-ships are often drawn across.

Heimskringla, Magnus Barelegs' Saga, in *E.S.*, ii, 112-13.

7 The correct reading is 'nine'.
8 Malcolm II, 1005-34.
9 Thorfinn's tenure of the earldom cannot have exceeded fifty years, from his father's death in 1014 to his own in 1064 or 1065.
10 The king at the time was Edgar.
11 Between East Loch Tarbert and West Loch Tarbert. (Tarbert = *isthmus*)
12 i.e. to the south of Tarbert, showing that Magnus crossed from east to west. While Kintyre had been an area of Norse settlement earlier, there is no evidence that it formed part of the Norse dominions after this date, and the tale that it was at this point annexed by Norway is not acceptable.

12

EXTRACTS FROM
THE ANGLO-SAXON CHRONICLE

*These brief annalistic entries were made contemporaneously,
or almost so, and can be taken as reliable.*

1072. In this year king William led a ship-force and a land-
army to Scotland, and lay about that land with ships on the
sea side; and he himself with his land-army went in over the
Forth. And he found there naught of which he was the better.

And king Malcolm came and made peace with king William,
and gave hostages, and was his man;[1] and then [William]
went home with all his army.

S.A., 95.

1093-94. And then [on the death of Malcolm and Margaret]
the Scots chose as king Donald, Malcolm's brother, and drove
out all the English who were with king Malcolm before.

When Duncan, king Malcolm's son, who was in king
William's court, — inasmuch as his father had formerly given
him as a hostage to our king's father, and he had remained
here ever since, — heard that all this had so happened, he
came to the king and did such fealty as the king would have
of him, and so, with consent, went to Scotland with what aid
he could get of English and French, and deprived his kinsman
Donald of the kingdom, and he was received as king.

But afterwards some of the Scots gathered themselves
together and slew almost all his followers; and he himself
escaped with few.

Thereafter they were reconciled, on the condition that he
should never again introduce English or French into the land.

1094. In this year also the Scots deceived and slew Duncan,
their king; and thereafter took to themselves again as king, a
second time, his paternal uncle Donald, by whose direction
and instigation [Duncan] was betrayed to death.

1097. Also in this same year, soon after St Michael's mass,
Edgar Etheling went with an army into Scotland, with king
[William's] aid, and in a hard-fought battle won the land, and

1 The meeting apparently took place at Abernethy, and one of the hostages
was Duncan, Malcolm's eldest son by his first wife.

13

drove out king Donald; and in fealty to king William set up
there as king his kinsman Edgar, who was the son of king
Malcolm and queen Margaret.

S.A., 117-19.

EARLY *NOTITIAE* OF LAND GRANTS

*The earliest charter by a S ottish king which has survived is
one issued by Duncan II in 1094 (p. 16 below). Yet that
charter, and several by Edgar and Alexander I, are not in
Scotland, but at Durham. It would therefore be extremely
hazardous to assert that no charters were issued before those
which have chanced to survive. For the period before and
after the date from which charters are extant, there are
certain notes of land-grants. Those which are in the Book of
Deer are in Gaelic and have been the subject of much discussion as evidence for the structure of a pre-feudal organisation
of society. Those in the Register of the Priory of St. Andrews
are in Latin. It is to be observed that the wording of one of
the latest entries in the Book of Deer suggests that the scribe
had a Latin charter in front of him, and that the Register of
the Priory of St. Andrews entries include a grant by Edgar, a
king who certainly issued charters. It is therefore impossible
to be sure that charters did not lie behind some of the other*
notitiae. *The* notitiae *at any rate show that kings and other
great magnates, cleric and lay, were disponing land before
the period for which charters are extant.*

From the Book of Deer
(i) undated

Muiredach, son of Morgann, who was a *mormaer* and a
toísech, gave *Pett Mec-Gartnait* and the field of *Toche Temni.*
Matain, son of Cairell, gave a *mormaer's* portion in Altrie,
and Cú Lí, son of Baíthín, gave a *toísech's* portion. . . .
Malcolm, son of Cinaed [Malcolm II], gave a king's portion
in Biffie and in *Pett Mec-Gobroig*, and the two davochs of
upper *Ros abard*. . . . Cainnech and Domnall and Cathal

14

'quenched'[1] all the grants from beginning to end in favour
of God and of Drostán [to be held] in perpetuity, free from
[the exactions of] *mormaer* and *toísech*.

(ii) 1131-2

Gartnait, son of Cainnech, and Ete, daughter of Gille-Míchéil,
gave *Pett Mec Gobroig*, for the consecration of a church in
honour of Christ and of the Apostle Peter, to Colum Cille
and to Drostán, free from all exactions, and under bond to
Cormac, bishop of Dunkeld. The eighth year of the reign of
David. Witnesses:[2] Nechtan, bishop of Aberdeen, Léot,
abbot of Brechin, . . . Ruaidrí, *mormaer* of Mar, Mataidín,
brithem,[3] . . . Domangart, *fer léginn*[4] of Turriff.

(iii) 1131 x 1158

Colbán, *mormaer* of Buchan, and his wife Eva, daughter of
Gartnait, and Donnchad, son of Síthech, the *toísech* of *Clann
Morgainn*, 'quenched'[5] all the grants in favour of God and of
Drostán and of Colum Cille and of the Apostle Peter

Original in Cambridge University Library; facsimile in *Nat. MSS. Scot.*i,
No.1; ed. and trans. J. Fraser, *Scottish Gaelic Studies*, v, 51-66. Cf.
Kenneth Jackson, *The Gaelic Notes in the Book of Deer*.

From the Register of the Priory of St. Andrews[6]
(i) 1040 x 1057

Macbeth, son of Finlach, and Gruoch, daughter of Bodhe, king
and queen of Scots, granted Kyrkenes to Almighty God and
to the culdees of the island of Lochleven for prayers and inter-
cessions. . . .

(ii) *ante* 1055

Maldunus, bishop of St Andrews, granted the church of
Markinch with all its land, honourably and devoutly, to God
and St Serf and the culdees of the island of Lochleven.

1 Literally 'drowned'.
2 Here the scribe lapses into Latin (*Testibus ipsis*), suggesting that he was
working from a Latin charter.
3 Judge. Sometimes rendered 'brehon'.
4 Reader, almost in the sense in which the word is used of a university
teacher.
5 Literally 'drowned'.
6 The text of those *notitiae* is reproduced in Lawrie, *Early Scottish Charters*.

(iii) 1070 x 1093

King Malcolm and Queen Margaret of Scotland devoutly
granted the township of Ballecristin to Almighty God and the
culdees of Lochleven, with the same liberty as previously.

(iv) 1097 x 1107

Edgar, son of Malcolm, king of Scotland, granted in alms to
Almighty God and the foresaid culdees, Petnemokane with
all its liberties, as was noted before in the preceding entry
[*i.e.*, the grant by Macbeth and Gruoch].

1094 CHARTER OF DUNCAN II TO DURHAM

I, Duncan, son of King Malcolm and manifest king of Scotland
by inheritance, have given in alms to St. Cuthbert and his
servants[1] Tiningeham, Aldeham, Scuchale, Cnolle, Hather-
uuich and from Broccesmuthe[2] all the service which Bishop
Fothad[3] had therefrom; and I have given these things in
such fulness, with sac and soc, as St. Cuthbert ever had
most fully from those of whom he holds his alms; and I have
given them for myself and for the soul of my father and for
my brothers and for my wife and for my children; and since
I wished this gift to be enduring to St. Cuthbert I obtained
the consent of my brothers.[4] Anyone, however, who
wishes to destroy this grant, or take from the servants of St.
Cuthbert anything in it, shall have the curse of God, of St.
Cuthbert and myself. [The marks of King Duncan, ten witnesses and a clerk are appended, and the charter bears Duncan's
seal.]

> Original at Durham; facsimile, transcript and trans-
> lation in *Nat. MSS. Scot.*, i, No. ii; text in *E.S.C.*,
> No. xii; facsimiles in Fraser, *Haddington Book*, and
> James Anderson, *Diplomata Scotiae*.

1 The monks of Durham.
2 Tynninghame, Auldhame, Scoughall, Knowe, Hedderwick, Broxmouth.
3 'Fodanus' in the charter. He was the last of the old line of bishops of St.
Andrews, who died in 1093.
4 Presumably the sons of Malcolm by Margaret, who were Duncan's half-
brothers.

The points of interest in this charter are that (a) Edgar admitted that he held his kingdom by gift of William Rufus, whose lordship he acknowledges; (b) he was recognised as king by Rufus while Donald Bane still ruled, and may at this time have had possession of Lothian; and (c) he refers to Duncan II as one of his brothers, contrary to the view soon to be advanced that Duncan was illegitimate. The authenticity of the charter has been questioned, but it is cogently defended by Professor A.A.M. Duncan in an article which trenchantly concludes: 'It is doubtful if we can sustain for much longer the thesis that there was no Norman Conquest of Scotland' (S.H.R., xxxvii, 103-35).

In the name of the Father and of the Son and of the Holy Ghost, Amen. Be it known to all the faithful of Christ, present and to come, that I, Edgar, son of Malcolm, King of Scots, holding the whole land of Lothian and the kingdom of Scotland by gift of my lord, William, King of the English, and by inheritance from my father, with consent of my foresaid lord King William and of my adherents, for the souls of my father and my mother and of my brothers Duncan and Edward and for the safety of my own body and soul and for all my predecessors or successors, give to God Almighty and the church of Durham and St. Cuthbert the glorious bishop and to Bishop William and the monks serving God and to serve for ever in the same church, the *mansio*[1] of Berwick and with it the following *mansiones* [Graden, Birgham, Edrom, Chirnside and other lands in Berwickshire] : these above written *mansiones* I give to God and St. Cuthbert with all lands, woods, waters, tolls and shipwrecks and all customs which pertain to the said *mansiones* and which my father had in them, free and stable, to be freely disponed for ever according to the will of the bishop of Durham. [The marks of Edgar, Alexander, his brother, Edgar the Atheling and several other persons were appended, and the charter bore the seal of King Edgar.]

Original not extant; transcripts in the archives at Durham; Latin text in *E.S.C.*, No. xv.

1 It would be hazardous to translate *mansio* as 'manor', with its technical connotation. Possibly the meaning is no more than that of 'estate' in modern usage.

c.1105
CHARTER OF THOR THE LONG TO DURHAM

To all sons of Holy Mother Church, Thor the Long gives greeting in the Lord. Know ye that Edgar, my lord, King of Scots, gave to me Ednam, lying waste, which I occupied with his help and with my own goods, and I have built a church in honour of St. Cuthbert, which church, with a ploughgate of land, I have granted to God and St. Cuthbert and his monks, to be possessed by them for ever. This grant I have made for the soul of my lord, King Edgar, and for the souls of his father and mother and for the salvation of his brothers and sisters, and for the redemption of Lefwine,[1] my beloved brother, and for the safety of my own body and soul. And if anyone shall presume, by any violence or device, to take away this my grant from the saint aforesaid and the monks serving him, may God Almighty take away from him the life of the kingdom of heaven and may he undergo everlasting punishment with the devil and his angels. Amen.

Original at Durham; facsimile in Anderson, *Diplomata*; Latin text in *E.S.C.*, No. xxiv.

1 Lefwine had perhaps been taken prisoner during the First Crusade.

1119 POPE CALIXTUS II
TO THE BISHOPS OF SCOTLAND

At this stage the pope was supporting the claim of the archbishop of York to jurisdiction over Scotland, where there was no archbishop.

Bishop Calixtus, servant of the servants of God, to all the bishops throughout Scotland, suffragans of the church of York, greeting and apostolic benediction. A certain grave and perilous presumption is said to prevail in your parts, to wit that, without consulting your metropolitan and other fellow-bishops, one is consecrated as bishop by another. . . . Therefore by apostolic authority we command you that none be consecrated henceforth as bishop in your churches except by your metropolitan the archbishop of York, or by his permission. Moreover we instruct and command your fraternity that setting every pretext aside you offer canonical obedience to our venerable brother Thurstan, consecrated archbishop of York by God's grace, and as if by the hands of St Peter; even as in the time of Gerard, archbishop of the same church, was commanded by the lord of holy memory our predecessor, Pope Paschal. And if you obey our commands may the divine mercy keep you and lead you to eternal life.

S.A., 137.

c. 1124
CHARTER OF DAVID I TO ROBERT DE BRUS

David, by the grace of God King of Scots, to all his barons, men and friends, French and English, greeting. Know ye that I have given and granted to Robert de Brus Estrahanent [*i.e.*, Annandale] and all the land from the boundary of Dunegal of Stranit [Nithsdale] to the boundary of Randolph Meschin; and I will and grant that he should hold and have that land and its castle well and honourably with all its customs, namely with all those customs which Randolph Meschin ever had in Carduill [Carlisle] and in his land of Cumberland on that day in which he had them most fully and freely. Witnesses: Eustace Fitzjohn, Hugh de Morville, Alan de Perci, William de Somerville, Berengar Engaine, Randolph de Sules, William de Morville, Hervi son of Warin and Edmund the chamberlain. At Scone.

Original in the Archives of the Duchy of Lancaster; facsimiles in *Nat. MSS. Scot.*, i, No. xix, and Fraser, *Annandale Book;* text in *E.S.C.*, No. liv.

19

1128 x 1136 DAVID I's
CHARTER TO ABBEY OF HOLYROOD

In the name of our Lord Jesus Christ, and in honour of the
Holy Rood, and of Saint Mary the Virgin, and of all the
Saints, I, David, by the grace of God king of Scots, of my
royal authority, and with the assent of Henry my son and
the bishops of my kingdom, and with the confirmation and
testimony of the earls and barons, the clergy and the
people also assenting, of divine prompting, grant all the
things underwritten to the Church of the Holy Rood of
Edinburgh, and in perpetual peace confirm them. These
therefore are what we grant to the aforesaid Church and to
the canons regular serving God therein in free and perpetual
alms: To wit, the Church of the Castle with all its appendages and rights; And the trial of battle, water, and hot iron,
as far as belongs to ecclesiastical dignity; and with Salectun[1]
by its right marches; and the Church of Saint Cuthbert,
with the parish and all things that pertain to that church,
and with the Kirkton by its right marches, and with the
land in which that Church is situate; and with another land
that lies under the Castle, to wit, from the spring that
rises near the corner of my garden, by the road that leads to
the Church of Saint Cuthbert, and on the other side under
the Castle until you come to a crag which is under the Castle
towards the east; and with the two chapels which pertain to
the same Church of Saint Cuthbert, to wit Crostorfin[2] with
two oxgates and six acres of land, and that chapel of Libertun
with two oxgates of land, and with all the tithes and rights,
as well of the living as of the dead, of Legbernard,[3] which
Macbetber gave to that Church, and which I have granted;
And the Church of Hereth[4] with the land that belongs to
that Church, and with all the land that I have added and
given to it, as my servants and good men walked its bounds
and gave it over to Alwin the Abbot, with one saltpan in
Hereth, and twenty-six acres of land. Which Church and land
aforenamed, I will that the canons of the Holy Rood hold

1 Saughton.   3 Leadburn.
2 Corstorphine.   4 Airth.

20

and possess for ever freely and quietly; and I strictly forbid
that any one unjustly oppress or trouble the canons or their
men who live in that land, or unjustly exact from them any
works or aids, or secular customs. I will moreover that the
same canons have liberty of making a mill in that land, and
that they have in Hereth all those customs, rights and easements, to wit in waters and fishings, in meadows and pastures,
and in all other necessary things, as they best held them on
the day in which I had it in my domain; And Broctun[5]
with its right marches; and Inverlet,[6] that which is nearest
the harbour, with its right marches, and with that harbour,
and with the half of the fishing, and with a tithe of the
whole fishing which belongs to the Church of Saint
Cuthbert; And Petendrei,[7] with its right marches; and
Hamere[8] and Ford, with their right marches; and the
hospital, with one plough of land; And forty shillings from
my burgh of Edinburgh yearly; and a rent of a hundred
shillings yearly for the clothing of the canons, from my cain
of Perth, and this from the first ships that come to Perth for
the sake of trade; and if it happen that they do not come, I
grant to the aforesaid Church, from my rent of Edinburgh
forty shillings, and from Stirling twenty shillings, and from
Perth forty shillings; And one toft in Stirling, and the draught
of one net for fishing; and one toft in my burgh of Edinburgh
free and quit of all custom and exaction; And one toft in
Berwick, and the draught of two nets in Scypwell; and one
toft in Renfrew of five roods, and the draught of one net for
salmon, and to fish there for herrings freely; And I forbid
that any one exact from you or from your men, any customs
therefor. I grant moreover to the aforesaid canons from my
chamber yearly, ten pounds to the lights of the Church, and
to the works of that Church, and to repairing those works
for ever. I charge, moreover, all my servants and foresters
of Stirlingshire and of Clackmannan, that the Abbot and
Convent have free power in all my woods and forests, of
taking as much timber as they please and wish for the building of their church and of their houses, and for any purpose
of theirs. And I enjoin that their men who take timber for

5 Broughton.   7 Pittendreich, near Lasswade.
6 Inverleith, i.e. Leith.   8 Whitekirk.

21

their purposes in the said woods, have my firm peace, and so that ye do not permit them to be disturbed in any way; And the swine, the property of the aforesaid Church, I grant in all my woods to be quit of pannage. I grant moreover to the aforesaid canons the half of the fat, tallow and hides of beasts slaughtered in Edinburgh and a tithe of all whales and sea-beasts which fall to me from Avin to Colbrandespade;[9] And a tithe of all my pleas and gains from Avin to Colbrandespade; And the half of my tithe of my cain, and of my pleas and gains of Kentyr and Argyll, and all the skins of rams, ewes, and lambs of the Castle and of Linlitcu which die of my flock; And eight chalders of malt, and eight of meal, and thirty cart loads from the bush of Libertun; And one of my mills of Dene, and a tithe of the mills of Libertun and Dene, and of the new mill of Edinburgh; And of Craggenemarf, as much as I have in my domain, and as much as Uuieth the White gave them in alms of the same Crag. I grant likewise to them leave to establish a burgh between that church and my burgh; and I grant that their burgesses have common right of selling their wares, and of buying, in my market freely and quit of claim and custom in like manner as my own burgesses; and I forbid that anyone take in their burgh bread, ale, cloth or any ware by force or without the consent of the burgesses. I grant moreover that the canons be quit of toll and of all custom in all my burghs, and throughout all my land, to wit, of all things that they buy and sell. And I forbid that any one take pledge on the land of the Holy Rood, unless the Abbot of that place shall have refused to do right and justice. I will moreover that they hold all that is above-written, as freely and quietly as I hold my own lands; and I will that the Abbot hold his court as freely, fully, and honourably, as the Bishop of Saint Andrews, the Abbot of Dunfermline, and the Abbot of Kelso hold their courts. These being witnesses, Robert, bishop of Saint Andrews, John, bishop of Glasgow, Henry my son, William my nephew, Edward the Chancellor, Herebert the Chamberlain, Gillemichael the earl, Gospatric the brother of Dolfin, Robert of Montague, Robert of Burnevile, Peter of Brus, Norman the sheriff, Oggu, Leising, Gillise, William of Graham, Turstan of Crectun,

9   From the River Avon to Cockburnspath.

Blein the archdeacon, Aelfric the chaplain, Waleran the chaplain.

Original in archives of City of Edinburgh; facsimile, transcript and translation in *Nat. MSS. Scot.*, i, No. xvi; *E.S.C.*, No. cliii.

c.1150 KING DAVID I AND THE CULDEES

An innovator like David I, bent on the introduction to Scotland of new monastic orders, had to provide for the extinction or absorption of the outdated communities of culdees, who did not obey a recognised regula *or rule. He dealt more leniently with the culdees of St. Andrews than with those of Lochleven.*

(i)

David, King of Scots, to his bishops, abbots, earls, sheriffs and all good men of his whole land, greeting. Know ye that I have granted and given to the canons of St. Andrews the island of Lochleven in order that they may establish an order of canons there; and the culdees who may be found there, if they are willing to live according to a rule (*regulariter*), shall remain in peace with them and under them, but if any of them wish to resist this, I will and command that he be expelled from the island.

E.S.C., No. ccxxxii.

(ii)

David [*etc.*]. Know ye that I have given and granted to the prior and canons of the church of St. Andrew the Apostle that they may receive the culdees of Kilrimont [St. Andrews] as canons among them with all their possessions and revenues if they wish to become canons, and if they do not wish to become canons those who are now alive are to have and hold their possessions for their lives, and after their deaths there shall be established in place of them as many canons in the church of St. Andrews as there are culdees, so that all their possessions, and all their lands and alms which they have, may be converted to the uses of the canons of the foresaid church in as perpetual, free and quiet alms as any church in my kingdom holds most fully and quietly.

E.S.C., No. ccxxxiii.

c.1150 CHARTER BY
DAVID I TO WALTER DE RIDDALE

David, King of Scots, to the bishops, abbots, justiciars, barons, sheriffs, provosts, ministers and all men of his whole land, French and English, etc., greeting. Know ye, both present and to come, that I have given and granted to Walter de Riddale, Whitimes and half of Eschetho and Lilislive, by their right marches and with all their appendages rightly to them pertaining, in wood, plain, meadows, pastures, waters and shielings which are on the west of Richeldun, to be held by him and his heirs of me and my heirs in fee and heritage freely, by the service of one knight, as any of my barons who are his neighbours, freely holding his fee, most fully and freely has and holds. . . .

E.S.C., No. ccxxii.

c.1160–1258 GRANTS TO RELIGIOUS HOUSES

These extracts have been selected to illustrate the diverse properties and rights granted and the manifold interests of the religious orders.

(i)

[Malcolm IV, in confirming the possessions and liberties granted to the abbey of Scone by David I, mentions the following:]
the teind of the whole parish of Scone, in grain, cheese and fish and all other things from which teind is rendered; at the

Queen's Ferry free passage for the abbot and canons of Scone
and their own men and stock without payment of any toll or
charge; freedom to take material in the king's woods throughout the whole of Scotland, where it is most convenient for
them, for the construction of the church of Scon and their
houses . . . ; the serfs (*nativos homines*) of the lands and
churches foresaid and their offspring, except those who,
being freed and discharged by the said canons, have lawfully
departed from them . . . ; and from every ploughgate of the
whole land of the foresaid church of Scon, for the said canons'
conveth,[1] each year at the feast of All Saints, one cow,
two swine, four measures of meal, ten thraves of oats, ten hens,
12 sheep, ten bundles of candles, four pennyworths of soap
and 20 half-measures of cheese.

Regesta Regum Scotorum, i, 264.

(ii)

Malcolm, King of Scots, etc. Let all present and to come know
that I have granted, and by this my charter confirmed, to
God and the church of Neubotle and the monks serving God
there a saltpan in Kalentyr, gifted by King David, my grandfather, and common easement in pastures and waters, and
fuel for the same saltpan in the wood of Kalentyr, with
common pasture, in perpetual alms, free and quit of all
custom and secular exaction.

Ibid., 176-7.

(iii)

To all sons of holy mother church, Richard de Moreville, constable of the king of Scotland, and William, his son and heir,
greeting. Know ye that we have granted and by this our present charter confirmed to God and the church of St Mary of
Melrose and the monks serving God there, for the souls of us
and of all our ancestors and successors, a place in Witelei
within the margin of the forest, to make a cowshed for 100
(that is, six score) cows, or a sheepfold, whichever shall seem
better and more useful to them . . . and a house in which they
may make a fire for the brethren and their herds, and also a
house in which they may place their hay. These three houses
to be made in the foresaid place of Witelei we have granted

1 A due collected by a superior in lieu of the obligation of his dependents
to entertain him on his journeyings.

in pure and perpetual alms to the said monks to be possessed
for ever.

Register of Melrose, No. 106.

(iv)

I, Philip, Count of Flanders and Vermandois, wish it to be
known to those present and those to come that, for the salvation of my soul and of the souls of my ancestors, I have
granted to the brothers of Melrose and of their houses every
kind of liberty of travelling safely through all my land.

Ibid., No. 14.

(v)

To all sons of Holy Mother Church, Seyr de Quency, Earl of
Winchester, greeting. Know ye that I have given and by this
my charter confirmed to God and the church of St. Mary of
Neubotle and the monks serving God there, in pure and perpetual alms, for the increase of the alms which my father
Robert granted to them in the territory of Travernent, namely
all the half of the marsh extending from the west eastward
to the burn of Wygtrig, to wit that part which is nearest to
their cultivation; moreover, the coal-heuch and quarry
between the forenamed burn of Wigtrig and the marshes of
Pontekyn [*i.e.,* Pinkie] and Invereske, and in the ebb and
flow of the sea. And I will and command that none of my
men within the bounds of the grange of Preston have any
common, either in pasture, coal-heuch or quarry, without
the consent or goodwill of the same monks.

Register of Newbattle, No. 66.

(vi)

To all who shall see or hear this writ, Malise, earl of
Strathearn, everlasting greeting in the Lord. Know ye all that
I, moved by charity, for the salvation of my soul and of
those of my ancestors and successors, have given, granted and
by this my charter quit-claimed of me and my heirs for ever
to God and to St John, Apostle and Evangelist, and to the
abbot and convent of Inchaffray, in pure and perpetual alms,
John, called Starnes, son of Thomas, son of Thora, with all
his offspring.

Charters of Inchaffray, No. 1xxxviii.

After being taken prisoner on a raid into England, King William 'the Lion' was forced to accept Henry II as feudal overlord of Scotland and to subject the Scottish Church to the English.

William, king of Scots, has become the liege man of the lord king against every man, for Scotland and for all his other lands; and has done him fealty as to his liege lord, as his other vassals are accustomed to do to him. Likewise he has done homage to king Henry, his son; and fealty, saving his faith to the lord king, his father.

And all bishops and abbots, and the clergy of the land of the king of Scots, and their successors, shall do to the lord king as to their liege lord, fealty for all for which he wishes to have it, as his other bishops are accustomed to do to him; and to king Henry, his son, and to their heirs.

And the king of Scots, and David, his brother, and his barons and his other vassals, have granted to the lord king that the church of Scotland shall make to the church of England henceforth such subjection as she ought to make to her, and used to make in the time of the kings of England, his predecessors.

Likewise Richard, bishop of St. Andrews, and Richard, bishop of Dunkeld, and Geoffrey, abbot of Dunfermline, and Herbert, prior of Coldingham, have granted also that the church of England shall have that right in the church of Scotland which by right she ought to have; and that they will not oppose the right of the church of England. . . .

And for the sure observance of this agreement and compact, by the king of Scots and his heirs to the lord king and to Henry, his son, and his heirs, the king of Scots has delivered to the lord king the castle of Roxburgh, and the castle of Berwick, and the castle of Jedburgh, and the castle of the Maidens,[1] and the castle of Stirling, at the mercy of the lord king. . . .

Moreover for the fulfilment of the aforesaid agreement and compact, the king of Scots has delivered up to the lord king his brother David as hostage, and earl Duncan, and earl

1   Edinburgh Castle.

27

Waldeve [and several others].

And when the castles have been rendered, William, king of Scots, and David his brother shall be released . . .

> The original is not extant and the text is known only from later transcripts and entries in chronicles. The full text and a translation are in E.L.G. Stones, *Anglo-Scottish Relations*, 1-5, the text in Lawrie, *Annals*, No. xlv, and a translation in *S.A.*, 260-3.

1176 POPE ALEXANDER III
TO THE BISHOPS OF SCOTLAND

Despite the undertaking given in the treaty of Falaise, the Scottish churchmen continued to resist the claims of English archbishops to authority in Scotland, and at a council at Northampton in 1176 they were able to play with some effect on the rivalry of Canterbury and York. In the same year the pope went a long way towards accepting the Scottish case.

Naturally it distresses you greatly, it distresses us also, that our dearest son in Christ, Henry, illustrious King of the English, has compelled you to swear to obey the English church; since this reflects injury toward God and contempt for us, and [is] to the debasement of ecclesiastical liberty, which it is not for any king, or prince, to control with regard to churches or ecclesiastics. And we refuse to permit that your liberty be diminished, and have straitly enjoined our venerable brother the archbishop of the church of York, legate of the apostolic see, not to exercise metropolitan right over you until it be learned, under examination of the Roman pontiff, whether you owe subjection to him by metropolitan right. And we have heedfully warned the aforesaid king, reasoning with him as we ought against the reception of the aforesaid oaths, that he should not compel you to offer him obedience nor afford to this his consent or favour. We therefore command your fraternity and enjoin that you attempt not to obey by metropolitan right any but the Roman pontiff, by pretext of these oaths or for any other reason, until in our presence, or in that of our catholic successor, if the aforesaid archbishop wishes to drag you into court concerning this, the controversy between you and him be terminated by the due conclusion. Given at Anagni, the third before the Kalends of August.

S.A., 267-8.

1189   QUITCLAIM OF CANTERBURY

Richard Coeur-de-Lion, seeking finance for the third crusade, sold back to William, for 10,000 merks, the rights his father had acquired by the Treaty of Falaise; and thereby, remarked a patriotic Scottish chronicler, King William 'by God's assistance worthily and honourably removed a heavy yoke of domination and of servitude from the kingdom of the Scots'.[1]

Richard, by the grace of God king of the English, . . . to the archbishops, bishops, abbots, earls and barons, justiciars, sheriffs and all his bailiffs and vassals, greeting.

Know ye, that we have restored to our dearest cousin William, by the same grace king of Scotland, his castles of Roxburgh and Berwick[2] as his own by hereditary right, to be possessed by him and his heirs for ever.

Moreover we have freed him from all compacts which our good father Henry, king of the English, extorted from him by new charters and by his capture; so to wit that he do to us fully and entirely whatever Malcolm, king of Scotland, his brother, did to our predecessors of right, and of right ought to have done; and that we do to him whatever our predecessors did of right to Malcolm aforesaid, and ought to have done; namely, in the matter of conduct when he comes to court and while he stays at court, and when he returns from court, and in his provisionings and in all liberties, dignities and honours rightfully due to him. . . .

1 Melrose Chronicle, in *E.S.*, ii, 322.
2 Edinburgh had been restored earlier, when William agreed to accept a bride of Henry's nomination.

Moreover concerning the lands which he has in England, whether in demesne or in fee, to wit in the earldom of Huntingdon and in all others, let him and his heirs possess them for ever in the same liberty and fullness as the foresaid King Malcolm possessed or ought to have possessed them; unless the foresaid King Malcolm or his heirs shall have since granted anything in fief; yet so that whatever has since been granted in fief, the services of those fiefs shall pertain to him and his heirs.

And the land which our father granted to King William aforesaid, we wish him and his heirs to possess by perpetual right in the same liberty with which he gave it to him.

We have restored also to him the allegiance which our father had received of his vassals, and all the charters which our father had of him through his capture. And if perchance any should be retained by oversight or be found, we command that they be wholly without validity.

And the oft-named King William has become our liegeman for all the lands for which his predecessors were liegemen of our predecessors; and he has sworn fealty to us and to our heirs.

The original, in Reg. Ho., is largely illegible, but the text is known from a later transcript and from chronicles. Facsimile, transcript and translation in *Nat. MSS. Scot.*, i, No. xlvi, text and translation in Stones, *op. cit.*, 6-8, text in Lawrie, *Annals*, No. cxxviii, and translation in *S.A.*, 308-9.

1218 'FILIA SPECIALIS'
BULL OF HONORIUS III

This bull, liberating the Scottish Church from subjection to any archbishop, was a reissue of bulls granted by Celestine III (1191-98) and Innocent III (1198-1216).

Honorius, bishop, servant of the servants of God, to his dearest son in Christ Alexander, illustrious king of Scots, and his successors forever. While all the faithful ought to find at the apostolic see patronage and favour, yet it is fitting that those should more especially be cherished by the defence of its protection whose faith and devotion have been tried in many things, that they may be so much the more incited to the fervour of love for it, and be subdued by the more devout affection of reverence for it, as they know that they have more surely attained a pledge of its benevolence and grace. For this reason, dearest son in Christ, considering the reverence and devotion towards the Roman church which we know you and your predecessors to have had from times long past, by the page of this present writing (following the example of Celestine and Innocent, our predecessors of happy memory, popes of Rome) we most strictly forbid that it be permitted to anyone except the pope of Rome or a legate sent from his side to publish a sentence of interdict or excommunication in the kingdom of Scotland, because the Scottish church (in which these episcopal sees are known to exist — St Andrews, Dunblane, Glasgow, Dunkeld, Brechin, Aberdeen, Moray, Ross and Caithness) is subject to the apostolic see as a special daughter, with no intermediary; and if such a sentence be pronounced, we decree it invalid. We add, also, that it be not permitted to any henceforth who is not of the kingdom of Scotland to exercise the office of legate in it unless one whom the apostolic see has specially sent from its body for that purpose. We forbid, too, that disputes which may arise in the same kingdom about its possessions be carried to trial by judges placed outside the kingdom, unless on appeal to the Roman church. And if any writings come to light which have been obtained contrary to the decree of this liberty, or chance in future to be obtained, without mention made of this concession, let nothing result to the prejudice of you or your successors, or of your kingdom, concerning the grant of this privilege. Besides, the liberties and immunities granted by the Roman church to you and your kingdom and the churches in that kingdom, and hitherto observed, we confirm and decree that they remain unimpaired in time to come, saving the authority of the apostolic see. Let it be permitted to no man at all to infringe this writing of our grant, prohibition and confirmation, or venture rashly to transgress it. But if any presume to attempt this, let him know that he shall incur the wrath of Almighty God and of the blessed Apostles Peter and Paul. . . . Given at the Lateran by the hand of Ranerius, vice-chancellor of the holy Roman church, on the eleventh before the Kalends of December, the 7th indiction, the year of the Lord's incarnation MCCXVIII, and the third year of the pontificate of Honorius III.

Original in Reg. Ho., facsimile, transcript and translation in *Nat. MSS Scot.*, i, No. xlvii.

1225 AUTHORISATION
OF A PROVINCIAL COUNCIL

Honorius, bishop, servant of the servants of God, to his venerable brethen all the bishops of the kingdom of Scotland, greeting and apostolic benediction. Certain of you lately brought to our ears the knowledge that since you had not an archbishop by whose authority you might be able to hold a provincial council, it results that in the kingdom of Scotland, which is so remote from the Apostolic See, the statutes of the General Council[1] are disregarded and very many irregularities committed which remain unpunished. Now, since it is improper to omit the holding of provincial councils, in which zealous consideration, under the fear of God, should be given to the correction of transgressions and the reformation of morals, and the canonical rules be read over and recorded, especially the rules decreed by that same general council, by apostolic warrant to you we command that since you are known not to have a metropolitan, you hold a provincial council by our authority. Dated at Tivoli, the nineteenth day of May in the ninth year of our pontificate.

Patrick, *Statutes of the Scottish Church*, 1.

The bull merely authorised 'a provincial council', but it was evidently interpreted to mean that a council should be held annually, and the Scots made arrangements accordingly, though in practice meetings seem to have been irregular and comparatively infrequent.

We, the prelates of the Scottish church, . . . ordain that every year all bishops and abbots and priors of priories shall

1 The Fourth Lateran Council (1215).

32

religiously assemble . . . for the holding of a council on a
certain day to be duly intimated to them by the conservator
of the council; so that they may be able to remain at the
same council for three days, if need be. . . .

And we ordain firstly that every year the duty of preaching
be laid on one of the bishops one after the other, [to be per-
formed] at the next council by himself or by another to be
proposed [by him], beginning with the bishop of Saint
Andrews; and that by choice of the others one of the bishops
be appointed conservator of the statutes of the council[2] . . .

Patrick, 9.

2 His title later became 'Conservator of the privileges of the Scottish Church.'

1237 TREATY OF YORK

*The recurrent claims of the Scottish kings to the three
northern English counties were surrendered in return for
security in lands of a specified value in Northumberland and
Cumberland.*

The said Alexander, king of Scots, remitted and quit-claimed
for himself and his heirs to the said Henry, king of England,
and his heirs in perpetuity the said earldoms of
Northumberland, Cumberland and Westmorland [and fifteen
thousand merks of silver which King John, father of Henry,
received from William, former king of Scots, father of
Alexander, for certain agreements entered upon between the
said kings which were not observed by King John, as
Alexander, king of Scotland, says, and all agreements made
about marriages between Henry, king of England, or Richard,
his brother, and Margaret or Isabella, sisters of the said
Alexander, king of Scotland].

In return for this remission and quitclaim the said Henry,
king of England, gave and granted to the said Alexander,
king of Scots, two hundred librates of land within the said
earldoms of Northumberland and Cumberland if the said
two hundred librates can be found in these earldoms outside
towns where castles are situated, and, if any is lacking, it shall

be made up in suitable places nearest the said earldoms of Northumberland and Cumberland; to be had, held and retained in demesne by the said Alexander, king of Scots, and his heirs the kings of Scots, of the said Henry, king of England, and his heirs; rendering therefor annually one falcon to the king of England and his heirs at Carlisle through the hands of the constable of the castle of Carlisle, whoever he may be, on the feast of the Assumption of the Blessed Mary, for all services, customs and other demands which might be exacted for the same lands. . . .

And the said king of Scots has done his homage for these lands to the said king of England, and has sworn fealty to him.

The original is not extant, but the text survives in a contemporary transcript in P.R.O. Text and translation in Stones, 19-26, and text in *Foedera*, i, 233.

1266   TREATY OF PERTH

Any effective· Norwegian control of the western isles had long ceased, and power there had come to lie with chieftains of mixed Celtic and Scandinavian race who owed little allegiance· to either Norway or Scotland. After the failure of King Haakon the Old to reassert Norwegian authority, in the campaign which included the action at Largs in 1263, Norway was prepared to cede the western isles, including Man.

This settlement and final agreement for terminating the disagreements, complaints, losses, damage and disputes concerning the isles of Man and the Sudreys and of the rights thereof was made, with the help of divine providence, between magnificent and illustrious princes the lords Magnus IV, by the grace of God illustrious King of Norway, by his solemn envoys . . . , on one side, and the lord Alexander III, by the same grace illustrious King of Scots, personally compearing there with the clergy and greater magnates of his realm, on the other, in this form, viz:

That the said lord Magnus, King of Norway, . . . granted,

resigned and quit-claimed . . . for himself and his heirs for
ever, Man with the rest of the Sudreys and all other islands
on the west and south of the great sea, with all right which
he and his progenitors had of old therein or he and his heirs
shall have in future. . . . ; to be held, had and possessed by
the said lord Alexander III, King of Scots, and his heirs, with
demesne-lands, homages, rents, services and all rights and
pertinents of the said islands, without retention, along with
the right of patronage of the bishopric of Man (saving, in all
and by all, the right, jurisdiction and liberty of the church of
Nidaros,[1] if it have any, in the bishopric of Man); and
excepting the islands of Orkney and Yhetland, which the said
king of Norway has reserved specially to his domain, with
their demesne-lands, homages and rents, services and all their
rights and pertinents within their borders; in such wise that
all the men of the said islands which are ceded, resigned and
quit-claimed to the said lord king of Scots, as well lesser as
greater, shall be subject to the laws and customs of the realm
of Scotland and be judged and dealt with according to them
henceforth, but for the misdeeds or injuries and damage
which they have committed hitherto while they adhered to
the said king of Norway they be no wise punished or mol-
ested in their heritages in those islands but stand peacefully
therein under the lordship of the king of Scots as other free
men and lieges of the said lord king who are known to enjoy
the most free justice unless they do anything else on account
of which they ought to be justly punished according to the
approved laws and customs of the realm of Scotland; if they
should wish to remain in the said islands under the lordship
of the said lord king of Scots, they may remain in his lordship freely and in peace, but if they wish to retire they may
do so, with their goods, lawfully, freely and in full peace;
so that they be not compelled either to remain or to retire
contrary to the laws and customs of the realm of Scotland
and their own will.

Therefore the foresaid lord Alexander, king of Scots, . . .
and his heirs . . . shall give and render for ever to the said
king of Norway and his heirs and their assignees within the
octave of the nativity of St John the Baptist, in Orkney, that

1 The archbishop of Nidaros (Trondheim) was metropolitan of the see of
Man and the Isles.

is, in the land of the lord king of Norway, in the church of St Magnus, into the hand of the bishop of Orkney or the bailie of the said lord king of Norway thereto specially deputed by him, or, if the bishop or bailie be not found there, shall deposit in the said church, in the custody of the canons thereof (for the use of the said lord king of Norway) — who shall give to them letters of discharge and receipt — the sum of a hundred merks good and lawful sterling yearly, to be counted according to the manner and use of the Roman court and the realms of France, England and Scotland; and also 4,000 merks sterling to be counted in the same way within the next four years at place and term foresaid, namely, 1,000 merks in the octave of the nativity of St John the Baptist in the year of grace 1267, with 100 merks of the foresaid annual, [and likewise for 1268, 1269 and 1270, after which the 100 merks of annual only] . . . .

If it happen (which God forbid!) that the men of the king of Norway suffer shipwreck in the kingdom or domain of the king of Scotland, or contrariwise, it shall be lawful for them, either in person or by others, freely and quietly to gather their ships, broken or shattered, along with all their goods, and to have them, to sell and to dispose of them, without any claim, as long as they have not abandoned them. And if anyone, contrary to this act of common agreement, seizes anything fraudulently or violently from these goods or ships, and is convicted thereof, let him be punished as a plunderer and breaker of the peace as he deserves. . . .

A.P.S., i, 420.

1278 HOMAGE OF
ALEXANDER III TO EDWARD I

The long-contested question of the nature of the homage done by Scottish kings to England was raised again on 28 October 1278.

At Westminster, Alexander, king of Scotland, did homage to

the Lord Edward, king of England, son of King Henry, in these words: 'I become your man for the lands which I hold of you in the kingdom of England for which I owe homage to you, saving my kingdom.' Then said the Bishop of Norwich: 'And saving to the king of England, if he has right to your homage for the kingdom.' To whom at once and openly the king replied, saying: 'To homage for my kingdom of Scotland, no one has right save God alone, nor do I hold it save of God alone.' Then Robert de Brus, Earl of Carrick, did fealty for the said lord king of Scotland, swearing upon his soul in these words: 'So may God and these holy things help me, my Lord, the king of Scotland, who is here, will be faithful to you in life and limbs and earthly honour, and will conceal your counsels.' And then the king of Scotland added, according to the form of homage which he did above, 'for the lands which I hold of you in the kingdom of England.' And the king of Scotland granted that, saving his kingdom, he would render to the king of England the services used and wont from those lands for which he had done homage to him.

Register of Dunfermline, No. 321.

1284 ACKNOWLEDGMENT OF THE MAID
OF NORWAY AS HEIR OF ALEXANDER III

To all the faithful of Christ to whom the present writ shall come, Alexander Comyn, Earl of Buchan, constable and justiciar of Scotland, Patrick Earl of Dunbar, Malise Earl of Strathearn, Malcolm Earl of Lennox, Robert de Brus, Earl of Carrick, Donald Earl of Mar, Gilbert Earl of Angus, Walter Earl of Menteith, William Earl of Ross, William Earl of Sutherland, Magnus Earl of Orkney, Duncan Earl of Fife, John Earl of Atholl, Robert de Brus, senior, James, Steward of Scotland, John de Balliol, John Comyn, William de Soulis, then justiciar of Lothian, Ingeram de Gynis, William de Moray, son of Walter de Moray, knights, Alexander de Balliol, Reginald le Chene, senior, William de St Clair, Richard Syward, William de Brechin, Nicholas de Hay, Henry de Graham,

Ingeram de Balliol, Alan son of the Earl, Reginald le Chene, younger, J. [. . .] de Lindesay, Patrick de Graham, [. . . tus] de Maxwell, Simon Fraser, Alexander de Argyll, Angus son of Donald and Alan son of Roderick, barons of the realm of Scotland, greeting in the Lord.

Know ye that, since it has pleased the Most High that our lord Alexander, eldest son of [king] Alexander, has gone the way of all flesh with no lawful offspring surviving directly from the body of the said king, we bind ourselves and our heirs straitly by the presents to our said lord king and the heirs descended from his body directly or indirectly who by right ought to be admitted to succeed to him and in the faith and fealty by which we are bound to them we firmly and faithfully promise that if our said lord king happens to end his last day in this life leaving no lawful son or sons, daughter or daughters of his body or of the body of the said Alexander his son, we each and all of us will accept the illustrious girl Margaret, daughter of our said lord king's daughter Margaret, of good memory, late queen of Norway, begotten of the lord Eric, illustrious king of Norway, and lawful offspring descended from her, as our lady and right heir of our said lord king of Scotland, of the whole realm of Scotland, of the Isle of Man and of all other islands belonging to the said kingdom of Scotland, and also of Tynedale and Penrith[1] with all other rights and liberties which belong or ought to belong to the said lord king of Scotland . . . and against all men . . . we shall maintain, sustain and defend [her] with all our strength and power.

Original in Reg. Ho.; printed in *A.P.S.*, i, 424.

1 These lands constituted the 200 librates conceded by England in 1237 (p. 33 above).

1289   TREATY OF SALISBURY

When Alexander III died in 1286, his heir, according to the declaration of 1284, was his little grand-daughter, child of his daughter and King Erik of Norway. But, in spite of the agreement of 1284, trouble was evidently stirred up by some who would have contested her claim, and in 1289 it was still uncertain when, or whether, she could safely be brought to Scotland. King Erik, out of interest for her welfare and prospects, consulted Edward I of England, and at Edward's request representatives of Scotland went south to meet representatives of England and Norway and discuss the situation.

The foresaid queen and heir shall come to the kingdom of England or Scotland before the Feast of All Saints next to come [1 November 1290], free and quit of all contract of marriage and betrothal: and this the foresaid Norwegian envoys promised in good faith that they would do and cause to be done within the foresaid term, so far as in them lies, unless the queen shall have therein some reasonable and allowable excuse. . . .

The said king of England promised in good faith that if the foresaid lady shall come into his hands or keeping free and quit of all contract of marriage and betrothal, then, when the kingdom of Scotland shall have been well settled and in peace, so that the lady herself may come there safely and remain there, and when the king of England shall be so requested by the people of the realm of Scotland, the said king will send the same lady to the realm of Scotland, as free and quit of all contracts, of which mention is made above, as he received her.

Provided that the good people of Scotland, before they receive the lady, shall give sufficient and good surety to the king of England aforesaid that they will in no wise marry the foresaid lady save with his ordinance, will and counsel, and with the assent of the king of Norway, her father.

And the foresaid Scottish envoys likewise promised in good faith, for themselves and for others of the kingdom of Scotland, that they would settle the land of Scotland before the said lady comes there; and they would give security that she should be able to come there with safety, as into her own kingdom, and freely to stay there of her own will, as true lady, queen and heir of that land. . . .

Rymer, *Foedera*, i, 719-20.

39

Edward I was already, in 1289, planning the marriage of Margaret to his son, Edward. In 1290 the Scots welcomed this prospect, urged King Erik to send his daughter to England and, in the Treaty of Birgham, formally agreed to the marriage, with certain safeguards for Scotland's integrity — though with qualifications which might make these safeguards illusory.

We, after due consideration of the peace and tranquillity of both kingdoms, and that mutual friendship should continue between their peoples for all time, have granted in the name and on behalf of our said lord [Edward I] and his heirs that the rights, liberties and customs of the same kingdom of Scotland in all things and in all ways shall be wholly and inviolably preserved for all time throughout the whole of that kingdom and its marches. Saving the right of our said lord, and of any other whomsoever, which has pertained to him, or to any other, on the marches, or elsewhere, over these things in question before the time of the present agreement, or which in any right way ought to pertain in future.

We expressly will and grant in the name of our said lord and his heirs, and in our name, that, failing offspring of the foresaid Edward and Margaret, or either of them, in the event that the foresaid kingdom [of Scotland] ought of right to revert to the nearest heirs, it shall revert and be restored to them, wholly, freely, absolutely and without any subjection, — if perchance in any way that kingdom shall happen to come into the hands of our said lord king or his heirs, — and in such a way that, by reason of these presents, nothing shall accrue or be lost in any way to our lord king, his heirs, or any other. . . .

We promise nevertheless in the name and on behalf of our said lord king and his heirs that the kingdom of Scotland shall remain separate and divided from the kingdom of England by its right boundaries and marches, as has hitherto in the past been observed, and that it shall be free in itself and without subjection; saving the right of our said lord, and of any other whomsoever, which has pertained to him, or to any other, in the marches or elsewhere . . . before the time of the present agreement, or which in any right way ought to pertain in the future. . . .

We expressly grant, for our said lord and his heirs, that the chapters of cathedral, collegiate, and conventual churches which hold their own elections shall not be compelled to pass outwith the same kingdom of Scotland to seek leave to elect, or to present the persons elected, or to swear fealty or oath to the king of Scotland. And that no one holding in chief of the foresaid king of Scotland shall be compelled to pass outwith the kingdom to do homage or fealty, or to make payment for relief [of his lands]. . . .

No one of the kingdom of Scotland shall be held to answer outwith that kingdom for any agreement entered into, or for any crime committed, in that kingdom, or in any other cause, contrary to the laws and customs of that kingdom; as has hitherto been reasonably observed. . . .

No parliament shall be held outwith the kingdom and marches of Scotland on matters touching that kingdom or its marches or the position of those who inhabit that kingdom. Neither shall any tallages, aids, hostings, or maltote be exacted from the foresaid kingdom, or placed upon the people of the same kingdom, except to meet the expenses of the common affairs of the kingdom and in those cases where the kings of Scotland were wont to demand the same. . . .

We protest also in these writings that all the foregoing is so to be understood that by reason of the present deed the rights of neither kingdom are to be in any way increased or decreased; neither are the rights of either of the kings, but each is to have his own position freely.

Stevenson, *Documents illustrative of the History of Scotland*, i, No. cviii.

1290 LETTER OF
BISHOP WILLIAM FRASER TO EDWARD I

The Maid of Norway set out for Scotland, but on 7 October, when this letter was written, there were rumours — which turned out to be true — that she was dead.

41

To the most excellent Prince and most revered Lord, Lord
Edward, by the grace of God most illustrious King of England,
Lord of Ireland, and Duke of Aquitaine, his devoted chaplain,
William, by divine permission humble minister of the church
of Saint Andrew in Scotland, wisheth health and fortunes
prosperous to his wishes with increase of glory and honour.
As it was ordered lately in your presence, your ambassadors
and the ambassadors of Scotland who had been sent to you
and also some nobles of the kingdom of Scotland met at
Perth on the Sunday next after the feast of Saint Michael
the Archangel to hear your answer upon those things which
were asked and treated by the ambassadors of Scotland in
your presence. Which answer of yours being heard and
understood the faithful nobles and a certain part of the
community of Scotland returned infinite thanks to your
Highness. And your foresaid ambassadors and we set ourselves to hasten our steps towards the parts of Orkney to
confer with the ambassadors of Norway for receiving our
Lady the Queen, and for this we had prepared our journey.
But there sounded through the people a sorrowful rumour
that our said Lady should be dead, on which account the
kingdom of Scotland is disturbed and the community distracted. And the said rumour being heard and published, Sir
Robert de Brus, who before did not intend to come to the
foresaid meeting, came with a great following to confer
with some who were there. But what he intends to do or
how to act, as yet we know not. But the Earls of Mar and
Atholl are already collecting their army; and some other
nobles of the land join themselves to their party and on that
account there is fear of a general war and a great slaughter
of men, unless the Highest, by means of your industry and
good service, apply a speedy remedy. My Lords the Bishop
of Durham, Earl Warenne and I heard afterwards that our
foresaid Lady recovered of her sickness, but she is still weak;
and therefore we have agreed amongst ourselves to remain
about Perth, until we have certain news by the knights who
are sent to Orkney, what is the condition of our Lady —
would that it may be prosperous and happy; and if we shall
have the accounts which we wish concerning her and which
we await from day to day, we will be ready to set forth for
those parts, as is ordained, for carrying out the business
committed to us to the best of our power. If Sir John de Balli‹

comes to your presence we advise you to take care so to treat with him that in any event your honour and advantage be preserved. If it turn out that our foresaid Lady has departed this life (may it not be so), let your excellency deign if you please to approach towards the March, for the consolation of the Scottish people and for saving the shedding of blood, so that the faithful men of the kingdom may keep their oath inviolate, and set over them for King him who of right ought to have the succession, if so be that he will follow your counsel. May your excellency have long life and health, prosperity and happiness. Given at Leuchars on Saturday the morrow of Saint Faith the Virgin, in the year of our Lord 1290.

Nat. MSS Scot., i, No. 1xx.

1291 SUBMISSION OF
THE CLAIMANTS TO EDWARD I

The claims of the competitors for the throne were submitted to King Edward, who insisted on being acknowledged as sovereign lord of Scotland.

To all who shall see or hear these letters, Florence Count of Holland, Robert de Brus Lord of Annandale, John Balliol Lord of Galloway, John de Hastings Lord of Abergavenny, John Comyn Lord of Badenoch, Patrick de Dunbar Earl of March, John de Vesci for his father, Nicholas de Soules and William de Ross, greeting in God. Seeing that we profess to have right to the kingdom of Scotland, and to set forth, maintain and declare such right before that person who has most power, jurisdiction and reason to try our right; and the noble Prince, Sir Edward by the grace of God King of England, has shown to us, by good and sufficient reasons, that to him belongs, and that he ought to have, the sovereign lordship of the said kingdom of Scotland, and the cognizance of hearing, trying and determining our right; We, of our own will, without any manner of force or constraint, will, concede

43

and grant to receive justice before him as sovereign lord of the land; and we are willing, moreover, and promise to have and hold firm and stable his act, and that he shall have the realm to whom right shall give it before him. In witness of this thing we have put our seals to this writing. Made and given at Norham, the Tuesday next after the Ascension [5 June], the year of grace one thousand two hundred and ninety-first.

On the following day the competitors went a step further, and conceded that Edward should have possession of Scotland until he gave his award.

We will, concede, and grant that he, as sovereign lord, in order to effect the things aforesaid, have sasine of the whole land and of the castles of Scotland until right be done and performed to the claimants, in such manner that, before he have the sasine aforesaid, he give good and sufficient security to the claimants and to the guardians and to the community of the kingdom of Scotland, to make restitution of the same kingdom and of the castles, with all the royalty, dignity, lordship, franchises, customs, rights, laws, usages, and possessions, and all manner of appurtenances, in the same state in which they were when sasine to him was given and delivered, to that person who shall, by judgment, have the right to the kingdom, reserving to the King of England the homage of him who shall be king, so that the restitution be made within two months after the day when the right shall be tried and declared. And that the issues of the same land in the meantime received be safely deposited and well kept in the hands of the Chamberlain of Scotland who now is, and of him who shall be associated with him on the part of the King of England, and under their seals, saving the reasonable maintenance of the land and of the castles and of the officers of the kingdom.

Nat. MSS Scot., ii, No. v; the second letter appears separately in vol. i, No. 1xxi.

Under John Balliol, Edward I's nominee, Scotland felt to the full its humiliating position as a vassal kingdom, and on 23 October 1295 made an alliance with France, another country which was actively hostile to the English. The treaty was confirmed by Balliol on 23 February following when the 'communities' of the burghs of Aberdeen, Perth, Stirling, Edinburgh, Roxburgh' and Berwick, as well as clerical and lay magnates, appended their seals in token of their approval. The treaty provided for the marriage of Edward, son of John Balliol, to the niece of King Philip of France, but the more significant clauses related to promises of mutual assistance against England.

In order that the foresaid injurious efforts of the king of England may the more conveniently be repressed and that the said king [Edward] be the more quickly compelled to withdraw from his perverse and hostile incursions . . . , the said king of Scots shall take care to begin and continue war against the king of England at his own cost and expense with all his power and with all the power of his subjects and of his kingdom, as often as it be opportune. . . . The prelates of Scotland, as far as it be lawful to them, with the earls, barons and other nobles and also the *universitates ac communitates villarum*[1] of the kingdom of Scotland shall make war against the said king of England in the same manner as is above expressed, with all their strength. . . . The prelates, earls, barons and other nobles and also the *universitates communitatesque notabiles* of the said kingdom of Scotland shall direct to us as soon as may be their letters patent hereon fortified with their seals.

It was also agreed . . . that if it happen the foresaid king of England to invade . . . the kingdom of Scotland by himself or by another, after war has been begun by the king of Scots at our request, or after this present agreement or treaty has been entered upon between us by occasion thereof, we, provided we be forewarned thereof on the part of the same king of Scots within a suitable time, shall give him help by occupying the said king of England in other parts, so that he shall thus be distracted to other matters from the foresaid

1 *i.e.*, the corporations and communities of the burghs.

invasion which he has begun. . . . If, however, the foresaid
king of England happens personally to leave England or goes
out of it with a notable number of infantry or cavalry while
war lasts between him and us, . . . then especially the said
king of Scotland with all his power shall take care to invade
the land of England as widely or deeply as he can.

[The king of France was not to commit the Scots to conclude their operations, nor was he to agree to conclude his
own operations without including the Scots in any peace or
truce; and the king of Scots was not to enter into a peace or
truce which did not embrace the French.]

A.P.S., i, 451-3 (partly from a MS. in the P.R.O. and partly from the French archives).

1290 x 1300 EXTRACTS FROM
RENTAL OF ABBEY OF KELSO

*These extracts from what is in effect a survey of the abbey's
properties and estates illustrate several features of land tenure
and agrarian management.*

The monks of the said monastery hold in temporality in the
sheriffdom of Roxburgh the grange of Reveden, with its
'toun'[1], in free alms; there they have a demesne which they
cultivate with five ploughs, and there they can have a flock
of about 280 ewes and pasture for their oxen.

They have there eight husbandlands and one oxgang, each
of which did the following seasonal services, namely each
week in summer one carriage[2] with one horse to Berwick, the
horse to carry three bolls of grain or two bolls of salt or one
and a half bolls of coal; and each week in winter the same
carriage, but the horse to carry only two bolls of grain or one
and a half bolls of salt or one boll and a firlot[3] of coal. And
every week when they performed this carriage to Berwick
each husbandland did one day's work of the labour enjoined

1 A group of houses in which tenants and others lived.
2 *i.e.*, a service of carrying.
3 A firlot was one quarter of a boll.

on it; and in the weeks when they did not go to Berwick
they did two days' cultivating, except in harvest-time,
when they did three days' work. . . .

They have there nineteen cot-holdings[4], eighteen of which
pay each twelve pence a year and do each six days' service in
harvest-time, receiving their meals and giving help with the
gathering and shearing of the sheep; and the nineteenth
cot-holding pays eighteen pence and does nine days' work.

There used to be two brewhouses there which rendered
two merks a year.

They have a mill there which used to render nine merks a
year. . . .

In Molle they have at Altonburn 50 acres of arable land
and meadow, with pasture for 300 sheep, with free entry and
exit, and for ten oxen and four other draught-animals. . . .

They have at Senegideside in the said holding seven acres
of land for their shepherd to dwell in, and pasture in Berehope
for 700 sheep. . . .

They have at Stapelaw four acres of land which Adam de
Roule and Iveta, his wife, gave to them. They have also four
acres at Lathelade in which they may place their folds and
enclose their sheep when they are away from Berehope.

They have a grange in the same tenement, which is called
Ileshow, where they can cultivate with two ploughs and have
in pasture 20 oxen, 20 cows, 250 ewes and 200 barren[5]
sheep.

They have the town of Bolden, in which are 28 husbandlands, each of which used to pay yearly 6s. 8d. at Whitsunday
and Martinmas and render these services: each husbandman
with his wife and family reaping in harvest-time for four
days and likewise doing a fifth day's work in harvest-time
with two men; each is to carry peats in a cart from Gordon
to the Pullis for one day, and each to carry one cartload of
peats from the Pullis to the abbey in summer — and no
more. Each husbandman is to do carriage by one horse from
Berwick once a year and they are to have their victual from
the monastery when they do this service. Each of them used
each year to cultivate at the grange of Newton one acre and

4 A cot-holding, held by a cottar, contained only a small piece of land,
much less than the husbandland of the normal agricultural tenant, and cottars
may be presumed to have hired themselves out as labourers.
5 Sheep not with lamb.

47

a half, and he is to harrow with one horse for one day, and each of them is to find one man for gathering the sheep and another man for shearing, without victual. They are to answer likewise of forinsec service[6] and other suits and to carry grain in harvest-time with a cart for one day, to carry the abbot's wool from the barony to the abbey and to find carriage beyond the moor towards Lesmahago.

Register of Kelso, ii, 455-6, 458, 461.

6 Traditional service over and above that defined in the terms on which a tenant held his land.

1310 DECLARATION OF
CLERGY IN FAVOUR OF KING ROBERT I

The reign of King Robert is dated from March 1306, but he was for long a king without a kingdom and one whose claims were challenged. It is evident that from the outset he had the support of some notable clergy, but there are many difficulties in the way of·believing that a document drawn up as early as February 1309/10 in fact commanded the wide assent which it professes to do.[1]

To all the faithful in Christ to whose knowledge the present writing shall come, the Bishops, Abbots, Priors, and the rest of the clergy in the Kingdom of Scotland greeting in the Author of Salvation. Be it known to you all that when between the Lord John de Balliol, sometime raised to be King of Scotland in fact by the King of England, and the deceased Lord Robert de Brus of worthy memory, grandfather of the Lord Robert the King who now is, a ground of dispute had arisen which of them, to wit, was nearest by right of blood to inherit and reign over the Scottish people; the faithful people without doubt always held, as from their predecessors and ancestors they had learned and believed to be true, that the said Lord Robert, the grandfather, after the death of

1 There are also several features in the original· MSS. of the Declaration which cause suspicion (*S.H.R.*, xxiii, 280-93).

King Alexander and his grand-daughter, the daughter of the
King of Norway, was the true heir, and ought, in preference
to all others, to be advanced to the government of the
kingdom, although, the enemy of the human race sowing
tares, by the various machinations and plots of his rivals,
which it would be tedious to narrate at length, the thing has
turned contrariwise; on account of whose overthrow, and
the want of kingly authority, heavy calamities have thenceforth resulted to the Kingdom of Scotland and its inhabitants,
as experience, the mistress of events, hitherto often repeated,
has manifestly declared. The people, therefore, and commons
of the foresaid Kingdom of Scotland, worn out by the stings
of many tribulations, seeing the said Lord John, by the King
of England, on various pretexts, taken, imprisoned, stripped
of his kingdom and people, and the Kingdom of Scotland
by him also ruined and reduced to slavery, laid waste by a
mighty depopulation, and overwhelmed by the bitterness of
frequent grief, desolated from the want of right government,
exposed to every danger, and given up to the spoiler, and the
people stripped of their goods, tortured by wars, led captive,
bound, and imprisoned; by immense massacres of the innocent,
and by continual conflagrations, oppressed, subjugated and
enslaved, and on the brink of total ruin, unless by divine
guidance steps should very quickly be taken for the restoration and government of the kingdom thus marred and desolated: by the providence of the Supreme King, under whose
government kings rule and princes bear sway, being no longer
able to bear so many and so great heavy losses of things and
persons more bitter than death, often happening for want of
a captain and faithful leader, with divine sanction agreed
upon the said Lord Robert, the King who now is, in whom
the rights of his father and grandfather to the foresaid kingdom, in the judgment of the people, still exist and flourish
entire; and with the concurrence and consent of the said
people he was chosen to be King, that he might reform the
deformities of the kingdom, correct what required correction,
and direct what needed direction; and having been by their
authority set over the kingdom, he was solemnly made King
of Scots, and with him the faithful people of the kingdom
will live and die as with one who, possessing the right of
blood, and endowed with the other cardinal virtues, is fitted

to rule, and worthy of the name of King and the honour of the kingdom, since, by the grace of the Saviour, by repelling injustice, he has by the sword restored the realm thus deformed and ruined, as many former princes and kings of the Scots had by the sword restored, acquired, and held the said kingdom when often ruined in times bygone, as is more fully contained in the ancient glorious histories of the Scots, and as the warlike toils of the Picts against the Britons and of the Scots against the Picts, expelled from the kingdom, with many others anciently routed, subdued and expelled by the sword, manifestly testify; and if any one on the contrary claim right to the foresaid kingdom in virtue of letters in time past, sealed and containing the consent of the people and the commons, know ye that all this took place in fact by force and violence which could not at the time be resisted, and through multiplied fears, bodily tortures, and various terrors, enough to confound the senses and distract the minds of perfect men and fall on the steadfast. We, therefore, the Bishops, Abbots, Priors and the rest of the clergy aforesaid, knowing that the premises are based on truth, and cordially approving the same, have made due fealty to our said Lord Robert, the illustrious King of Scotland, and we acknowledge, and by the tenor of these presents publicly declare, that the same ought to be rendered to him and his heirs by our successors for ever; and in sign of testimony and approbation of all the foregoing, not compelled by force, induced by fraud, or falling through error, but of pure and lasting and spontaneous free will, have caused our seals to be affixed to this writing. Given in the General Council of Scotland, celebrated in the Church of the Friars Minor of Dundee, the twenty-fourth day of the month of February, in the year of the Lord one thousand three hundred and nine, and in the year of the said reign the fourth.

There are two versions of this document, both in Reg. Ho. The one here reproduced appears in facsimile, transcript and translation in *Nat. MSS. Scot.*, ii, No. xvii.

1315   CHARTER BY
ROBERT I TO SIR COLIN CAMPBELL

Robert, by the grace of God King of Scots, to all good men
of his whole land, greeting. Know ye that we have given,
granted and by this our present charter confirmed to our
beloved and faithful Sir Colin, son of Neil Cambel, for his
homage and service, the whole land of Louchaw and the land
of Ardscodyrthe, with the pertinents: to be held and had by
the said Colin and his heirs of us and our heirs in fee and
heritage and in a free barony by all their right bounds and
marches, in wood and plain, meadows and pastures, moors
and marshes, peataries, ways and paths, in waters, lakes, fish-
ponds and mills and with patronage of churches, in huntings
and hawkings and with all their other liberties, commodities,
easements and rightful pertinents, as well not named as named,
as freely and quietly, fully and honourably, as any of our
barons in Argyll hold or possess their baronies of us: the said
Colin and his heirs providing for us and our heirs, in return
for the said lands, one ship of forty oars in our service, with
all its pertinents and sufficient men, at the expense of the
same Colin and his heirs, for forty days, as often as they shall
be forewarned; and when we will that our host be held throughout the land, the said Colin and his heirs are to do forinsec
service for the said barony, as our other barons of Argyll
have done for their baronies. In witness whereof to this our
present charter we have ordered our seal to be appended.
Witnesses: Bernard, Abbot of Arbroath, our Chancellor [*etc.*].
At Arbroath, the 10th day of February in the 9th year of our
reign.

Facsimile in Anderson's *Diplomata*.

1315, 1318   SETTLEMENT OF SUCCESSION

*Bruce had no son until the future David II was born in 1324.
The military and political situation demanded a king, rather
than a queen regnant, and in 1315 the king's brother,*

Edward, was recognised as his heir in preference to his daughter, Marjory. Three years later, when both Edward and Marjory were dead, the succession had to be settled afresh.

(i)

In the year 1315 on [27 April], at Ayr, in the parish church of that place, the bishops, abbots, priors, deans, archdeacons and the rest of the prelates of churches, the earls, barons, knights and the rest of the community of the realm of Scotland, cleric and lay, gathered together to treat, discuss and ordain upon the state, defence and permanent security of the kingdom of Scotland, unanimously agreed and ordained in the following manner:

That each and all of them, cleric and lay, would obey and faithfully support in all things, as their king and liege lord, against all mortals, the magnificent prince their liege lord, Lord Robert, by the grace of God illustrious king of Scotland, now reigning, and the heirs male of his body lawfully to be begotten.

They also ordained with the consent of the said lord king and of his daughter Marjory, heir apparent on the day of the present ordinance, that if it happen (which God forbid) that the said lord king close the last day of his life without any surviving male heir begotten of his body, the noble man Lord Edward de Brus, brother german of the said king, as a vigorous man and as most highly skilled in warfare for the defence of the right and liberty of the realm of Scotland, and the heirs male to be lawfully begotten of his body, shall succeed the said lord king in the realm. And all the foresaid clergy and laymen will obey them in all things as king and lord in succession as is expressed above in relation to the person of the lord king and his heirs.

They ordained with the consent of the said king and of the said Lord Edward, his brother, that, failing the said Lord Edward and the heirs male lawfully descended from his body (which God forbid), the succession of the said kingdom of Scotland shall revert to the foresaid Marjory, whom failing to the nearest heir lineally descended from the body of the lord King Robert, without challenge of any man, until, with the consent of the said lord king or, whom failing (which God forbid), with the consent of the greater part of the community of the realm, the said Marjory shall be joined

52

in marriage.

They ordained that if the foresaid lord king should die, leaving as heir male a minor, or the said Lord Edward, his brother, should die in a like manner, . . . the noble man Lord Thomas Randolph, Earl of Moray, shall have guardianship of the heir and the realm until such time as it shall appear to the community of the realm, or to the greater part thereof, that the heir himself is able to undertake the rule of his realm.

They moreover ordained that if the said Marjory should die in widowhood leaving her heir a minor, . . . the said earl shall have guardianship of the heir and the realm as is expressed above in the cases of the heirs of the lord king and his brother, if the said earl shall assent thereto. If the said Marjory chance to die leaving no heir of her body and if no heir of the lord King Robert's body is surviving (which God forbid), the said earl shall have guardianship of the kingdom until he can conveniently call together the prelates, earls, barons and others of the community of the realm to ordain and discuss concerning the lawful succession and government of the kingdom. . . .

A.P.S., i, 464-5.

(ii)

[On 3 December 1318] it was ordained and by the unanimous consent of each and all [of the prelates, earls, barons and the rest of the community of the kingdom] it was agreed that if it happen (which God forbid) that the said lord king should close his last day with no male heir lawfully begotten of his body surviving, Robert, son of the Lady Marjory of good memory, daughter of the said lord king, lawfully begotten of the noble man Lord Walter, Steward of Scotland, her husband, shall fully succeed the same lord king in his kingdom as his nearest lawful heir: whom all the above shall obey in all things and faithfully support, as was above expressed of the person of the lord king.

The lord king, with the unanimous consent of one and all of the community, has assigned the guardianship or care of the said Robert, or of other heir begotten of the body of the lord king, together with the custody of the whole kingdom and people, if at the time of the decease of the lord king the heir shall be of minor age, to the noble man Sir Thomas Randolph, earl of Moray and lord of Man; and if, in the meantime, the said earl shall have chanced to die (which God forbid), to the noble man Sir James of Douglas; until such time as it shall seem to the community of the realm, or to the greater and wiser part thereof, that the said Robert, or other heir of the lord king, as above expressed, is able himself to undertake the rule of the kingdom and the people.

A.P.S., i, 465.

1316–7 CONFIRMATION BY ROBERT I TO BERNARD DE HAUDEN

This charter shows what the obligations of military service on a crown tenant involved and how they could be partially commuted for a money payment.

Robert etc. Know ye that we etc. have confirmed to Bernard de Hauden and his heirs, in place of the ward which he is obliged to do in our castle of Roxburgh (of that service which pertains to the fee of one knight, in virtue of which they are obliged to do ward), that they should give to us each year at Whitsunday 20s.: but if perchance emergency or war should arise through which they have to do their ward in our said castle, and they remain there for forty days, they are to be quit for that year of the payment of the said 20s.: and if they go in the army, in obedience to our precept, and cross the water of Forth towards the north or our march towards the south, they are to be quit for that year of the foresaid 20s.: however, whether they do their ward or pay the said money or go in the army, and an emergency occurs, they are to enter our said castle to defend it or pass to the army should need arise: and if a common aid be imposed throughout our whole land and they pay the aid which pertains to their fee, for that year they are to be quit of paying the said 20s. and of doing ward in the said castle.

Registrum Magni Sigilli, i, app. I, No. 55.

1320   LETTER OF BARONS OF SCOTLAND
TO POPE JOHN XXII
otherwise called
THE DECLARATION OF ARBROATH[1]

To our most Holy Father in Christ, and our Lord, John, by
Divine Providence chief Bishop of the most holy Roman and
Universal Church, your humble and devoted sons: Duncan
Earl of Fife, Thomas Randolph Earl of Moray, Lord of Man
and Annandale, Patrick of Dunbar, Earl of March, Malise
Earl of Strathearn, Malcolm Earl of Lennox, William Earl of
Ross, Magnus Earl of Caithness and Orkney, William Earl of
Sutherland, Walter, Steward of Scotland, William of Soulis,
Butler of Scotland, James Lord of Douglas, Roger of Mowbray,
David Lord of Brechin, David of Graham, Ingelram of Umfravil,
John of Menteith, Guardian of the earldom of Menteith,
Alexander Fraser, Gilbert of Hay, Constable of Scotland,
Robert of Keith, Marischal of Scotland, Henry of St Clair,
John of Graham, David of Lindsay, William Oliphant, Patrick
of Graham, John of Fenton, William of Abernethy, David of
Wemyss, William Muschet, Fergus of Ardrossan, Eustace of
Maxwell, William of Ramsay, William Mowat, Allan of Moray,
Donald Campbell, John Cambrun, Reginald le Cheyne,
Alexander of Seton, Andrew of Leslie, Alexander of Straton,
and the rest of the barons and freeholders, and whole
community, of the kingdom of Scotland, send all manner of
filial reverence, with devout kisses of your blessed and happy
feet.

Most holy Father and Lord, we know and gather from
ancient acts and records, that in every famous nation this of
Scotland hath been celebrated with many praises: This nation
having come from Scythia the greater, through the Tuscan
Sea and the Hercules Pillars, and having for many ages taken
its residence in Spain in the midst of a most fierce people,
could never be brought in subjection by any people, how
barbarous soever: And having removed from these parts,
above 1,200 years after the coming of the Israelites out of
Egypt, did by many victories and much toil obtain these
parts in the West which they still possess, having expelled the
Britons and entirely rooted out the Picts, notwithstanding of

1 The translation is based on one published in 1689.

55

the frequent assaults and invasions they met with from the Norwegians, Danes, and English; And these parts and possessions they have always retained free from all manner of servitude and subjection, as ancient histories do witness.

This kingdom hath been governed by an uninterrupted succession of 113 kings, all of our own native and royal stock, without the intervening of any stranger.

The true nobility and merits of those princes and people are very remarkable, from this one consideration (though there were no other evidence for it) that the King of Kings, the Lord Jesus Christ, after His Passion and Resurrection, honoured them as it were the first (though living in the outmost ends of the earth) with a call to His most Holy Faith: Neither would our Saviour have them confirmed in the Christian Faith by any other instrument than His own first Apostle [in calling] [2] (though in rank the second or third) St Andrew, the most worthy brother of the Blessed Peter, whom He would always have to be over us, as our patron or protector.

Upon the weighty consideration of these things our most Holy Fathers, your predecessors, did with many great and singular favours and privileges fence and secure this kingdom and people, as being the peculiar charge and care of the brother of St Peter; so that our nation hath hitherto lived in freedom and quietness, under their protection, till the magnificent King Edward, father to the present King of England, did under the colour of friendship and alliance, or confederacy, with innumerable oppressions infest us, who had in mind no fraud or deceit, at a time when we were without a king or head, and when the people were unacquainted with wars and invasions. It is impossible for any whose own experience hath not informed him to describe, or fully to understand, the injuries, blood and violence, the depredations and fire, the imprisonments of prelates, the burning, slaughter and robbery committed upon holy persons and religious houses, and a vast multitude of other barbarities, which that king executed on this people, without sparing of any sex or age, religion or order of men whatsoever.

But at length it pleased God, who only can heal after

2 The word 'vocatione', though necessary for the sense, is not in the version preserved in the Reg. Ho., but appears in the version engrossed in the *Scotichronicon* and was presumably in that which reached the pope.

wounds, to restore us to liberty, from these innumerable calamities, by our most serene prince, king, and lord Robert, who, for the delivering of his people and his own rightful inheritance from the enemy's hand, did, like another Joshua or Maccabeus, most cheerfully undergo all manner of toil, fatigue, hardship, and hazard. The Divine Providence, the right of succession by the laws and customs of the kingdom (which we will defend till death) and the due and lawful consent and assent of all the people, made him our king and prince. To him we are obliged and resolved to adhere in all things, both upon the account of his right and his own merit, as being the person who hath restored the people's safety in defence of their liberties. But after all, if this prince shall leave these principles he hath so nobly pursued, and consent that we or our kingdom be subjected to the king or people of England, we will immediately endeavour to expel him, as our enemy and as the subverter both of his own and our rights, and we will make another king, who will defend our liberties: For so long as there shall but one hundred of us remain alive we will never give consent to subject ourselves to the dominion of the English. For it is not glory, it is not riches, neither is it honours, but it is liberty alone that we fight and contend for, which no honest man will lose but with his life.

For these reasons, most Reverend Father and Lord, We do with earnest prayers from our bended knees and hearts, beg and entreat Your Holiness that you may be pleased, with a sincere and cordial piety, to consider that with Him whose Vicar on earth you are there is no respect nor distinction of Jew nor Greek, Scots nor English, and that with a tender and fatherly eye you may look upon the calamities and straits brought upon us and the Church of God by the English; and that you may admonish and exhort the king of England (who may well rest satisfied with his own possessions, since that kingdom of old used to be sufficient for seven or more kings) to suffer us to live at peace in that narrow spot of Scotland beyond which we have no habitation, since we desire nothing but our own, and we on our part, as far as we are able with respect to our own condition, shall effectually agree to him in every thing that may procure our quiet.

It is your concernment, Most Holy Father, to interpose in this, when you see how far the violence and barbarity of the pagans is let loose to rage against Christendom for punishing of the sins of the Christians, and how much they daily encroach upon the Christian territories. And it is your interest to notice that there be no ground given for reflecting on your memory, if you should suffer any part of the Church to come under a scandal or eclipse (which we pray God may prevent) during your times. Let it therefore please Your Holiness to exhort the Christian princes not to make the wars betwixt them and their neighbours a pretext for not going to the relief of the Holy Land, since that is not the true cause of the impediment: The truer ground of it is, that they have a much nearer prospect of advantage, and far less opposition, in the subduing of their weaker neighbours. And God (who is ignorant of nothing) knows with how much cheerfulness both our king and we would go thither, if the king of England would leave us in peace, and we do hereby testify and declare it to the Vicar of Christ and to all Christendom.

But if Your Holiness shall be too credulous of the English misrepresentations, and not give firm credit to what we have said, nor desist to favour the English to our destruction, we must believe that the Most High will lay to your charge all the blood, loss of souls, and other calamities that shall follow on either hand, betwixt us and them. Your Holiness in granting our just desires will oblige us in every case where our duty shall require it, to endeavour your satisfaction, as becomes the obedient sons of the Vicar of Christ.

We commit the defence of our cause to Him who is the Sovereign King and Judge, we cast the burden of our cares upon Him, and hope for such an issue as may give strength and courage to us and bring our enemies to nothing. The Most High God long preserve your Serenity and Holiness to His Holy Church.

Given at the Monastery of Arbroath in Scotland, the sixth day of April in the year of Grace 1320, and of our said king's reign the 15th year.

Original in Reg. Ho.; facsimile and text in *A.P.S.*, tion in Lord Cooper, *Supra Crepidam*, and in Sir James Fergusson, *The Declaration of Arbroath*.

An indenture between Robert I and his parliament, on 15 July 1326, for the levy of an extraordinary tax, indicates the presence of representatives of the burghs.

The present indenture bears witness that . . . Robert, by the grace of God the illustrious King of Scots, holding his full Parliament at Cambuskenneth, and the earls, barons, burgesses and all the other free tenants of his kingdom convening there, it was declared by the same Lord the King that the lands and rents, which used of old to belong to his Crown, had by divers donations and transfers, made on the occasion of war, been so diminished that he had not maintenance becoming his station without the intolerable burdening and grievance of his commons: Wherefore, he earnestly requested of them that, as he had sustained many hardships both in his person and in his goods for the recovery and protection of the liberty of them all, they would be pleased, from the gratitude that became them, to find a way and manner whereby he might be suitably maintained as became his station and with less grievous burden of his people; who, all and each, earls, barons, burgesses, and free tenants as well within liberties as without, holding of our Lord the King or of any other superior within the realm mediately or immediately, of what condition soever they were, considering and confessing that the foresaid reasons of our Lord the King were true, and how very many other advantages had in their times accrued to them through him, and that his request was reasonable and just, after a common and diligent discussion of the premises, unanimously, thankfully and cheerfully granted and gave to their Lord the King aforesaid annually, at the terms of Martinmas and Whitsunday proportionally, for the whole time of the life of the said King, the tenth penny of all their fermes and rents, as well of their demesne lands and wards as of their other lands whatsoever within liberties and without, as well within burghs as without, according to the old extent of lands and rents in the time of our Lord of good memory, Alexander, by the grace of God the illustrious King of Scots last deceased, to be faithfully made by his officers, the destruction of war alone excepted, in which case a deduction shall be made from the tenth penny above granted, according to the amount of the rent which for the reason foresaid can not be levied from the lands and rents foresaid, as shall be found by an inquest to be faithfully made by the sheriff of the place: provided that all such money shall be wholly applied to the use and profit of our said Lord the King, without any remission to be made to any one whatsoever; and if he shall make a donation or remission from such money before it be conveyed into the King's treasury and fully paid, the present grant shall be null and of no force nor effect. . . . On the other hand our Lord the King, weighing and considering with satisfaction the gratitude and goodwill of his people, has graciously granted to them that, from Martinmas next to come, namely, the first term of making payment, he shall not impose any collections nor take any prises or carriages,[1] unless when on a journey or in passing through the kingdom, after the manner of his predecessor King Alexander aforesaid, for which prises and carriages full payment shall be made on the nail; and that all large purveyances of the King, with their carriages, shall be made entirely without prise; and that the King's officers shall make payment in hand, without delay, for everything in making such large purveyances, according to the common market price of the country. Also it was consented and agreed between our Lord the King and the community of his kingdom that, upon the death of the said King, the grant of the tenth penny aforesaid shall immediately cease. . . . In testimony of all which, to the one part of this indenture, remaining in the hands of the said earls, barons, burgesses and free tenants, is affixed the common seal of the realm, and to the other part, remaining in the hands of our Lord the King, the seals of the earls, barons and the other greater free tenants, along with the common seals of the burghs of the kingdom, in the name of themselves and of the whole community, are of common consent affixed.

Facsimile, transcript and translation in *Nat. MSS. Scot.*, ii, No. xxvii; text in *A.P.S.*, i, 475 (cf. 483-4).

1 'Prises' were exactions, and 'carriages' the compulsory provision of men and vehicles for transport.

Bruce's struggle for the recognition of his kingdom's independence was successfully concluded by an agreement which was made on 17 March 1327/8 with English commissioners who had come to Holyrood and which was confirmed by Edward III at Northampton on 4 May following.

Firstly, that good peace, final and perpetual, be between the said kings, their heirs and successors, and their kingdoms and lands, and between their subjects and peoples, on the one part and the other, in the form which follows –

And for the assurance and confirming of this peace it is treated and accorded that a marriage be made, at the earliest that it can be duly made, between David, eldest son and heir of the said king of Scotland, and Joan, sister of the foresaid king of England, who as yet are of so tender age that they cannot make contract of matrimony; and, for the assurance of the said marriage, an oath is made on the souls of the said kings, by the persons named below, and of the prelates and other great men of the kingdom of Scotland.

And that the foresaid king of Scotland shall give and assign to the said Joan, in places suitable in his kingdom of Scotland, £2,000 of land and of rent by year. . . .

And, if it happen that God does His will of the said Joan before the said marriage be completed or accomplished, that then the said king of England, his heirs or his successors, have the marriage of the said David for another nearest and most suitable of their blood, and that she to whom he shall be so married have the said £2,000 of land. . . .

And, if it happen that God does His will of the said David before the said marriage be completed or accomplished, that then the said king of England . . . have the marriage of the next heir male of the foresaid king of Scotland for the said Joan. . . .

Item, it is treated and accorded that the said kings, their heirs and successors, shall be good friends and loyal allies, and that the one shall aid the other in suitable manner as good allies: saving on the part of the king of Scotland the alliance made between him and the king of France. But if it happen that the said king of Scotland . . . by reason of the said alliance or for any other cause whatever make war upon the said king of England, . . . that the said king of England . . . may make war on the foresaid king of Scotland. . . .

Item, it is treated and accorded that if any levy war in Ireland against the said king of England, . . . the foresaid king of Scotland . . . shall not assist the said enemies of the said king of England; also . . . that if any levy war against the foresaid king of Scotland . . . in the Isle of Man or in the other islands of Scotland, the said king of England . . . shall not assist the said enemies.

Item, . . . that all writs, obligations, instruments and other muniments touching the subjection of the people or of the land of Scotland to the king of England, the which are annulled and voided by the letters of the said king of England, and all other instruments and privileges touching the freedom of Scotland that can be found in good faith with the king of England, be given up and restored to the foresaid king of Scotland at the earliest that they can well be, according as they shall be found, so that of this delivery there be made an indenture of each writ, obligation, instrument and muniment that shall be delivered. . . .

Item, . . . that the said king of England shall assist in good faith, that the processes, if any are made in the Court of Rome and elsewhere by the authority of our Holy Father the Pope against the said king of Scotland, his realm and his subjects, cleric or lay, be dismissed, with their effect; and this to do and accomplish he shall send his special letters of prayer to the pope and the cardinals.

Item, . . . forasmuch as the said king of Scotland, the prelates and other great men of his realm, are bound to the said king of England in £20,000 sterling, to be paid in three years at three terms at Tweedmouth, and for the making of this payment have submitted themselves to the jurisdiction of the papal *camera* . . . , nevertheless the said messengers and procurators of the king of England in his name will and grant for certain reasons that no execution, condemnation or denunciation be made by any judge of the papal *camera* against the said king of Scotland or the others bound, until the end of two months after each term of the said three terms. . . .

Original in Reg. Ho. Facsimile, transcript and translation in *Nat. MSS. Scot.*, ii, No. xxvi; text and translation in Stones, *op. cit.*, 164-70.

1329 CHARTER BY
ROBERT I TO THE BURGH OF EDINBURGH

Robert, by the grace of God King of Scots, to all good men of his whole land, greeting. Know ye that we have given, granted and set in feu-ferm and by this our present charter confirmed to the burgesses of our burgh of Edinburgh our foresaid burgh of Edinburgh, with the harbour of Leith, its mills and the rest of its pertinents: to be held and had by the same burgesses and their successors of us and our heirs freely, quietly, fully and honourably, by all its right bounds and marches, with all the commodities, liberties and easements which were wont rightly to pertain to the said burgh in the time of King Alexander of good memory, our predecessor last deceased: rendering therefor yearly, the said burgesses and their successors to us and our heirs, fifty-two merks sterling[1] at Whitsunday and Martinmas by equal portions. In witness whereof we have ordered our seal to be appended to this our present charter. Witnesses: Walter of Twynham, our Chancellor, Thomas Randolph, Earl of Moray, Lord of Annandale and Man, our nephew, James, Lord of Douglas, Gilbert Hay, our Constable, Robert Keith, our Marischal of Scotland, and Adam More, knights. At Cardross, the 29th day of May in the 24th year of our reign.

> Original in the archives of the city of Edinburgh; text and translation in *Charters and other documents relating to the City of Edinburgh* (Scottish Burgh Records Society).

1 £34. 3s. 4d. A similar feu charter to Aberdeen in 1319 stipulated for a payment of £213. 6s. 8d., and one to Berwick in 1320 for £333. 6s. 8d.

1357 TREATY OF BERWICK

David II, leading an invasion of England in 1346, had been captured at Neville's Cross. By a treaty made on 3 October 1357 by English and Scottish commissioners it was agreed that he should be 'liberated from prison and ransomed' on the following terms.

63

That is to say for one hundred thousand merks sterling to be paid during the ten years next following the making of this agreement by these instalments, that is to say the ten thousand merks of the first payment at the Feast of the Nativity of St John the Baptist next to come [24 June], and other ten thousand merks on the Feast of the Nativity of St John the Baptist thereafter next following, and so from year to year ten thousand merks on the same Feast of the Nativity of St John until the said sum of one hundred thousand merks shall have been fully paid. . . .

A truce shall be confirmed and observed by sufficient surety of letters and oaths between the king of England and all his good people in England and in Scotland, and also in the Isle of Man, and the king of Scotland and all the other people of Scotland and their adherents, by land and by sea, in all parts and places, without fraud or guile, until the said sum shall have been fully paid. And that Edward Balliol and John of the Isles and all other allies and adherents of the king of England shall be included in the said truce. . . .

In case of default of payment at any of the said terms, the said king of Scotland, without other request or delay, shall come to England and give himself up as a prisoner of the king of England in the castle of Newcastle on Tyne within the three weeks next following the said term at which payment is in default, to remain a prisoner until payment of the arrears be made. .

A.P.S., i, 518-21.

1357 LEGISLATION FOR GOOD GOVERNMENT

These acts, passed in the year of David II's return from captivity, reflect some of the perennial problems of Scottish administration and represent a programme which successive kings strove to carry out but which was not fulfilled in its entirety until the seventeenth century. They should be compared, in particular, with the legislation of James I (pp. 76-81 below).

Item, that [the king] appoint good and sufficient sheriffs and coroners who know and are able to exercise their offices and to do justice to every man, as is fitting; and who also have good and sufficient bailies and officers for whom they must answer. And if any have been infeft in these offices of old, and shall be unable in their own persons to exercise those offices, then in that case they shall present to the lord king other good and sufficient officers to exercise the said offices in their places, for whom they must answer.

Item, it is ordained that the said lord our king, during his lifetime, shall call back into his hands all lands, rents and possessions, and customs, given and granted by him to any persons of any estate whatsoever; and that all lands, rents and possessions which of old were wont to pertain to the demesne and royal crown shall remain in the hands of the king wholly and for ever without any alienation whatever, and he shall live on them; so that the community of the kingdom, already burdened with the payment of the king's ransom, may not be further burdened for his expenses. And that the lord king renew the oath which he formerly took at his coronation, namely, that he will not alienate his demesne lands, possessions or rents whatsoever pertaining to the crown; and that, without mature counsel, whatever has been revoked of lands and wardships or rents shall not be alienated. . . .

Item, that firm peace shall be observed and kept everywhere throughout the whole realm among all the subjects of our lord the king who are within his peace, so that no one henceforth make war against his neighbours under the full pain of forfeiture. And that this be proclaimed publicly in the present council. . . .

Item, that all burghs and burgesses shall freely enjoy all their rights, liberties and privileges which they were wont to have in time of peace. And that henceforth no one presume to oppress them unjustly, either within burghs or without, under the pain of breaking the king's protection. . . .

Item, that all foreign merchants, from wheresoever they come, be allowed to enter peacefully to buy and to sell, as was lawfully wont before; and that all good coinage of the king of England, of gold or silver, be accepted throughout the kingdom of Scotland at the true value at which it is current in England.

A.P.S., i, 492.

1363–4 PROPOSALS FOR
SETTLEMENT WITH ENGLAND

Both during his captivity and after his release David was prepared to consider an arrangement whereby his successor on the Scottish throne would not be his statutory heir Robert the Steward, his nephew, but a member of the English royal house. Tentative proposals for a personal union of the two kingdoms, with safeguards for Scottish integrity, were formulated in November 1363 but were rejected by the Scottish parliament in the following March.

The king of Scotland should sound the estates of his realm as to whether they would agree and decide that, if the said king of Scotland should die without an heir[1] begotten of his body, the said king of England and his heirs, the kings of England, should succeed to the kingdom of Scotland in heritage. [Should this be accepted,] the king of England shall cause to be handed over the town, castle and surroundings of Berwick, the town and castle of Roxburgh and the castles of Jedburgh and Lochmaben, all with their respective surroundings, and all other lands occupied and held by the English[2] in which King Robert, father of the said king of Scotland, was vest and seised at the time of his death. It is agreed that the whole sum of money due for the ransom shall be discharged, the hostages released and obligations and bonds relating to the ransom surrendered. . . . The name and title of the realm of Scotland shall be preserved and maintained with honour and with due distinction, without union or annexation with the realm of England; and the king shall be styled, in his letters and otherwise, 'King of England and of Scotland'. After having been crowned king of England, the king shall come to the realm of Scotland to be crowned as king at Scone, on the royal seat, which he is to cause to be given up by England. . . . At his coronation he shall swear to maintain the freedom of the holy Church of Scotland, so that it shall be subject to no archbishop but only to the apostolic see; to maintain the laws, statutes and customs of the kingdom of Scotland as established under the good kings of Scotland of the past; and that he will

1 Later in the document the phrase is 'heir male'.
2 In 1334 Edward Balliol, as vassal king of Scotland, had surrendered Berwick and the southern counties to Edward III.

66

in no way summon or constrain the people of Scotland to
compear in England or elsewhere outwith where they ought;
. . . and that no bishoprics, dignities or other benefices in the
Scottish Church shall be conferred on any save Scotsmen. . . .
[He shall also swear that all officers of state, sheriffs, provosts,
bailies, constables and other officers shall be Scotsmen; that
he will hold and maintain the prelates, earls, barons and all
freeholders in their franchises, lands, rents and possessions;
and that he will impose no new exactions upon the realm of
Scotland.] Finally, the king of Scotland shall try out these
proposals on his people and shall inform the king of England
and his council of their will, within fifteen days after Easter
next to come [7 April 1364] or earlier if conveniently
possible.

A.P.S., i, 493-4.

In the parliament held at Scone on 4 March 1363[/4] . . . there
having assembled and compeared the prelates and nobles of
the kingdom who ought to be and could conveniently be
there present, certain matters were explained and read . . .
which had been touched upon and spoken of between the
council of the king of England and others who had lately been
with our lord the king in London, on the acceptance of which
matters peace would thereupon be obtained and confirmed.
And it was there expressly replied by the three estates that
they were in no manner willing to accept, nor in any
wise willing to assent to, those matters which had been sought
by the king of England and his council as is above noted. . . .

A.P.S., i, 492-3.

1364   GENERAL CHARTER TO BURGHS

David, by the grace of God king of Scots, to all good men of
his whole land, cleric and lay, greeting: Know ye that we, with
[consent of our] council, have granted to our beloved
Scottish burgesses free leave to buy and sell everywhere within the liberties of their own burghs, but forbidding any of
them to buy or sell within the bounds of the liberty of

another [burgh] without licence. Also we forbid any bishop, prior or other churchman, any earl, baron or other layman, of whatever rank, to buy or sell wool, skins, hides or other merchandise under any pretext, save only from [or to] the merchants of the burghs within whose liberties they live; and so that the merchants may buy, we order them to display, and to offer to the merchants, effectually and without fraud, all such merchandise at the market-place and cross of the burgh, and to pay there the king's customs. Also we forbid any foreign merchants, coming with ships and merchandise, to sell any kind of merchandise except to the merchants of our burghs, or to buy anything except through the hands of the merchants of the burghs, under pain of our royal punishment.[1] And we confirm by the tenor of our present charter that these privileges, liberties and constitutions shall endure for all time.

Records of the Convention of Royal Burghs, i, 540.

1 The meaning of *defensio* may well be specifically forfeiture.

1373   SETTLEMENT OF SUCCESSION

On the death of David II (1371), Robert the Steward succeeded, in terms of an act of 1318,[1] and immediately after his coronation his eldest son, John, Earl of Carrick (later Robert III), was acknowledged as his heir. There was, however, some doubt about the legitimacy of the Steward's family by his first wife, Elizabeth Mure, and in order to secure them against the descendants of his second, and unquestionably legal, marriage to Euphemia Ross, an act was passed on 4 April 1373 which amounted to an entail of the crown.

King Robert, holding his parliament at Scone, and wishing and desiring to avoid to the best of his ability the uncertainty of the succession and the evils and misfortunes which, in very many kingdoms and places, arise and in times past have arisen from the succession of female heirs, and to avoid these for himself and his people, especially in times to come,

1 pp. 53-4.

Of deliberate counsel, and with the consent and assent of
the prelates, earls, barons and the rest of the magnates and
nobles and of all others of the three estates or communities
of the whole realm there assembled,

Declared, ordained and enacted that the sons of the king,
of his first and second wives, now born, and their heirs male
only, shall succeed in turn to the said king in his kingdom
and in the right of reigning in the manner and under the form
and conditions underwritten, namely,

That the lord John, earl of Carrick and Steward of Scotland,
the first-born son of the same king, for the right of whose
succession a declaration had been fully made in the immediately preceding parliament, and his heirs male only, shall,
after his death, succeed him in the kingdom and in the right
of reigning; and failing the said lord John and his heirs male
(which God forbid), the lord Robert, earl of Fife and Menteith,
the second-born son of the same lord king by his first wife, and
his heirs male only, shall in turn and immediately succeed to
the kingdom and the right of reigning; and failing also the
said lord Robert and such heirs of his (which God forbid), the
lord Alexander, lord of Badenoch, the third-born son of the
same lord king by the same wife, and his heirs male only, shall,
after their death, in turn and immediately, likewise succeed
to the kingdom and the right of reigning; and failing likewise
the said lord Alexander and his foresaid heirs (which God
forbid), the lord David, earl of Strathearn, son of the same lord
the king by his second wife, and his heirs male only, shall in
turn and immediately likewise succeed to the kingdom and
the right of reigning; and failing likewise the said lord David
and his heirs aforesaid, Walter, son of the same lord king,
brother-german to the said lord David, and his heirs male
only, shall likewise succeed to the kingdom and the right of
reigning; and the foresaid five brothers and their heirs male
descending from them happening finally and wholly to fail
(which God forbid), the true and lawful heirs of the royal
blood and kin shall thenceforward succeed to the kingdom
and the right of reigning.

Original in Reg. Ho.; text in *A.P.S.*, i, 549.

Neither the ageing Robert II (1371-90) nor the infirm Robert III (1390-1406) possessed the energy which the times required and which alone could have established effective government under a new royal house lacking both the prestige and the wealth which might have enabled it to meet the challenge of its mighty subjects. In the last two decades of the fourteenth century there are many illustrations of prevailing disorder and on 27 January 1398/9 a general council at Perth passed this act.

Quhare it is deliveryt that the mysgouvernance of the reaulme and the defaut of the kepyng of the common law sulde be imput to the kyng and his officeris: and tharfore gife it lykeis oure lorde the kyng til excuse his defautes he may at his lykyng gerre[1] calle his officeris to the quhilkis he hes giffyn commission and accuse thaim in presence of his consail: and thair ansuere herde the consail sal be redy to juge thair defautes, syn na man aw to be condampnyt quhil[2] he be callit and accusit.

Item sen it is wele sene and kennyt that oure lorde the kyng for seknes of his person may nocht travail to governe the realme na restreygne trespassours and rebellours it is sene to the consail maste expedient that the duc of Rothesay be the kyngis lieutenande generally throch al the kynrike for the terme of thre yhere, hafande ful powere and commission of the kyng to governe the lande in all thyng as the kyng sulde do in his person gife he warre present: that is to say to punys trespassours, till restreygne trespassis and to trete and remitte with the condicions efter folowande, that is to say that he be oblygit be his letteris and suorne til governe his person and the office til hym committit with the consail general and in the absence of thaim with the consail of wyse men and lele, of the quhilkis there arre the namys: in the firste the duc of Albany, the lorde of Brechyn, the byschopis of Andriston, Glasgu and Aberden, the erlys of Douglas, of Ross, of Moref and Crauforde, the lorde of Dalketh, Schir Thomas the Hay, constable, Schir Wilyhem of Keth, marchal, Schir Thomas of Erskyne, Schir Patrik the Graham, Schir John

1 cause.   2 until.

of Levynston, Schir Wilyhem Stewart, Schir John of Remorgny, Adam Forstar, the abbot of Halyrudehous, the archiden of Louthyan and Maister Water Forstar; the quhilkis consail general and special sal be obligit be thair letteris and suorne til gife hym lele consail for the common profite, nocht hafande ee[3] to fede[4] na freyndschyp, ande in efter the said duc be suorne til fulfyl efter his power all the thyngis that the kyng in his crownyng wes suorne for til do to haly kyrke and the pupyl syn in to thir thyngis he is to ber the kyngis power, that is to say the fredume and the rycht of the kirke to kepe undamyste the lawys and the lovable custumes to gerre be kepit to the pupil, manslaerys, reiferis, brynneris and generaly all mysdoeris thruch strynthe till restreygnhe and punyse and specialy cursit men, heretikis and put fra the kyrke at the requeste of the kyrke to restreygne, and that the kyng be obliste that he sal nocht lette his office na the execucion of it be na contremandmentis as sumquhile has bene seyne and gife ocht be done in the contrare be letteris or ony other maner thruch our lorde the kyngis bydding that contremandment be of na valu na of effect na the forsaid lieutenant be nocht haldyn tyl ansuere suylke contremandmentis na be nocht essoynyhet thruch vertu of thaim that he doys nocht his office.

> This act, printed (with a facsimile) in *A.P.S.*, i, 572-3, is taken from a transcript in the handwriting of perhaps two generations later, and it is not certain that the precise terminology of 1399 has been preserved.

3 eye.
4 feud.

1399 CHARTER BY
ROBERT III TO GEORGE LESLEY

This document is inserted simply as a style, taken at random to illustrate the processes of conveyancing under a fully developed feudal system of landholding.

Robert, by the grace of God King of Scots, to all good men of his whole land, cleric and lay, greeting. Know ye that we have granted to our beloved cousin George of Lesley, knight, and Elizabeth, his spouse, our niece, heritably, all and whole the barony of Fytkill, with the pertinents, lying in the sheriffdom of Fyff; which barony, with the pertinents, belonged heritably to our beloved cousin Alexander of Lesley, Earl of Ross, who, not led by force or fear nor falling into error but of his pure and free will, upgave and purely and simply resigned the same into our hands by his letters patent, in presence of most of the magnates of our realm, barons, knights and nobles, and for him and his heirs entirely discharged for ever all right and claim which he had, or could have, in the said barony with the pertinents: to be held and had all and whole the foresaid barony with the pertinents by the said George and Elizabeth, his spouse, the survivor and the heirs lawfully begotten or to be begotten between them, whom perchance failing by the true and lawful nearest heirs whomsoever of the said George, of us and our heirs in fee and heritage for ever by all right ancient bounds and divises, in woods, plains, moors, marshes, ways, paths, meadows, parks and pasturages, mills, multures and their sequels, hawkings, huntings and fishings, smithies and brewhouses, with pit and gallows, *sok, sak, tholl, theme, infangandethefe* and *outfangandthefe*,[1] with tenandries and services of free tenants, with courts, escheats and the issues of courts and with all manner of other liberties, commodities, easements and rightful pertinents whatsoever pertaining to the said barony with the pertinents or in any manner able to pertain thereto in the future, as well not named as named, as well under the earth as above the earth, near and far, freely, quietly, fully, wholly and honourably, well and in peace: the said George and Elizabeth his spouse and the survivor and the heirs lawfully begotten or to be begotten between them, whom perchance failing the true, lawful and nearest heirs whomsoever of the said George, rendering to us and our heirs, from the said barony with the pertinents, yearly at the term of Whitsunday, at the mercat cross of Cupar, a pair of gloves in name of blench ferm if it be asked only, for the wards, marriages and reliefs, suits of court and all manner of other secular services, exactions or

1 These ancient Anglo-Saxon terms were repeated as words of style long after they had ceased to have any meaning.

demands which in time to come can be exacted in any manner or required by us or our heirs from the said barony with the pertinents. In witness whereof we have ordered our seal to be appended to this our present charter. Witnesses: the venerable fathers in Christ Walter and Gilbert, our chancellor, bishops of St. Andrews and Aberdeen, our dearest first-born David, Duke of Rothesay, Earl of Carrick and Steward of Scotland, Robert, Duke of Albany, Earl of Fife and Menteith, our beloved brother, Archibald, Earl of Douglas, Lord of Galloway, James of Douglas, Lord of Dalkeith, and Thomas of Erskyne, our beloved cousins, knights. At Perth the 5th day of February in the 9th year of our reign.

Facsimile in Anderson's *Diplomata*.

1423   TREATY OF LONDON

James I had been captured by the English when on his way to France by sea in 1406 and remained a prisoner until released on the following terms.

Inprimis that the said lord James, king of Scots, or his heirs or successors kings of Scots, shall well and faithfully pay to the foresaid lord Henry, king of England and France, or his heirs or successors, or their deputes, in the Church of St Paul, London, in England, for the maintenance and expenses of the same lord king James during the time he has been in the kingdom of England and elsewhere in the company of the kings of England and the time he shall be in England until the day on which he shall have entered the kingdom of Scotland, or on which he shall be deemed to have entered, forty thousand pounds of good and legal money of England, to wit, in the foresaid Church of St Paul, ten thousand merks of the foresaid money within six months reckoned from the first day of his entry into the kingdom [of Scotland], or from the first day on which he shall be deemed to have entered; and each year thereafter following . . . ten thousand merks until the said forty thousand pounds shall have been fully and wholly paid. . . .

Item, that on the first day of the month of March next to come, the commissioners of the foresaid Henry, king of England and France, deputed or to be deputed thereto, and the foresaid James, king of Scots, and the ambassadors for and on behalf of the foresaid kingdom of Scotland, or others to be appointed in their places, shall meet in the church of Durham, namely in order that the said King James and the commissioners of the foresaid kingdom of Scotland may hand over and deliver to the commissioners of the foresaid king of England and France, on the same first day, or at least before the last day of the same month of March, the persons who are to be given over and delivered as hostages for the handing over of the said king James, and as security for the observance of the appointment. Item that the said king James or the commissioners of the kingdom of Scotland aforesaid, shall really and in effect hand over and deliver to the foresaid commissioners and deputes of the foresaid king of England and France, or of his heirs or successors, kings of England, before the foresaid last day of March, in the city of Durham, for security for the payment of the said forty thousand pounds and the keeping of this appointment, the persons of the hostages whose names are contained in the schedule annexed to the presents or other hostages of like value in temporal property and rents who are to be acceptable to the foresaid commissioners of the foresaid king of England or his heirs and successors; and in handing over the hostages the ambassadors and commissioners of the kingdom of Scotland aforesaid shall swear, each severally touching the holy gospels of God, that the persons thus to be handed over as hostages are indeed the persons agreed upon as hostages and not other individuals impersonating them or pretending to be them.

Item, that within the same month of March the foresaid king James or the ambassadors or commissioners of the foresaid kingdom of Scotland shall deliver and hand over to the commissioners of the said Henry, king of England and France, or his heirs and successors, four letters obligatory of the four underwritten burghs or towns of the kingdom of Scotland, sealed with the common seals of the said burghs or towns, according to the form laid down in the schedule annexed hereto, saving always any change in the names of the same

towns or burghs and of their provosts, bailies or rulers, namely
One of the burgh of Edinburgh.
One of the burgh of Perth, commonly called St Johnston.
One of the burgh of Dundee.
One of the burgh of Aberdeen.

Rotuli Scotiae, ii, 241.

1424–28   LEGISLATION OF JAMES I

From the fourteenth century to the sixteenth, almost reign by reign, the Acts of the Parliaments of Scotland *contain statutes indicative of an understanding of the existence of constitutional, judicial, economic and social problems and of a readiness to try to solve them. There is insufficient evidence to show how far the statutes were observed, and the very repetition of some of them may itself suggest that the proposed solutions were ineffective. Certainly a good deal of this legislation is significant mainly of good intentions.*

Several of the acts of James I are printed below. The first seven of them reflect a general concern for ordered govern-ment and for the enforcement of the law, but others have points of special interest. Nos. 8 and 9 are directed to the recovery and conservation of the financial resources of the crown, in the shape of the customs, the mails or rents payable from royal burghs, and the royal lands. Nos. 10-12[1] were designed to curb transactions by ambitious clerics who sought appointments from the papal court, to the prejudice of the rights of the lawful patrons, and who spent Scottish money in furthering their ends. Nos. 13 and 14 were intended to divert the king's subjects from un-profitable sports like football to practice in archery, which would serve for the defence of the realm. No. 15, in legislating about beggars, indicated certain rules which long obtained in Scottish poor law. No. 16, for uniformity of law throughout the realm, may have been directed especially at Galloway, where peculiar local laws seem to have survived,

1 The numbering beyond No. 9 is editorial, and not that of the *Acts of the Parliaments.*

*but it had its relevance to the Highlands as well. In No. 17
we find the concept of a standing central court for civil
justice and the germ of the idea which ultimately produced
the Court of Session, though the final solution was to be
found in a development from the council and not, as suggested
here, from the three estates in parliament. Nos. 18 and 19 relate to the composition of parliaments and general councils.
In the first of them the king insisted on the personal attendance of all barons and freeholders as well as prelates and earls,
but in the second provision was made instead for representation
of small barons and free tenants by shire commissioners. No. 20,
relating to crafts in burghs, was an attempt to solve a persistent
problem: it appears from acts of 1426 and 1427 that, while
deacons of crafts could have useful functions in supervising
workmanship, there were suspicions about the conspiratorial
nature of the meetings of craftsmen which they convened —
suspicions which were to be voiced again in 1493 and 1555;
the act of 1428 provided that 'wardens' of the crafts were to
be appointed by the burgh council.*

1424

1 In the first to the honour of God and halikirk that
the halikirk and the ministeris of it joise and bruk[2] thar aulde
privilegis and fredomys and that na man let[3] thame to set
thar landis and teyndis under all payne that may folowe be
spirituale law or temporall.

2 Item that ferme and sikkir[4] pece be kepit and haldin
throu all the realme and amangis all and sindry liegis and
subjectis of our soveran lorde the kyng. And that na man tak
on hande in tyme to cum to amuff[5] or mak weire aganis
otheris under all payne that may folowe be course of common
lawe.

3 Item it is statut and ordanyt that na man opinly or
notourly rebell aganis the kyngis persone under the payne
of forfautour of lif landis and guidis.

4 Item it is statut and ordanyt that gif ony disobeyis till
inforse the kyng aganis notoure rebellouris aganis his persone
quhene thai be requiryt be the kyng and commandit thai
salbe chalangit be the kyng as fautouris[6] of sik rebellyng bot
gif thai haif for thame resonable excusacioun.

2 enjoy.	3 hinder.	4 firm and sure.
5 move.	6 favourers.	

5 Item it is statut that na man of quhat estate degre or condicioun he be of rydande or gangande in the cuntre leide nor haif ma personis with him na may suffice him or till his estate and for the quhilkis he will mak full and redy payment. And gif ony complaynt be of sik ridaris or gangaris the kyng commandis his officiaris of the lande that quhar thai happin to be till arest thame and put thame under sikkir borowis[7] quhill the kyng be certifyit tharof and haif saide his will quhat salbe done to sic trespassouris.

6 Item it is ordanyt that thar be maide officiaris and ministeris of lawe throu all the realme that can and may halde the law to the kingis commonis and sik as has sufficiently of thar awin quhar throughe thai mai be punyst gif thai trespass. And gif ony be infeft of sik officis of befor and ar nocht sufficient to minister to thame in propir persone that utheris be ordanyt in thar stedis for the quhilkis thai that has sik officis of the king in fee be haldin to answer to him gif thai trespass.

7 Item the parliament statutis and the kyng forbiddis that ony cumpanyis pas in the cuntre lyand apone ony the kingis liegis or thig[8] or sojorne horsis outher on kirkmen or husbandis of the lande. And gif ony complaynt be maid on sic trespassouris to the scheref of the lande that he arest sic folkis and chalange thame as brekaris of the kyngis pece taxand the kingis scathis apone thame. And gif thai be convyct of sic trespassis that thai be punyst and fynde borowis[9] bath till assithe[10] the kyng and the party plenyeande. And gif sik trespassouris takis ony skaythe in the aresting of thame it salbe imput to thame self and in case that na complaynt be maide to the schref the schref sall inquyre at ilke hede court that he haldis gif ony sik faltouris be within his schrefdome. And gif ony beis fundin that thai be punyst as is befor writtyne.

8 Item it is consentyt throu the hail parliament that all the gret and smal custumys and buroumaillis of the realme byde and remane with the king till his leving. And gif ony maner of persone makis ony clame till ony part of the saide custumis that he schawe to the king quhat he has for him and the king sall mak him ansuer with avisment of his counsall.

---

7 sure pledges.
8 beg, presumably with violence.
9 pledges.
10 satisfy or compensate.

9 Item anentis the landis and rentis the quhilkis war of befor tyme our soverane lorde the kingis antecessouris it is sene speidful that the king charge all and sindrie schrefis of his realme to gar inquyre be the best eldest and worthiest of thar bailyereis quhat landis possessionis or annuell rentis pertenys to the king or has pertenyt in his antecessouris tymes of gude memour David Robert and Robert his progenitouris and in quhais handis thai nowe be and at ilk schref gar retour the inquest under his seil and thair seilis that beis apone it. And gif it likis the king he may ger[11] summonde all and sindry his tenandis at lauchfull day and place to schawe thar charteris and evidentis and swa be thar haldingis he may persave quhat pertenys to thame.

A.P.S., ii, 3-4.

10 Item it is statut be the haill parliament and the king forbiddis that na clerk pass nor sende procuratour for him over the see but[12] special leif of our lorde the king askit and obtenyt.

11 Item in lykewys it is statut be the haill parliament and the king forbiddis that ony clerk of his realme in tyme to cum purches ony pensione out of ony benefice secular or religious under all payne that he may tyne[13] aganis the kingis maiestie or rais ony pensioun grantit in tyme bygane in ony maner of wayis under the panis forsaide.

12 Item it is ordanit that na man haf out of the realme golde nor silver bot he pay xl d. of ilk punde of custum to the king under the payne of tynsal[14] of all gold and silver at beis fundyn and x lb. to the king for the unlawe.

13 Item it is statut and the king forbiddis that na man play at the fut ball under the payne of iiij d. . . .

A.P.S., ii, 5.

14 Item it is ordanyt that all men busk thame[15] to be archaris fra thai be xij yeris of eilde. And that in ilk x lib. worth of lande thar be maid bowmerkis and specialy nere paroche kirkis quhare upone haly dais men may cum and at the lest schute thrise about and haif usage of archary. . . .

A.P.S., ii, 6.

11 cause.
12 without.
13 lose.

14 loss.
15 equip themselves.

15 Item it is ordanyt that na thiggar be thollyt to thigg[16] nother in burgh nor to land betuix xiiii and lxx yeris of age bot thai be sene be the consall of the toun or the commonis of the cuntre that thai may nocht wyn thar leffing otherwayis and thai that sa beis fundyn sall have a certane takyn[17] to landwart of the schireff and in burowis of the aldermen and balyeis and all uther personys haifande na taikynnis nother of lande na of burghe salbe chargyt be oppin proclamatioune to laubour and to pass to craftis for wynning of thar leving and that under payn of birninge on the cheyk and bannyssing of the cuntre.[18]

A.P.S., ii, 8.

1426

16 It is ordanit be the king with the consent and deliverance of the thre estatis that all and sindry the kingis liegis of the realme leif and be governyt undir the kingis lawis and statutis of this realme alanerly and undir na particulare lawis na speciale prevalegis na be na lawis of uther cuntreis nor realmis.

A.P.S., ii, 9.

17 Item oure soverane lorde the king withe consent of his parliament has ordanit that his chancellare and with him certane discret personis of the thre estatis to be chosyn ande depute be oure soverane lorde the king sall syt fra hyne furthe thre tymis in the yere quhare the king likis to commande thaim, quhilk sal knaw, examyn, conclude and finally determyn all and sindry complayntis, causis and querellis that may be determynit befor the kingis consal. The quhilk personis sal hafe thare expensis of the partiis fundyn fautyce[19] and of thar unlawis[20] or uthir ways as beis plesande to our soverane lorde the king.

A.P.S., ii, 11.

16 no beggar be suffered to beg.
17 token.
18 The substance of this act was repeated in James II's reign, and again in James V's, when this addition was made: 'that na beggaris be tholit to beg in ane parochine that ar born in ane uther and that the hedismen of ilk parochine mak taikynnis and geve to the beggaris thairof and that thai be sustenit within the boundis of that parochine and that nane uther be servit with almous within that parochine bot thai that beris that takin alanerlie' (*A.P.S.*, ii, 347-8).
19 at fault.
20 fines.

18 Item the king and the hail parliament hes ordanit ande
statute that all prelatis erlis baronnis and frehaldaris of the
king within the realme sen thai are haldyn to geif thare
presens in the kingis parliament ande general consale fra thin
furth be haldyn till appere in propir persone ande nocht be
a procuratoure bot gif that procuratour allege ande prufe
lauchfull cause of his absens.

A.P.S., ii, 9.

1428

19 Item the king with consent of his hail consal general
has statute and ordanit that the smal baronnis and fre tenandis
nede nocht to cum to parliament nor general consalys swa
that of ilk schrefdome thare be sende chosyn at the hede
court of the schrefdome twa or ma wismen efter the largeness
of the schrefdome, outetane[21] the schrefdomis of Clakmannan
and Kynross of the quhilkis ane be sende of ilk ane of thaim,
the quhilk salbe callit commissaris of the schire.

Ande be thir commissaris of all the schiris sall be chosyn a
wise and ane expert mann callit the common spekar of the
parliament the quhilk sal propone all and sindry nedis and
causis pertening to the commonis in the parliament or generall
consal. The quhilkis commissaris sal haf ful ande playn powere
of al the laif[22]. of the schrefdome under the witnessing of the
schreffis sele and with the selis of divers baronnis of the
schire to here treit ande finally to determyn all causis to be
proponit in consale or parliament.

The quhilkis commissaris and spekaris sal have thare costage
of thaim of ilk schire at aw comperance in the parliament or
consal.. . . .

All bischoppis abbotis prioris dukis erlis lordes of parliament
and banrentis, the quhilkis the king wil, be reservit and
summonde to consalis and to parliamentis be his special
precep.

A.P.S., ii, 15.

20 Anentis the men of craftis in burowis, it is sene spedfull
ande the king with the hail consal has ordanit for a yere that
of every craft thare salbe chosyn a wardane be the consal of
the burgh the quhilk wardane with consale of uthir discret

21 except.
22 remainder.

men unsuspect assignyt til hym be the said consal sal examyn
ande pryse the mater and the werkmanschip of ilk craft and
sett it to a certane price, the quhilkis gif ony brekis the said
wardane sal punyss the brekaris in certane payn, quhame gif
he punyss nocht the alderman, balyeis and consal of the
burgh sall punyss in certane payn, quhame gif thai punyss
nocht the king sal hafe a certane payn of the burgh: the payn
of the brekaris of the price salbe the eschet of the samyn
thing of the quhilk the price beis brokyn of, . . . the payn of
the prisar gif he be negligent and punyss nocht salbe the unlaw
of the borow court, . . . the payn of the alderman, balyeis
and the consal of the burgh that beis negligent . . . salbe in
x lib. to the king . . . : the quhilk ordinance salbe extendit to
masonis, wrychtis, smythis, talyeouris, webstaris and all
uthiris elik generally quhais feis and handilling sal be prisit
as it is befor saide. And attour to landewart in scherefdomis
ilk baron sal ger pryse in thare baronryis ande punyss the
trespassouris as the wardane dois in the borowis, ande gif
the barone dois nocht the scheref sal punyss the barone, ande
gif the scheref dois nocht thai salbe in amerciament to the
king . . .

A.P.S., ii, 15

1455   ACT OF ANNEXATION

*There came to be a well understood practice that a Scottish
king, usually in his twenty-fifth year, passed an act of
revocation by which he recalled to the crown all gifts of
lands and revenues which had been made, to the possible
prejudice of the royal resources, during his minority. The
following act was made in James II's twenty-fifth year, but
special significance attaches to it in that it followed the
overthrow of the 'Black Douglases' and the forfeiture to the
crown of their vast possessions. Certain former Douglas
property was specified in the schedule, appended to the act,
of lands which were to remain inalienably with the crown.*

Forsamekill as the poverte of the crowne is oftymis the cause
of the poverte of the realme and mony uther inconvenientis
the quhilkis war lang to expreyme, be the avyse of the full
consale of the parliament it is statute and ordanyt that in ilk
part of the realme for the kingis residence quhar it sall happyn
him to be thar be certane lordschippis and castellys annext
to the crowne perpetualy to remane, the quhilk may not be
giffyn away nother in fee nor in franktenement till ony
persone of quhat estate or degre that ever he be but[1] avyse,
deliverance and decret of the haill parliament ande for great
seande[2] and resonable causis of the realme, and albeit it
happyn our soverane lorde that now is or ony of his successouris kingis of Scotlande till analy[3] or dispone apon the lordschippis and castellys annext to the crowne as is befor saide,
thai alienacionis or disposicionis salbe of nane avale, sa that
it salbe lefull to the king beyng for the tyme to ressaif thai
landis quhen ever him likis till his awne use but[1] ony process
of law and the takaris sall refunde all profettis that thai haif
takin up of thai landis agane to the king for all the tyme that
thai hade thame ande that our soverane lorde that now is be
sworne and in lik maner all his successouris kingis of Scotlande
in to thar coronacione to the keping of this statute and all
the poyntis tharof.

A.P.S., ii, 42.

1 without.
2 fitting.
3 alienate.

1462 TREATY OF WESTMINSTER-ARDTORNISH

*Overmighty subjects could not only weaken the crown and
make the task of government difficult; they could ally with
England and threaten the integrity of the realm. In the
minority of James III, the Lord of the Isles (who was also
Earl of Ross) became a pensioner of the English king and
entered into a pact for the partition of Scotland, with the
forfeited and exiled Earl of Douglas.[1]*

1 The treaty was sealed and signed at London on 13 February 1461/2 and

. . . It is appointed . . . that . . . John de Isle, erle of Rosse, Donald Balagh and John of Isles, son and heire apparent to the seid Donald, with all there subgettez, men, people and inhabitantes of the seid erldom of Rosse and Isles aboveseid, shall at feste of Whittesontide next commyng become and be legemen and subjettes unto the seid most high and Christen prince Kynge Edward the Fourthe, his heires and successours, kynges of Englond . . . and do homage unto hym. . . . And in semble wyse the heires of the seid John, th'erle, Donald and John shall be and remaigne for ever subjettis and liegemen unto the seid kynge Edward, his heires and successours, kynges of Englonde. . . .

Item the seid John th'erle, Donald and John and eche of them shall be always redy after the seid feste of Whitteson-tide upon convenable and resounable warnyng and com-maundement . . . to do diligente and effectuall service with and to all them [*sic*] uttermest myght and power in suche werres as the seid most high and myghty prynce, his heires and successours, kynges of England . . . shall move or arreise or [cause to be] moved or arreised in Scotlande or ayenste the Scottes in Irlande or ayenst the kynges ennemyes or rebelles there. . . .

Item the seid John, erle of Rosse, shall from the seid feste of Whittesontyde next comyng yerely duryng his lyf have and take for fees and wages in tym of peas of the seid most high and Christen prince C merc sterlyng of Englysh money, and in tyme of werre . . . he shall have wages of CC li. sterlyng . . . yerely and after the rate [i.e., *pro rata*] of the time that he shall be occupied in the seid werres. [*Donald is to have £20 in peace and £40 in war, and John, his son, £10 and £20.*]

Item . . . if it so be that hereafter the seid reaume of Scotlande or the more part thereof be conquered, subdued and brough[t] to the obeissaunce of the seid most high and Christen prince and his heires or successours . . . be th'assistence . . . of the seid John . . . and Donald and of James, erle of Douglas, then (the seid fees and wages . . . cessyng) the same erles and Donald shall have . . . all the possessions of the seid reaume beyonde [the] Scottyshe See [i.e., the Firth of Forth], they to be departed egally betwix them, eche . . . to holde his parte of the seid most Cristen prince. . . .

ratified by Edward IV at Westminster on 17 March. Ardtornish was the residence of the Lord of the Isles. In the *Rotuli Scotiae* the date is given, wrongly, as 1462/3.

Item if so be that by th'aide . . . of the seid James, erle of Douglas, the seid reaume . . . be conquered . . . he shall have, enjoye and inherite all his owne possessions . . . on this syde the seid Scottyshe See . . . to holde them of the seid most high and Christen prince. . . .

Rotuli Scotiae, ii, 405-7.

1467-87 ACTS CONCERNING BURGHS

An act of 1467, confirmed in 1487, forbade craftsmen to operate as merchants unless they renounced their crafts. Hitherto burgh government had, so far as we know, been vested mainly in the merchants, but an act of 1469 provided for some representation of the crafts in the election of officers. At the same time, the ancient method of popular election of councillors was laid aside in favour of nomination of the new council by the old, and in 1474 it was further provided that four members of the old council should continue to sit with the new.

1467   It is statute and ordanit that na man of craft use merchandise be himself, his factouris or servandis, bot gif[1] he lefe and renunce his craft but[2] colour or dissimulacioun.

A.P.S., ii, 86, c. 2.

1469   Item as tuiching the electioune of alderman bailyis and utheris officiaris of burowis because of gret truble and contensione yeirly for the chesing of the samyn throw multitud & clamor of commonis sympil personis, it is thocht expedient that nain officiaris na consail be continuit eftir the kingis lawis of burowis forthir than a yeir. And at[3] the chesing of the new officiaris be in this wise that is to say that the aulde counsail of the toune sall cheise the new counsail in sic noumyr as accordis to the toune. And the new counsail & the aulde of the yeir before sall cheise all officiaris

1 but if, *i.e.* unless.
2 without.
3 that.

pertenying to the toune as alderman bailyis dene of gild and
utheris officiaris. And that ilka craft sall cheise a persone of
the samyn craft that sall have voce in the said electioune of
the officiaris for that tyme in like wise yeir be yeir.

A.P.S., ii, 95, c. 5.

1474 Item it [is] statute and ordanit in burowis nocht with-
standing the actis maide of before that thair salbe of the
aulde consale of the yer befor foure worthy personis chosin
yeirly to the new consale at thair entre to syt with thame for
that yere and have power withe thame to do justice.

A.P.S., ii, 107, c. 12.

1487 It is statut and ordanit that the act of parlment
tueching the craftsmen usand and deland with merchandise
micht be put to execucioun sa that he that is a craftisman
outher forbere his merchandise or ellis renunce his craift but [4]
ony dissimulacioun or colour, under the pain of eschete of
the merchandise that he usis occupyand his craift, and this
eschete to be inbrocht be the said serchouris to our soveran
lordis use, and compt thairof to be made in his chekker.

A.P.S., ii, 178, c. 13.

4 without.

1468-9 ACQUISITION OF
ORKNEY AND SHETLAND

*The treaty of Perth in 1266[1] had provided that, in return for
the cession of the Western Isles, Scotland should pay 100
merks annually to Norway. There is little evidence to show
how regularly the 'annual of Norway' was paid, but it was
evidently long in arrear when it was finally extinguished by
the treaty of 1468 which arranged for the marriage of James
III to Margaret, daughter of Christian, king of Denmark,
Norway and Sweden. By the same treaty, Christian pledged
his lands and rights in Orkney for 50,000 florins, part of*

1 p. 34 above.

his daughter's dowry of 60,000 florins. Then, as he succeeded in raising only 2,000 florins, and not 10,000, on 20 May 1469 he pledged Shetland for the remaining 8,000. The pledges extended only to the lands and rights of the Norwegian crown, but in 1470 James III acquired from Earl William Sinclair the earldom of Orkney, which henceforth, unlike the crown rights, pertained to the kings of Scots in heritage. As the Scots always rejected Danish offers to redeem the pledge, the royal lands and rights in Orkney and Shetland have also remained with the Scottish crown.

Christian . . . King of Denmark, Sweden and Norway . . . to all Christians. . . . We . . . (obtaining first the consent as well as the assent of the prelates, magnates and nobles of our kingdom of Norway and carefully considering, moreover, the profit and advantage of both kingdoms) do grant, deliver and by the tenor of the presents give, as part of the dowry of Margaret, our only daughter, to the foresaid Prince James . . . and Margaret, our daughter, his spouse, and their heirs and children only, the yearly pension of 100 merks sterling due every year to us and our heirs, kings of Norway for the time, in consideration of the islands of the Sudreys and Man; wholly remitting, moreover, all and sundry sums of money, damages, reparations and compensations due by reason of the pension foresaid and upon occasion of the contracts entered into by our predecessors, the former kings of Norway, and the kings of Scotland. . . .

For completion, moreover, of the whole dowry, we promise, undertake and pledge us, our heirs and successors, to the foresaid most excellent Prince James, most serene king of Scots, or his procurators, for the sum of sixty thousand florins of the Rhine, to be faithfully paid, of which sum we shall fully and faithfully pay ten thousand florins aforesaid and give satisfaction thereon in counted money, readily and effectually, to the foresaid procurators before their return to the kingdom of Scotland from our kingdom of Denmark; and for the sum of fifty thousand florins remaining of the whole sum aforesaid we, Christian, king of Norway, with consent and assent of the prelates, magnates and greater nobles of our realm of Norway aforesaid, give, grant, pledge and mortgage and place under assured pledge and security all and sundry our lands of the islands of the Orkneys with all and sundry rights, services and their rightful pertinents, pertaining or that in whatsoever manner may pertain to us and our predecessors, kings of Norway, by royal right; to be held and had all and whole our lands of the islands of the Orkneys aforesaid, with all and sundry customs, profits, freedoms, commodities and their other rightful pertinents whatsoever, as well named as not named, pertaining or that can rightfully pertain in any way in the future to the foresaid lands of Orkney, by the foresaid most excellent Prince James, king of Scots, our dearest son and ally, as part of the dowry with our foresaid daughter Margaret, ever and until whole and full satisfaction and payment is effectually made by us, our heirs and successors, kings of Norway, to the foresaid James, king of Scots, his heirs or successors, of the sum of fifty thousand florins of the Rhine remaining of part of the dowry. . . .

Further, . . . we, Christian, king of Norway, and we, the spokesmen and procurators of the most excellent Prince James, king of Scots, having power hereto, desiring to draw together in a stronger bond of alliance, for us, our heirs and successors and the magnates of our realms, scrupulously undertake on the word of a king to afford mutual friendship and the maintenance of the new alliance, help, aid and assistance, each in his turn, at the request of the other, against whatsoever prince or princes, nation or people (our allies before the date of the presents alone excepted), and by the tenor of the presents assuredly to maintain them, pledging hereto ourselves and our heirs and successors. . . .

In faith and witness of all and sundry the foregoing we, Christian, . . . have had our seal appended, and we, spokesmen aforesaid,[1] have had our seals appended, in double form, to the presents, at the town of Havn [Copenhagen] . . . on 8 September 1468. . . .

> The original of 1468, in the Register House, is imperfect, but the missing words can be supplied from the Danish copy, which was printed by Torfaeus in *Orcades seu rerum Orcadensium Historia* (1697), pp. 191 *et seq.* A complete text and translation appear in John Mooney, *Charters and other records of Kirkwall.*

1 i.e., the ambassadors of King James.

1472 ERECTION OF
ARCHBISHOPRIC OF ST. ANDREWS

Until 1472 the Scottish Church remained a province without a metropolitan. The erection of an archbishopric at St. Andrews was followed, twenty years later, by the erection of one at Glasgow, to which the sees of Dunkeld, Dunblane, Galloway and Argyll were subordinated, though Dunkeld and Dunblane were soon restored to St. Andrews.

We[1] . . . erect the foresaid church and episcopal seat of St Andrews as the metropolitan and archiepiscopal seat of the whole realm aforesaid, and we adorn it in like manner and distinguish it, by a gift of special grace, with the title of metropolitan dignity and archiepiscopal honour, and we assign to it Glasgow, Dunkeld, Aberdeen, Moray, Brechin, Dunblane, Ross, Caithness, Whithorn, Lismore, Sodor or the Isles and Orkney, the churches of the said realm, with their cities, dioceses, rights and all pertinents, and the whole aforesaid realm for its archiepiscopal province, and the prelates of the same churches for its suffragans and all the clergy of the cities and dioceses aforesaid for its provincials and we subject them to it in respect of archiepiscopal rights . . .

And we decree that to our venerable brother Patrick, bishop of St Andrews, and to his successors, bishops of St Andrews for the time, shall be assigned the pall and cross in token of the plenitude of pontifical office and the archiepiscopal dignity, and the church of St Andrews as metropolitan; and that the said present bishop and those who will be in their time bishops of St Andrews ought to be esteemed and in all future times called and named archbishops of St Andrews, ought to wear the archiepiscopal and metropolitan insignia, and be able to do, conduct, exercise, pursue and administer the rights, jurisdictions and all and sundry things which metropolitans can of right do and exercise in their cities, dioceses and provinces. . . .

We ordain that the archbishop and church of St Andrews aforesaid and also the beloved sons the chapter of the same church of St Andrew shall hold and enjoy all and sundry privileges, exemptions, immunities, graces and apostolic

1 These passages are extracted from a bull of Pope Sixtus IV, dated 13 August 1472.

indults and any other things which archbishops, metropolitan churches and their chapters can in any way use and enjoy by custom or of right; and that the foresaid suffragans, their clergy and people shall together show reverence and honour to their said archbishop and metropolitan. . . .

Robertson, Statuta Ecclesiae Scoticanae, i, cx.

1487   INDULT OF INNOCENT VIII

Friction had long been caused by the growing papal practice of making appointments to high offices in the Scottish Church, because the king insisted that, as bishops and abbots were often his councillors and officials, he should have a voice in their selection. In 1487 the pope, without giving up his right to appoint, undertook to take the king's recommendations into account. From this point the royal wishes were usually decisive in ecclesiastical promotions; in 1526 the Scottish parliament claimed formally that the king had the right of nomination, and in 1535 the pope admitted this.

[The popes, our predecessors, have been accustomed to give a hearing to the petitions of Catholic monarchs, and, in making provisions (in consultation with the cardinals) to cathedral churches and to monasteries of a yearly value exceeding 200 florins, gold of the camera, have proceeded with great deliberation, and, out of regard to the estate of the princes of the dominions where the benefices lie, have sometimes postponed the provision to permit the temporal power to indicate preference for a candidate.] Following in the footsteps of our predecessors, we are content and grant (as we have stated by word of mouth to our venerable brothers William, archbishop of St Andrews, and Robert, bishop of Glasgow, your envoys sent to us to offer the accustomed obedience to the holy see) that, on the occurrence of vacancies of churches and monasteries of this sort within your kingdom and dominions, we shall postpone the appointment for at least eight months, and meantime, during that period of eight months, await the letters and humble supplications thereon of you and your successors, kings of Scotland, remaining in the same faith and devotion, so that, on receiving intimation, we may the better be able to proceed to these provisions as we shall think expedient; urging our successors that in such provisions they take equal care to observe this practice.

Herkless and Hannay, Archbishops of St Andrews, i, 157-8.

1494   ARTICLES OF LOLLARDS OF KYLE

The few references to 'heresy' in the fifteenth century (including an act of James I against 'heretics and lollards') give us little real indication how far the influence of the English Wyclif and the Bohemian Hus had spread in Scotland. The accusation of the Lollards of Kyle in 1494 does, however, suggest that some extremely radical ideas had taken root and that they may not have died out before criticism of the existing religious system was reinforced by the teaching of Luther, which began in 1517.

In the year of God 1494, were summoned before the King and his Great Council, by Robert Blacader, called Archbishop of Glasgow, the number of thirty persons, remaining some in Kyle-Stewart, some in King's-Kyle, and some in Cunningham; amongst whom [were] George Campbell of Cessnock, Adam Reid of Barskimming, John Campbell of New Mylns, Andrew Shaw of Polkemmet, Helen Chalmers Lady Polkellie [and Marion] Chalmers Lady Stair. These were called the LOLLARDS OF KYLE. They were accused of the Articles following:

I First, That images are not to be had, nor yet to be worshipped.

II That the relics of saints are not to be worshipped.

III That laws and ordinances of men vary from time to time, and that by[1] the Pope.

IV That it is not lawful to fight, or to defend the faith.

---

1 without the authority of.

(We translate according to the barbarousness of their Latin and dictament.)

V That Christ gave power to Peter only, and not to his successors, to bind and loose within the Kirk.

VI That Christ ordained no priests to consecrate.

VII That after the consecration in the Mass, there remains bread; and that there is not the natural body of Christ.

VIII That tithes ought not to be given to ecclesiastical men (as they were then called).

IX That Christ at his coming has taken away power from kings to judge. (This article we doubt not to be the venomous accusation of the enemies, whose practice has ever been to make the doctrine of Jesus Christ suspect to kings and rulers, as that God thereby would depose them of their royal seats where, by the contrary, nothing confirms the power of magistrates more than does God's word. — But to the Articles.)

X That every faithful man or woman is a priest.

XI That the unction of kings ceased at the coming of Christ.

XII That the Pope is not the successor of Peter, but where he said, 'Go behind me, Sathan.'

XIII That the Pope deceives the people by his Bulls and his Indulgences.

XIV That the Mass profiteth not the souls that are in purgatory.

XV That the Pope and his bishops deceive the people by their pardons.

XVI That Indulgences ought not to be granted to fight against the Saracens.

XVII That the Pope exalts himself against God, and above God.

XVIII That the Pope can not remit the pains of purgatory.

XIX That the blessings of the bishops (of dumb dogs they should have been styled) are of no value.

XX That the excommunication of the Kirk is not to be feared.

XXI That in to no case is it lawful to swear.

XXII That priests might have wives, according to the constitution of the law.

XXIII That true Christians receive the body of Jesus Christ every day.

XXIV That after matrimony be contracted, the Kirk may make no divorcement.

XXV That excommunication binds not.

XXVI That the Pope forgives not sins, but only God.

XXVII That faith should not be given to miracles.

XXVIII That we should not pray to the glorious Virgin Mary, but to God only.

XXIX That we are no more bound to pray in the Kirk than in other places.

XXX That we are not bound to believe all that the doctors of the Kirk have written.

XXXI That such as worship the Sacrament of the Kirk (we suppose they meant the Sacrament of the altar) commit idolatry.

XXXII That the Pope is the head of the Kirk of Antichrist.

XXXIII That the Pope and his ministers are murderers.

XXXIV That they which are called principals in the Church, are thieves and robbers.

The text has been preserved by John Knox, who said that it had been extracted from 'the Registers of Glasgow'. The passages in brackets are Knox's own glosses and comments. Printed in Knox, *History of the Reformation*, ed. Dickinson, i, 8-9.

1496 EDUCATION ACT

The purpose lying behind this act was to strengthen the administration of justice by ensuring that the class who provided judges, either by inheritance or by appointment, should have knowledge of the law. Like many well-intentioned acts, it is mainly significant of good intentions.

It is statute and ordanit throw all the realme that all barronis and frehaldaris that ar of substance put thair eldest sonnis and airis to the sculis fra thai be aucht or nyne yeiris of age and till remane at the grammer sculis quhill thai be competentlie foundit and have perfite latyne and thereftir to remane thre yeris at the sculis of art and jure sua that thai

may have knawlege and understanding of the lawis. Throw
the quhilkis justice may reigne universalie throw all the realme
sua that thai that ar schireffis or jugeis ordinaris under the
kingis hienes may have knawlege to do justice that the pure
pepill sulde have na neid to seik our soverane lordis principale
auditouris for ilk small iniure. And quhat baroune or frehaldar
of substance that haldis nocht his sone at the sculis as said is
haifand na lauchfull essonye[1] bot failyeis heirin fra knawlege
may be gottin thairof he sall pay to the king the soum of xx
pounds.

A.P.S., ii, 238, c. 3.

1 excuse.

1502 TREATY OF
PERPETUAL PEACE WITH ENGLAND

*When a marriage was arranged between James IV and
Margaret, elder daughter of Henry VII, England and Scotland
entered into this treaty, ratified by Henry on 31 October and
by James on 17 December. The clause requiring papal confirmation was fulfilled by a bull of Alexander VI, dated
28 May 1503, so that either party breaking the treaty would
incur excommunication.*

Keeping in view the . . . alliance which presently exists
between our said most illustrious princes for the term of their
lives and that of the survivor and for a year after the survivor's
death, and also the marriage [between James and Margaret]
to be contracted before Candlemas next, [the Scottish and
English commissioners] wish . . . that there be a true, sincere,
whole and unbroken peace, friendship, league and alliance . . .
from this day forth in all times to come, between them and
their heirs and lawful successors. . . .
Neither of the kings aforesaid nor any of their heirs and
successors shall in any way receive or allow to be received
by their subjects any rebels, traitors or refugees suspected,
reputed or convicted of the crime of treason. [And if such

persons do come to either kingdom, they are not to receive any countenance, but, on the request of their sovereign, they are to be put in ward and to be handed over within twenty days.]

[In the event of any king, prince or other person invading or disturbing either realm or making usurpation of its rights, the prince of the other realm shall come to its assistance with his forces.]

[Provision is made for the comprehension of the existing allies of Scotland and England if they so desire.]

Although it happen the said king of England or his heirs and successors aforesaid or any of them to levy war against any of the said princes comprehended herein, then the king of Scotland . . . shall wholly abstain from making any invasion of the kingdom of England, its places and dominions, as well by himself as by his subjects, but it shall be lawful to the king of Scotland to give help, assistance, favour and succour to the same prince against whom war has been levied on the part of the king of England, for his defence alone and not otherwise. [And a reciprocal provision is made for the case of the king of Scotland making war on an ally of the king of England.]

It is agreed . . . that each of the foresaid princes shall, before 1 July 1503, obtain at his own expense and cost a rescript or letters apostolic . . . whereby all and sundry the contents of the present treaty are by the authority of the apostolic see approved and confirmed. And moreover each of the princes aforesaid, their heirs or successors, shall, before the said 1 July, . . . require the sacred apostolic see and the supreme pontiff to impose sentence of excommunication . . . on either of the said two princes and on their heirs and successors who shall violate, or permit to be violated, the present peace or any clause of the present treaty. . . .

Foedera, xii, 793-8.

1502, 1505 EXTRACTS FROM
CROWN RENTALS

Information somewhat similar to that obtained from the records of the abbey of Kelso in the late thirteenth century (p. 46 above) comes in the early sixteenth from the rentals of crown lands. The rentals are voluminous, and deal with properties in many parts of the country; only two brief samples can be given here.

(i)

From the Rental of the lordship of Methven, made at Stirling, 12 April 1502

Westir Ardete, 53s. 4d. and 18 poultry: set for the terms of three years to Robert Thomesoune for 13s. 4d., John Cummyn for 1 merk, James Simpill for ½ merk, Jonet, late spouse of Ewan Neilsoune, and the said Ewan, for 20s., making 53s. 4d., with carriages and services, and the grassum[1] as much.

Estir Ardete set for terms as above to John Patrik, Walter Ker, deceased, Donald Gib, Simon Cummyn, Stephen Cumyn, John Andersoun, Patrick Gregoure, deceased, William Anderson, Thomas Burnne, Robert Atkin and Elizabeth Davidsoune, £6 in money and 12 poultry, grassum £6. . . .

Westir and Estir Busbeis set for terms as above to John Tiry, provost of [the collegiate church of] Methven, for £5. 6s. 8d. in money and 24 poultry, and without grassum on account of the king's residence there.

Exchequer Rolls, xii, 640.

(ii)

From the account of the grange of Darnaway, 24 March 1505

In primis the first stak of aitis the pruf[2] was 2 ferlotis 2 peccis.[3] Item the secund stak aitis the pruf 5 ferlotis 3 peccis. Item the therd stak aitis pruf 6 ferlotis 2 peccis. Item the ferd stak aitis pruf 5 ferlotis 3 peccis. Item the fyft stak aitis pruf 1 boll 2 peccis. Item the 6 stak aitis pruf 3 bollis 3 ferlotis 1 pec. Item the 7 stak aitis pruf 2 bollis.

1 Payment for renewal of the tenancy.
2 I.e., a sample, evidently representing a proportion of the stack after threshing.
3 The measures of capacity were 1 chalder = 16 bolls, 1 boll = 4 firlots, 1 firlot = 4 pecks.

1 ferlot 1½ peccis. Item the 8 stak aitis pruf 5 ferlotis. Item the 9 stak aitis pruf 5 ferlotis 3 peccis. Item the 10 stak aitis pruf 2 bollis 3 ferlotis. Item the 11 stak aitis pruf 2 bollis 3 ferlotis. Summa of the pruf 20 bollis 2 ferlotis 1 pec ½ pec.

Expenses of the same

Item to 5 plewmen 5 celder atis. Item to the schiphird 14 bollis atis. Item to the bowman[4] 8 bollis atis. Item to Rannald for the yet kepen[5] 6 bollis atis. Item to Brande for the mokyn[6] 9 bollis aitis. Item to the nuris[7] to mak grotis[8] 1 boll aitis. Item to Walter Douglas kepand the place 5 ferlotis aitis. Item to Montnam 2 bollis aitis. Item to the smyth 5 ferlotis aitis. Item to the Jhone Ayr, wachman, 6 ferlotis aitis. Item to the vyndoustaris[9] 4 bollis aitis. Summa, 9 celdre 4 bolle. Item to the seid[10] 16 celdre 7 bolle 1 ferlota. . . . Item in 5 plewis 50 oxin. Item with Jhone McGilmwell, bowman, 3 ky with cauff, 4 young ky with cauff, 13 yeld ky,[11] twa ky with the nuris and the barne,[12] 5 ky with the schiphird, 2 of thaim with cauff. Item with Jhone McGillemoyll of 3 yeiris auldis 8 noyt.[13] Item with him of twa yeiris auldis 6 not. Item with him of cauffis 6. Item with the schiphird of ane yeir auld 2 styrkis. Item with ane of the ky that the nuris has 1 cauff. Item with Jhone McGillemoyll 1 bowyll. Item with Andro Mulisone and Jhone Brothy of 2 yeiris ald 1 ster.

The scheipe. Item with the schiphird 116 yowis. Item with him 42 wedderis. Item with him 64 oggis. Item with him of yeiris auldis 9 scheip. Summa totalis liffand 231 auld 10 young.

Ibid., 672-3.

4 man in charge of cattle.
5 gate-keeping.
6 mucking, or cleaning out the byre.
7 nurse: at Darnaway the king had a mistress and an illegitimate child.
8 husked grain.
9 winnowers.
10 for seed.
11 cows without calves.
12 bairn.
13 cattle.

1516 BONDS OF
MANRENT AND OF MAINTENANCE

*Scottish social relationships, where they were not defined by
the conditions of land tenure, were apt to be based on the
kin, or blood relationship, and the 'band' or bond. One type
of bond was the bond of manrent, whereby a lesser man
undertook to support a greater man, who reciprocated by
granting a bond of maintenance to the lesser man.*

(i) Bond of Manrent

Be it kend til al men be thir present lettres me Patrik Chene
of Essilmount to be bundyn and oblist, and be thir my
lettres and the fathe and treuth in my body bindis and
oblissis me and becummys man, til ane noble and potent
lorde Williame, Erll of Eroll, Lorde Hay and Constable of
Scotlande, and til his airis male gottin of his body, thai beand
of xiiij yeris of age, That I sal be lelle,[1] trew and afauld[2] to
him and to thame.[3] . . . Becauss my said gude lorde and mastir
has infeft me in his landis of Tawarty for all the dais of my
life for my seruice forsaide. To the obseruing keping and
fulfilling hereof I binde and obliss me to my said lorde and
mastir in the sickerast forme of obligatioune but fraude or
gile. And thir my lettres til endure for all the dais of my life.
In witnes of the quhilk thing to thir my lettres of manrent
I haue affixit my sele and subscriuit the samyne with my
hande At Slanis the xxiij day of May the yere of Gode jm vc
and sextene yeris.

Patrik Chene of Esilmount with my hand etc.
Spalding Club Miscellany, ii, 267.

(ii) Bond of Maintenance

Be it kend til al men be thir present lettres ws Williame, Erll
of Eroll, Lorde Hay and Constable of Scotlande to be bundyn
and oblist, and be thir our lettres and the fath and treuth in
our body stratlie bindis and oblissis us, to our lovit cusing
Patrik Chene of Essilmount, fforsamekill as he is becummyne
speciale man til us and our airis male for al the dais of his life,

1 loyal.
2 faithful.
3 The common form of words which follows here is not printed. For another
bond of manrent see p.161below.

as at more lyntht is contenit in his lettir of manrent maid til
ws tharupone, Herfor we binde and obliss us and our airis
as said is That we sal supple, maneteine and defende the said
Patrik in al and syndre his richteous caussis and querellis movit
and to be movit And be and do for him in al thingis as we
aucht to do for our speciale man, kynisman and seruande. To
the observyng, keping and fulfilling herof we binde and
oblissis us to the said Patrik in the sickerast forme of obligatioune, but[4] fraude or gile: And thir our lettres of manteinance
til the said Patrik for al the dais of his life til endure. In witnes
of the quhilk thing we haue affixit herto oure sele and subscrivit thir oure lettres with oure awne hande. At Slanis the
xxiiij day of Maij the yere of Gode a thousand vc and sextene
yeris. And this til endure alss wele and obseruit for his kin
frendis and seruandis as for him selue.

Wylyam Erll of Eroll.
Ibid., 268.

4 without.

1517   TREATY OF ROUEN

*In order to renew and strengthen the traditional alliance
between Scotland and France, John, Duke of Albany and
Governor of Scotland, concluded this treaty with Francis I.
The somewhat hypothetical prospects of a French bride
which the treaty offered to James V ultimately found fulfilment when he married the Princess Madeleine (b. 1520) in
1537.*

Firstly, the said lord kings . . . will not give passage, aid, favour,
assistance or welcome in their realms, countries, lordships,
harbours and seaports, either with victuals, artillery, men,
money or other commodity, to those who, by invasion, could
or would bring annoyance or hurt to the other. . . .
  If the king of England assail or make actual war on the
king of Scotland, his heirs and successors, or on the said lord
[king of France], his heirs and successors, from that hour
the said lord [king of France] and the said king of Scotland,

if he is of age, or his . . . regent . . . during his minority, being duly informed in writing, by sure account or by common report, will assist each other for the defence of their persons and countries, as follows:

That is to say, that for the first and the second times that the said king of England . . . makes war, as said is, on either of the kings, the said lord king [of France] . . . shall be bound to send to the said king of Scotland . . . 100,000 *ecus du soleil*, 500 lansquenets,[1] 500 infantry and 200 archers of the said lord's command. . . .

And further, if the king of England assail or make war on the said lord [king of France], as said is, as soon as the said king of Scotland . . . [or] his . . . regent . . . has been duly informed, as above, they shall be bound, with all their power and might and with the aid which the said lord sends to them, to break and make war on the king of England . . . , and if the said king of England assail and make the like war on the said king of Scotland, . . . the said lord, as soon as he has been informed as above, and in addition to the help above-mentioned, shall be bound for his defence, and to divert the war, to make war with all his power on the land and subjects which the same king of England holds and occupies beyond the sea. . . .

Further it has been agreed and concluded between us that whenever the said king of England would make war on the said lords [kings of France], the king of Scotland shall be bound to send to the said lord 6000 good soldiers of his realm at the expense of the said lord [king of France] if required.

[The king of France is not to desist from war after conquering the continental possessions of England, but is to pursue the war in England itself.]

Moreover . . . we have agreed that, if the promise of his eldest daughter made by the said lord king of France to the Catholic King [of Spain], or to his brother, does not take place, . . . the king of France shall have her betrothed and married to the said king of Scotland; and if the promise of his daughter made by the said lord king of France to the said Catholic King, or to his brother, does take place, and it pleases God to give to him another daughter, then, when she

1 Mounted men armed with lances.

shall have reached the age to contract marriage, the said king of France shall, if our Holy Mother the Church agrees, cause her to be betrothed and married to his said brother and cousin [the king of Scotland].

Teulet, *Relations Politiques*, i, 4-8.

1521 JOHN MAJOR ON SCOTTISH SOCIETY

John Major's History of Greater Britain *is, in part, a plea for better understanding between England and Scotland. His own experience of England led him, as it has led many anglicised Scots, to take a poor view of his native country, but his knowledge not only of England, but of France, suggests that his views should not be discounted. He set a fashion with his belief that security of tenure was the key to sound husbandry, and that opinion has never since been abandoned, despite much evidence to the contrary. His account of the divergence between Highlands and Lowlands does not appear to be exaggerated.*

In Scotland the houses of the country people are small, as it were cottages, and the reason is this: they have no permanent holdings, but hired only, or in lease for four or five years, at the pleasure of the lord of the soil; therefore they do not dare to build good houses, though stone abound; neither do they plant trees or hedges for their orchards, nor do they dung the land; and this is no small loss and damage to the whole realm. If the landlords would let their lands in perpetuity, they might have double and treble of the profit that now comes to them — and for this reason: the country folk would then cultivate their land beyond all comparison better, would grow richer, and would build fair dwellings that should be an ornament to the country. . . .

In both of the British kingdoms the warlike strength of the nation resides in its common people and its peasantry. The farmers rent their land from the lords, but cultivate it by means of their servants, and not with their own hands. They keep a horse and weapons of war, and are ready to take part in his quarrel, be it just or unjust, with any powerful lord, if they only have a liking for him, and with him, if need be, to fight to the death. . . .

Among the nobles I note two faults. The first is this: If two nobles of equal rank happen to be very near neighbours, quarrels and even shedding of blood are a common thing between them; and their very retainers cannot meet without strife. . . . The second fault I note is this: The gentry educate their children neither in letters nor in morals — no small calamity to the state. . . .

Further, just as among the Scots we find two distinct tongues, so we likewise find two different ways of life and conduct. For some are born in the forests and mountains of the north, and these we call men of the Highland, but the others men of the Lowland. By foreigners the former are called Wild Scots, the latter householding Scots. The Irish tongue is in use among the former, the English tongue among the latter. One-half of Scotland speaks Irish, and all these as well as the Islanders we reckon to belong to the Wild Scots. In dress, in the manner of their outward life, and in good morals, for example, these come behind the householding Scots — yet they are not less, but rather much more, prompt to fight; and this, both because they dwell more towards the north, and because, born as they are in the mountains, and dwellers in forests, their very nature is more combative. It is, however, with the householding Scots that the government and direction of the kingdom is to be found, inasmuch as they understand better, or at least less ill than the others, the nature of a civil polity. One part of the Wild Scots have a wealth of cattle, sheep, and horses, and these, with a thought for the possible loss of their possessions, yield more willing obedience to the courts of law and the king. The other part of these people delight in the chase and a life of indolence; their chiefs eagerly follow bad men if only they may not have the need to labour; taking no pains to earn their own livelihood, they live upon others, and follow their own worthless and savage chief in all evil courses sooner than they will pursue an honest industry. They are full of mutual dissensions, and war rather than peace is their normal condition. The Scottish kings have with difficulty been able to withstand the inroads of these men. From the mid-leg to the

101

foot they go uncovered; their dress is, for an over garment, a loose plaid, and a shirt saffron-dyed. They are armed with bow and arrows, a broadsword, and a small halbert. They always carry in their belt a stout dagger, single-edged, but of the sharpest. In time of war they cover the whole body with a coat of mail, made of iron rings, and in it they fight. The common folk among the Wild Scots go out to battle with the whole body clad in a linen garment sewed together in patchwork, well daubed with wax or with pitch, and with an over-coat of deerskin. But the common people among our domestic Scots and the English fight in a woollen garment. For musical instruments and vocal music the Wild Scots use the harp, whose strings are of brass and not of animal gut; and on this they make most pleasing melody. Our house-holding Scots, or quiet and civil-living people — that is, all who lead a decent and reasonable life — these men hate, on account of their differing speech, as much as they do the English.

A History of Greater Britain (Scot. Hist. Soc.), pp. 30-1, 47-50.

1525   ACT AGAINST HERESY

The teaching of Luther, whose protest against the traditional teaching of the Church began in 1517, soon reached Scotland by way of the east coast ports.

. . . Forsamekle as the dampnable opunyeounis of heresy are spred in diverse cuntreis be the heretik Luther and his discipillis and this realm and liegis has fermelie persistit in the halifaith sen the samin was first ressavit be thaim and never as yit admittit ony opunyeounis contrare the Cristin faith bot ever has bene clene of all sic filth and vice, therefore that na maner of persoun strangeare that hapnis to arrife with thair schippis within ony part of this realm bring with thaim ony bukis or werkis of the said Lutheris, his discipillis or servandis, desputt or reherse his heresyis or opunyeounis bot geif it be to the confusioun thairof [and that be clerkis in the sculis

alanerlie] [1] under the pane of escheting of thair schippis and
gudis and putting of thair persounis in presoun, and that this
act be publist and proclamit outthrow this realme at all
portis and burrowis of the samin sa that thai may allege na
ignorance thairof [and all uther the kingis liegis assistaris to sic
opunyeounis be punist in semeible wise and the effect of the
said act to strik apon thaim etc.[2]].

A.P.S., ii, 295, c. 4.

1 A marginal addition.
2 Addition made by lords of council, 4 September 1527.

1528   LETTERS OF FIRE AND SWORD

*A weak executive, with neither a standing army nor a police
force at its disposal, could not of itself suppress disorder or
punish violence. Recourse was therefore had to the device of
empowering families or clans to take action against others — a
device which amounted to setting a thief to catch a thief and
which was apt to raise as many problems as it solved.*

James, be the grace of God, King of Scottis, To our shirreffis
of Kincardin, Abirdene, Banf, Elgen, Fores, Narne, and
Inuernyss; and to our derrest bruthir, James, Erle of Murray,
our lieutenant generale in the north partis of our realme, and
to our louittis consignis [   ] Erle of Suthirland;
Alexander, Maistir of Sutherland; Johne, Erle of Cathnes;
Johne, Lord Forbes; Hew, Lord Fraser of Lovet; Johne Grant
of Freuchy; Ewin Alansone, capitane of the Clan Cammeroun;
Johne M'Kainze of Kintaill; Wellem Chesholme of [   ]
Vrquard, our shirref of Cromerty; Johne M'Ky of Strathnaver;
and all uthiris, frehaldaris, baronis, capitanis of Clannys, and
gentilmen, oure trew liegis, within our shirefdomis and
boundis abouewrittin, oure shirreffis in that parte, coniunctlie and seuerallie, specialie constitute, Greting:
Forsamekill as Johne M'Kinla, Thomas Makkinla, Ferquhar
M'Kinla, brethir, Donald Glass, Anguss Williamsone, his
bruthir William, Lauchlane M'Kintoschis son, throcht assistance and fortifying of all the kin of Clanquhattane, duelland
103

within Baienach, Petty, Brauchly, Strathnarne, and uther partis thairabout, committis daly rasing of fire, slauchtir, murthur, heirschippis, and waisting of the cuntre, sa that oure trew liegis in thair partis about thaim may nocht leif in peace, and mak ws seruice. And in speciale, the saidis personis and thair complices hes cumm laitlie to the landis pertening to James Dunbar of Tarbert, in the Bray of Murray, and thair hes rasit fire, slane and murtharit vj men and two wemen, and mutilate uthir v men, and maid plane heirschip[1] of nolt,[2] scheip, hors, gait,[3] swyne, cornis, and insycht gudis,[4] layand the land waist, and makand depopulation of the cuntre, and tendis in contemption of oure autorite to ourthraw all landis about thaim with thair maisterfull oppressioun, heirschippis, and destruction, and suffir na man to brouk[5] landis that thai may wyn to, and will na wayis obey to our lawis. And we and oure consale avisitlie considerand the grete harmys and con-temptionis done be the said kin of Clanquhattane, and thair assistaris, aganis the commoun wele, hes concludit and deter-mit to mak utir exterminatioun and destructioun of all that kin, thair assistaris and parte takaris. And thairfore it is our will, and we charge straitlie and commandis yow, our said˙ lieutenent, and shirreffis foirsadis, and your deputis, and utheris, our shirreffis in that parte abone exprimit, that incon-tinent thir oure lettres sene, ye pass all at anys, or as ye may cum to, as salbe ordourit be yow, our said lieutenent, with all your powaris and convocatioun of our liegis in thai partis, in feir of weir,[6] upon the said Clanquhattane, and invaid thame to thair uter destructioun, be slauchtir, byrning, drowning, and uthir wayis; and leif na creatur levand of that clann, except preistis, wemen, and barnis. And that ye tak to your self, for your laubouris, all thair gudis that may be apprehendit, and hald the symyn to your aune use; and thair attour ye sall haue reward of ws for your gude seruice in the premissis. And gif ony personis assistis to thame that is nochte of thair kin, or takis thair parte, that ye invaid thai assistaris, in lykewyse as the principale, to thair utir destructioun. For the quhilkis

1 spoliation.
2 cattle.
3 goats.
4 furnishings.
5 enjoy.
6 equipped for war.

inuasionis, slauchteris, birningis, taking of gudis, or uthir
skathis, done or to be done upon the said Clanquhattane, or
thair assisteris, thair sall neuir actioun nor cryme be impute
to you, nor utheris, our trew liegis, doaris, or committaris
thairof; nor accusatioun, nor restitutioun follow thairupon in
the law, nor by the law, in tyme to cum. Bot all schairpnes
done and to be done upon thame salbe haldin and repute
lauchfull and richtuuslie done, be command of ws and oure
consale, for the common wele of oure realme; and als that ye
tak the wemen and barnis of the said clan to sum partis of
the sey, nerrest land, quhair schippis salbe forsene on our
expenssis, to saill with thame furth of our realme, and land
with them in Jesland, Zesland, or Norway; becaus it were
inhumanite to put handis in the blude of wemen and barnis.
This ye do, and ilkane of yow for your awne parte, as ye lufe
the commoun wele of our realme, and will haue thank of ws
thairfore and ansueir to ws thairvpoun. The quhilk to do we
committ to yow, coniunctlie and seueralie, our full powar be
thir our lettres. Gevin under our signete, at Edinburgh, the
x day of Nouember, and of our regne the xvj yeir.

Spalding Club Miscellany, ii, 83-4.

1532 ESTABLISHMENT OF
COLLEGE OF JUSTICE

*A permanent central court of civil justice, developing from
the council, had taken shape in James IV's reign, and in the
later 1520s there was in effect a Court of Session staffed by
semi-professional judges. It remained to provide endowment,
and this was forthcoming as a result of negotiations between
James V and the pope. In, return for the right to levy a
perpetual tax on the Scottish Church, James undertook to
remain loyal to Rome and to institute a College of Justice.
But most of the judges named were already judges in the
Court of Session, the supposed innovation was something of
a pretence and most of the money from the church went to
other purposes, leaving only inadequate provision for judicial
salaries.*

Our soverane lord in this present parliament, the thre estatis
of this realme beand gaderit, exponit sene he and his noble
progenitouris, kingis of Scotland, and liegis of the samin, has
bene first, or at the leist with the first, that evir acceptit the
Cristin faith and bene maist obedient sonnis to our haly
faderis the papis of Rome and the auctorite apostolik, without
ony maner of smot, violacioun or defectioun, and our haly
faderis the papis of Rome has been verray gracius and benevolent to his hienes and realme with all maner of privilegeis
and benefitis, and maist of all Pape Clement now pape of
Rome has bene mair gracius and benevolent till his grace than
to all his forbearis; Quharfor to schaw him thankfull and
obedient sone to his halynes and the kirk of Rome it is divisit
statute and ordanit be his hienes with avise and consent of the
thre estatis of parliament that he sall keip, observe, manteine
and defend the auctorite, liberte and fredome of the sete of
Rome and halikirk and sall never mak nor statute ony actis,
constitucionis, do nor attempt nor suffir to be done nor
attemptit ony thing in contrare thairof; and geif in tymes
past ony thing has bene done or in tymes cuming sall happin
to be done incontrare the auctorite, fredome and liberte of
halykirk annullis and decernis the samin now as than and than
as now of nane avale, force nor effect and that nain of our
said soverane lordis liegis be bund or oblist to obey the
samin, salfand alwayis the actis foundit apon our haly fader
the papis privilegis or thaim that hes bene lang in lovable use
kepit and observit in our soverane lord that now is and his
maist noble progenitouris tymes.
Item . . . becaus our soverane is maist desyrous to have ane
permanent ordour of justice for the universale wele of all his
lieges and thairfor tendis to institute ane college of cunning
and wise men baith of spirituale and temporale estate for the
doing and administracioun of justice in all civile actionis, and
thairfor thinkis to be chosin certane persounis maist convenient
and qualifyit thairfore to the nowmer of xiiij persounis, half
spirituale half temporall, with ane president, the quhilkis
personis sall be auctorizat in this present parliament to sitt
and decyde apon all actiouns civile, and nane utheris to have
voit with thame onto the tyme that the said college may be
institute at mare lasare; and thir persounis to begynn and sitt
in Edinburgh on the morne efter Trinite Sonday quhill

Lammes and thaireftir to have vacance quhill the xix day of
October nixt thaireftir and than to begin and sitt quhill Sanct
Thomas evin effore Yule and thaireftir to begin apon the
morn efter the Epiphany[1] day and sitt quhill Palmsonday
evin and thairefter to begyn on the morn efter *Dominica in
albis*[2] and sitt quhill Lammes; and thir persounis to be
sworne to minister justice equaly to all personis in sic causis
as sall happin tocum before thaim with sic uthir rewlis and
statutis as sall pleise the kingis grace to mak and geif to thaim
for ordouring of the samin: the thre estatis of this present
parliament thinkis this artikle wele consavit and thairfor the
kingis grace with avise and consent of the saidis thre estatis
ordanis the samin to have effect in all punctis and now
ratifyis and confermes the samin; and has chosin thir persounis
underwrittin to the effect forsaid, quhais processis, sentencis
and decretis sall have the samin strenth, force and effect as
the decretis of the lordis of sessioun had in all tymes bigane:
providing alwayis that my lord chancelare being present in
this toun or uther place he sall have voit and be principale of
the said counsell and sic uther lordis as sall pleise the kingis
grace to enjone to thaim of his gret counsell to have voit
siclik to the nomer of thre or four, that is to say the abbot
of Cambuskynneth, president, Mr. R. Bothuile, Schir Jhone
Dingwell, Mr. Henry Quhite, Mr. Robert Schanwell, vicar of
Kirkcaldy, Mr. William Gibsone, Mr. Thomas Hay, Mr. Arthour
Boyis, the lard of Balwery, Schir Jhone Campbell, Mr. Adam
Otterburn, James Colvile of Est Wemys, the justice clerk,
Mr. Francis Bothuil, Mr. James Lauson, and thir lordis to
subscrive all deliverancis and nane utheris eftir that thai
begyn to sitt to minister justice.

A.P.S., ii, 335-6, cc. 1-2.

1 New Yere *deleted*.
2 First Sunday after Easter.

*Accounts of the condition of Scottish agriculture too often
overlook the fact that far-seeing landlords could insist on the
maintenance of certain standards and on the introduction of
some 'improvements'.*

Thir ar the claussis divisit be the Comptrollar and commissaris
chosin be the kingis grace for setting of his landis of Fiffe
and Stratherne in few and takkis,[1] to be insert in thair
charteris and to be observit and kepit be thaim and thair
successouris in tyme to cum.

In the first, that all and sindry quhatsumevir tenentis of
our soverane lordis landis of Fiffe that hes tane his landis for
ferme sall have ane gud, large yard, weil dykit and heggeit
with hawthorne, sawch,[2] allir[3] or esp,[4] with planting of
eschis,[5] planis, and elme, that is to say, for ilk mark of silvir
thre treis, and for ilk chalder of ferme quheit and beir yerlie
to plant xx treis, and for ilk chalder of aitis ten treis, for the
compleit circuling of thair yardis, with sawing of brome,
wphalding of woddis and schawis, quhar ony ar at this tyme,
or hes bene, or may be had be diking and haning;[6] and to
saw hemp and lint outwith thair caleyard, and nane within;
and that na tenant sall analy[7] nor wedsett[8] ony of his few
landis, in all nor in part, without speciale avise and consent
of the kingis grace, and that be resignatioun of the samin
maid in his hienes handis; and that every tenent big, wphald,
and sustene honest and sufficient houssis efferand[9] to the
quantite of thair maling.[10]

And quhar ony man hes fewis seperat be thaimselfis, for
silvir or ferme or part of baith [he] sall have [ane] honest
mansioun, with hall, chalmer, pantry, kiching, and uthir
office houssis substantiously biggit,[11] efferand[9] to the
quantite of thair maling,[10] berne, byre, dowcat,[12] planting of
treis, orchardis, or yardis, wele dikit, heggit or fowseit[13] and

1 leases.	7 alienate.	13 ditched.
2 willow.	8 mortgage.	
3 alder.	9 corresponding.	
4 aspen.	10 holding.	
5 ash trees.	11 built.	
6 caring for.	12 dovecote.	

sett about with treis precedand, and with uthir clausis as is
above writtin; and to hayne medowis in all placis quhair thai
may be had, with planting of allir, sawch and hesill in boggis
and humyde placis convenient thairfor, and to have stankis
and pondis for fische, quhar the samin may be gudly had,
with cunyngaris.[14]

Item, that every ane of the saidis tenentis be honestlie and
sufficientlie armit, and conforme to the actis of parliament
to pas with our soverane lord in his army or uthir particular
radis, as thai sall be chargit at all tymes.

Exchequer Rolls, xvii, 719.

14 rabbit-warrens.

1543 ACT AUTHORISING
VERNACULAR SCRIPTURES

*Almost immediately after the death of James V, in December
1542, a government came into power which was favourable
to the reformation and to the English alliance. It authorised
the circulation of the Bible in the vernacular (15 March
1542/3) and entered into treaties with England.*

Anent the writting gevin in be Robert lord Maxwell in presens
of my lord gouvernour and lordis of artiklis to be avisit be
thaim gif the samin be resonable or nocht of the quhilk the
tenour followis: It is statute and ordanit that it salbe lefull
to all our souirane ladyis lieges to haif the haly write baith
the new testament and the auld in the vulgar toung in Inglis
or Scottis of ane gude and trew translatioun and that thai
sall incur na crimes for the hefing or reding of the samin
providing alvayis that na man despute or hald oppunyeonis
under the panis contenit in the actis of parliament The lordis
of artiklis beand avisit with the said writting findis the samin
resonable and therfor thinkis that the samin may be usit
amangis all the lieges of this realme in our vulgar toung of
ane gude trew and just translatioun becaus thair was na law
schewin nor producit in the contrare And that nane of our

109

said souirane ladyis lieges incur ony crimes for haifing or
reding of the samyn in forme as said is nor salbe accusit thairfor in tyme tocum And that na personis despute argoun or
hald oppunionis of the samin under the saidis panis contenit
in the forsaidis actis of parliament.

A.P.S., ii, 415, c. 12.

1543   TREATIES OF GREENWICH

*One treaty provided for peace between England and Scotland
for the lifetimes of Henry VIII and Mary and for a year after
the death of the first to die. The second, from which
extracts follow, provided for the marriage of Mary to Prince
Edward, son of Henry. The treaties were concluded on
1 July, but were to be ratified later.*

We have agreed . . . that . . . Prince Edward, eldest son and
nearest apparent and undoubted heir of the unconquered and
most potent Prince Henry VIII, by the grace of God King of
England, France and Ireland, Defender of the Faith and
Supreme Head on Earth of the Church of England and Ireland,
as yet of less age and not six years old, shall marry . . . Mary,
Queen of Scotland, now also minor and not yet out of her
first year. . . .

[As soon as Mary completes her tenth year and reaches
her eleventh, she shall be taken in the next month to the
vicinity of Berwick to be shown to those whom Henry (if he
survive) or Edward shall send there so that they may accom-
pany her to the presence of the English king. Before her
departure from Scotland, the contract of marriage shall be
concluded by proxy.]

Notwithstanding any other effect hoped herefrom through
the marriage to follow, the kingdom of Scotland shall nevertheless retain the name of kingdom and be called the kingdom
of Scotland, with all its laws and lawful liberties of the same
kingdom, as they have always, from the beginning, been
rightly and continuously used and observed and approved in
the same kingdom of Scotland.

If, after the arrival of the most illustrious Lady Mary in England and the consummation of her marriage with the most illustrious Prince Edward, it happen (which God forbid) the said most illustrious prince to die without issue by . . . Mary, in that case the said . . . Mary is to have free faculty and power to return to the kingdom of Scotland . . . without any impediment or obstacle.

At the time when . . . Mary is brought to the kingdom of England by the present agreement a noble man James, Earl of Arran, governor of the kingdom of Scotland, who by that name shall meantime both uplift the fruits of the kingdom and intromit with the goods of the said queen, shall — both himself and his heirs and successors — be at that time freed and discharged by the . . . King of England and . . . Prince Edward, and be rendered quit of the fruits received and all the movable goods with which the said governor has intromitted, reserving only from those movable goods which then remain a convenient part and portion which is required to direct the person of the said . . . Mary into England. . . .

Within two months from the date of these presents the present treaty shall be sworn, confirmed and ratified.

Foedera, xiv, 792-96.

1543   DENUNCIATION OF
TREATIES OF GREENWICH

The real reason why the Scottish parliament, on 11 December 1543, repudiated the agreement with England was that the pro-English and reforming faction had been displaced and the Governor, Arran, had fallen under the influence of Cardinal David Beaton and others favourable to France and the papacy. But English action had given the Scots ample grounds for a technical justification of their volte-face, *as this document shows.*

The quhilk day anentis the artikle proponit tuiching the pece and contract of mariage laitlie tane and maid betuix the

ambassatoris of our soverane lady the quenis grace and the
commissaris of the king of Ingland betuix our said soverane
lady and Edward prince of Ingland, sone and apperand air to
the king of Ingland, gif the samyn suld be observit and keipit
or nocht: My lord governour and thre estatis of parliament
fyndis that the said peice was takin concludit and endit in
the begynnyng of the moneth of Julii last bypast betuix the
saidis ambassatoris and commissaris of bayth the realmes and
the selis to have bene interchengit betuix that and the first
day of September nixt therefter exclusive, and thane the said
peace was proclamit bayth in Ingland and Scotland, and
throw pretence tharof the merchandis of Scotland put thair
schippis and guidis to the see, and lang befor the said first
day of Semptember thai war takin be Inglismen and haldin
thame selfis, thair schippis and guidis as yit unrestorit bot
demanit as inimeis, nochtwithstanding the said pece and divers
message send for delivering of thame. Quharthrow the said
king of Ingland hes violate and brokin the said pece and thar-
for and becaus the said contract of marriage was grantit for
the said peice to have bene had observit and keipit betuix the
twa realmes, quhilk was nocht keipit bot brokin and violet be
the said king of Ingland as said is, and als becaus my lord
governour send bayth the contractis of pece and mariage
ratifiit, apprevit and sworn be him and selit with our soverane
ladeis gret sele according to the indentis befor the said first
day of Semptember, and causit the samyn to be deliverit to
the said king of Ingland, quha was requirit be the ambassatoris
send be my lord governour to have deliverit the saidis contractis
in siclik maneir ratifyit apprevit and sworn be him, and he
refusit to do the samyn: My lord governour and thre estatis
in parliament forsaid has declarit and declaris the saidis
contractis to be expirit in thame selfis and nocht to be keipit
in tyme cuming for the part of Scotland be law, equite and just
resoun.

A.P.S., ii, 431, c. 2.

1548 TREATY OF HADDINGTON

*After the defeat of the Scots at Pinkie in 1547, English armies
were in occupation of a number of strong points in south-
east Scotland, and the Scottish government could not, of its
own resources, eject them. France was prepared to help, but
only on conditions to which the Scots agreed in a treaty
made on 7 July 1548 at the nunnery outside Haddington,
where the Scots and French were besieging the English.*

The quhilk day Monsiour Dessy,[1] Lieutennent generall of the
navy and armie send be the maist Christin king of France for
support of this Realme at this present tyme, schew . . . how
that the said maist Christin king hes set his haill hart & minde
for defence of this Realme, desyrit in his said maisters name
for the mair perfyte union and indissolubill band of perpetuall
amitie lig & confederatioun the mariage of our soverane
Lady to the effect that the said maist Christin kingis eldest
sone and Dolphin of France may be conjunit in matrimonie
with hir grace, . . . observand and keipand this Realme and
liegis thairof in the samin fredome liberteis & lawis as hes
bene in all kingis of Scotlandis tymes bypast; and sall mantene & defend this Realme and liegis of the samin as he dois
the Realme of France and liegis thairof. . . . And thairfoir
desyrit my Lord Governour and thre Estatis of Parliament to
avise heirwith and gif thair determinatioun thairintill gif the
desyre foirsaid be ressonabill & acceptabill or not. The Quenis
grace our soverane Ladyis maist derrest mother being present,
my Lord Governour and thre Estatis of Parliament foirsaid all
in ane voice hes fundin and decernit and be censement of
Parliament concludit the desyre of the said Monsiour Dessy
Lieutennent in name of the said maist Christin king his
maister (Monsiour Dosell[2] his Ambassadour present in the
said Parliament confirmand the samin) verray ressonabill, and
hes grantit that our said Soverane Lady be maryit with the
said Dolphin at hir perfyte age, and presentlie gevis thair
consent thairto, swa that the said king of France keip manteine and defend this Realme, liegis of the samin, liberteis &
lawis thairof, as he dois his awin realme of France and liegis

1 Andre de Montalembert, sieur d'Esse.
2 Henri Cleutin, sieur d'Oysel et de Villeparisis et Saint-Aignan.

of the samin. . . .

My Lord Governour in our soverane ladyis name ratifeis
and apprevis in this present Parliament the determinatioun
and consent of the thre Estatis of the samin being present
concerning the mariage of our Soverane Lady with the
Dolphin of France conforme to the act of Parliament maid
thairupone, provyding alwayis that the king of France . . .
keip and defend this realme, . . . as his awin realme . . . and as
hes bene keipit in all kingis tymes of Scotland bypast, and to
mary hir upone na uther persoun bot upon the said Dolphin
allanerlie.

A.P.S., ii, 481-2.

1549, 1552, 1559
STATUTES OF REFORMING COUNCILS

*In three councils, attempts were made to reform the Scottish
Church without drastically altering its structure, and so go
some way to meet the criticisms of the reformers. The statutes
passed, from which a selection is given below, are probably
significant of intention rather than achievement, but they do
at least illustrate some of the prevalent evils.*

This synod exhorts that neither prelates nor their subordinate
clergy keep their offspring born of concubinage in their company, nor suffer them directly or indirectly to be promoted
in their churches, nor under colour of any pretext to marry
their daughters to barons or make their sons barons out of
the patrimony of Christ.

1549. Patrick, *Statutes of the Scottish Church*, 92.

Likewise it is statute that no cleric having the means of an
honourable livelihood according to his own calling engage in
secular pursuits, especially by trading, . . . or by leasing farms
from others allow himself to be withdrawn by farm work
from spiritual exercises to the neglect of his proper cure of
souls.

1549, repeated in 1559. Patrick, 92, 166.

Item all prelates and churchmen are to be exhorted to wear henceforth graver attire than they have been wont to do. . . .

1549. Patrick, 94.

It is enacted that parsons[1] of parish churches — who, in the judgment of the ordinary, shall be reckoned capable and suitable for preaching the elements of the faith to their parishioners — preach in person at least four times in the year.

1549, repeated in 1552 and 1559. Patrick, 103-4, 136, 171.

With respect to curates[2] of parish churches or ministers performing the pastoral duties, since very many of them throughout the whole realm of Scotland are discovered to be so very deficient as well in learning, morals and discretion as in other qualifications requisite for that office, the present convention has statute that . . . all curates be cited by their local ordinaries to appear . . . and undergo a due examination in all the requirements of their office.

1549. Patrick, 110.

[The council of 1552 authorised a new Catechism, which was to be read by priests to their congregations.] That those on whom this task is imposed by the present constitution may the better acquit themselves of it, with greater ease to themselves and greater devotion and profit on the part of the people, the said parsons, vicars or curates must not go up into the pulpit without due preparation, but they must prepare themselves with all zeal and assiduity for the task of reading by constant, frequent and daily rehearsal of the lesson to be read, lest they expose themselves to the ridicule of their hearers when, through want of preparation, they stammer and stumble.

Patrick, 146.

Item the present synod ordains and has decreed that all ruinous and dilapidated churches within the realm of Scotland shall be rebuilt and repaired in their walls, roofs, ornaments and all necessaries.

1559. Patrick, 168.

1 I.e., *rectores*, clerics drawing the bulk of the revenues of parishes but not normally resident in them.
2 I.e., persons having the cure of souls, irrespective of their precise title.

1557 FIRST BOND OF
LORDS OF THE CONGREGATION

The increased boldness of the reformers in the late 1550s was partly a reflection of political circumstances: Mary of Guise had become governor in 1554, and her administration of Scotland in the interests of France was highly unpopular. Yet the 'First Bond' on behalf of the 'Congregation' seems to have misfired. Although ample space was provided for signatures, only three earls, the son of one of them, and one laird, actually signed.

We, persaving how Sathan, In his membris the Antechristes of oure tyme, crewellie dois Raige seiking to downetring and to destroye the Evangell of Christ and his Congregatioune: awght according to our bownden dewtye to stryve in oure maisteres Cawss, even unto the deth: Being certane of the victorye, in HIM: The quhilk our dewtie being weill consyderit: WE do promis before the Maiestie of God, and his Congregatioune: that we (be his grace) sall with all diligence continewallie applie oure hoill power, substaunce, and oure very lyves to mentene sett forwarde and establische the MAIST BLISSED WORDE OF GOD, and his Congregatioune: And sall lawboure, at oure possibilitie, to haif faithfull ministeres purelie and trewlie to minister Christes Evangell and Sacramentes to his Peopill: We sall mentene thame, nwrys thame, and defende thame, the haill Congregatioune of CHRIST, and everye member therof, at oure haill poweres, and waring of oure lyves aganis Sathan and all wicked power that dois intend tyrannye or troubill aganis the forsaid Congregatioune. Onto the quhilk holie worde and Congregatioune we do joyne ws: and also dois forsaik and Renunce the Congregatioune of Sathan with all the superstitioune, abhominatioune, and Idolatrie thereof: And mareattour sall declare oure selfues manifestlie Innemies tharto: Be this oure faithfull promis, before God, testefyit to his Congregatioune, be oure Subscriptiones at thir presentes. At Edinburgh the [   ] day of December The yere of God ane thowsaunde fyve hundreth fiftie sevin yeres: God callit to wytnes. (*Signed:*) A. Erle of Ergyl,[1] Glencarne,[2] Mortoun,[3]

1 Archibald, Earl of Argyll.   2 Alexander, Earl of Glencairn.
3 James, Earl of Morton, afterwards Regent.

Ar. Lord of Lorn,[4] Jhone Erskyne.[5]

Original in Nat. Library of Scotland; facsimile and
transcript in *Nat. MSS. Scot.*, iii, No. x1.

4 Archibald, Lord Lorne, afterwards Earl of Argyll.
5 John Erskine of Dun, afterwards superintendent of Angus.

1559   THE BEGGARS' SUMMONS

The agitation in the burghs against the friars, who professed
poverty but were accused of engrossing alms which might
have relieved the needs of the genuine poor, found expression
in this document, posted at the doors of friaries throughout
Scotland and summoning the friars to quit before the next
Whitsunday term.

The Blynd, Cruked, Beddrelles,[1] Wedowis, Orphelingis,[2]
and all uther Pure, sa viseit be the hand of God, as may not
worke,
   To the Flockes of all Freires within this Realme, we wische
Restitutioun of Wranges bypast, and Reformatioun in tyme
cuming, for Salutatioun.
   Ye your selfes ar not ignorant (and thocht ye wald be) it
is now (thankes to God) knawen to the haill warlde, be his
maist infallible worde, that the benignitie or almes of all
Christian people perteynis to us allanerly; quhilk ye, being
hale of bodye, stark, sturdye, and abill to wyrk, quhat under
pretence of poverty (and neverles possessing maist easelie all
abundance), quhat throw cloiket and huded simplicitie (thoght
your proudnes is knawen) and quhat be feynyeit halynes,
quhilk now is declared superstitioun and idolatrie, hes thire
many yeiris, exprese aganis Godis word, and the practeis of
his holie Apostles, to our great torment (allace!) maist
falslie stowin[3] fra us. And als ye have, be your fals doctryne
and wresting of Godis worde (lerned of your father Sathan),
induced the hale people, hie and law, in seure hoip and beleif,

1 Bed-ridden.
2 Orphans.
3 stolen.

117

that to cleith, feid [   ]⁴ and nurreis yow, is the onlie
maist acceptable almouss allowit before God; and to gif ane
penny, or ane peice of breade anis in the oulk⁵ is aneuch for
us. Even swa ye have perswaded thame to bigge⁶ yow great
Hospitalis, and manteyne yow thairin [   ]⁴ force, quhilk
onlye pertenis now to us be all law, as biggit and dotat to the
pure of whois number ye are not, nor can be repute, nether
be the law of God, nor yit be na uther law proceding of
nature, reasoun, or civile policie. Quhairfore seing our number
is sa greate, sa indigent, and sa heavelie oppressed be your
false meanes, that nane takes cair of owre miserie; and that
it is better for us to provyde thire our impotent members,
quhilkis God hes geven us, to oppone to yow in plaine con-
troversie, than to see yow heirefter (as ye have done afore)
steill fra us our lodgeings, and our selfis, in the meantyme, to
perreis and die for want of the same. We have thocht gude
therfore, or we enter with yow in conflict, to warne yow, in
the name of the grit God, be this publick wryting, affixt on
your yettis⁷ quhair ye now dwell, that ye remove fourth of
oure saidis Hospitales, betuix this and the Feist of Witsunday
next,⁸ sua that we the onlie lauchfull proprietares thairof
may enter thairto, and efterward injoye thai commodities of
the Kyrk, quhilkis ye haif heirunto wranguslie halden fra us.
Certefying yow, gif ye failye, we will at the said terme, in
hale nummer (with the help of God, and assistance of his
sanctis in erthe, of quhais reddie support we doubt not),
enter and tak posessioun of our saide patrimony, and eject
yow utterlie fourth of the same.

*Lat hym therfore that before hes stollin, steill na mare;
but rather lat him wyrk wyth his handes, that he may be
helpefull to the pure.*

Fra the hale Citeis, Townes, and Villages of Scotland,
the Fyrst Day of Januare 1558.⁹

Knox, ii, 255-6.

4 This page at the end of the manuscript is badly torn down the right-hand side.
5 once a week.
6 build.
7 gates.
8 the normal term of removal.
9 I.e., 1559 by modern reckoning.

A rebellion, partly on patriotic and partly on religious grounds, had begun in the summer of 1559 against the French-dominated administration of Mary of Guise. In the autumn the insurgents had formally 'deposed' her and had transferred authority to a council under the presidency of James, Earl of Arran and Duke of Châtelherault, heir presumptive to the absent Queen Mary. But native forces found it impossible to achieve lasting success against the standing army of French soldiers, and the 'provisional government' of Scotland had to seek help from Queen Elizabeth of England.

[At Berwick on 27th February 1559/60 it was agreed between representatives of Elizabeth and representatives of Châtelherault,] secund personn of the realme of Scotland, and the remanent of the rest of the lordes of his parte joyned with him in this caus for maynteinance and defence of the auncient ryghteis and liberteis of their cuntree. . . .

That the Quenis Majestye having sufficientlie understanded alsweall by information sent from the nobilite of Scotland as by the manifest proceadingis of the Frenche that thei intend to conquer the realme of Scotland, supprese the liberties thairof and unyte the same unto the Crown of France perpetualie, contrarie to the laws of the said realme and to the pacts, othes, and promessis of France; and being thairto most humilie and earnestlie required by the said nobilite for and in the name of the hole realme:

Shall accept the said realme of Scotland, the said Duck of Chasteaulerault being declared by Acte of Parliament to be heyre apperand to the Crowne theirof, and the nobilite and subjectes of the same, into hir Majesties protection and maynteinaunce onelie for preservation of theym in their old fredomes and liberteis, and from conquest, during the tyme the mariage shall continew betuix the Queyn of Scottis and the Frenche King, and one yeir after: and for expelling owte of the same realme of such as presentlie goeth abowte to practise the said conquest.

Hir Majestie shall with all speyd send into Scotland a convenient ayd of men of warre on horse and foot to joyne with the power of the Scotishmen with artailye munition and all uthers instrumentis of warre mete for the purpose, alsweall by

sea as by land, not onelie to expel the present power of
Frenche within that realme oppressing the same but also to
stop as far as convenientlie may be all grytare forces of
Frenche to enter thairin for the like purpose, and shall continew hir Majesties ayde to the said realme, nobilite and subjectes of the same, until the French being ennemis to the
said realme be utterlie expelled thence. . . .

And yf in caise any fortes or strenthes within the said realme
be wonne out of the handes of the Frenche at this present or
any time hereafter, by Her Majesties ayde, the same shal be
immediatelie demolished by the Scottishmen, or delivered to
the Duck and his partye, at their optionn and choise. Neyther
shall the power of England fortifye within the grownde of
Scotland being owt of the bowndes of England, but by the
advyse of the said Duck, nobilite and estates of Scotland. . . .

[In return the Scots promise to support the English arms,
to resist conquest or annexation by France, and if England is
invaded by France to send 2,000 cavalry and 2,000 infantry
to England's aid.]

And fynalie, the said Duck, and nobilitie joyned with him,
certanelie perceaving that the Quenys Majestie of England is
theirunto onelie moved uppon respect of princelie honour
and neyghbowrheid for defence of the just freedome of the
Crowne of Scotland from conquest, and not of any other
sinister entent, doeth by these presentis testifye and declair
that thei nor any of theym meane by this compacte to with-
drawe any deu obedience from their Soverane Ladye the
Queyn, nor in any lefull thing to withstand the Frenche king,
being her husband and head, that during the mariage shall
not tend to the subversionn and oppressionn of the just and
auncient liberties of the said Kingdome of Scotland . . .

Foedera, xv, 569-71.

1560 TREATY OF EDINBURGH

*The war waged in Scotland in the early months of 1560,
mainly between the French soldiers of Mary of Guise and the*

forces sent from England to assist the reformers, was brought to an end by this agreement. The treaty was one between the English and the French, but it was accompanied by certain 'concessions' made to the Scots by the representatives of their absent queen, Mary, and her husband, Francis, now King of France.

[It was agreed between French and English representatives, at Edinburgh on 6 July 1560] that all military forces, land and naval, of each party shall withdraw from the realm of Scotland . . . and that all warlike preparations, namely in England and Ireland against the French or Scots and in France against the English, Irish or Scots, shall entirely cease. . . .

Since the realms of England and Ireland belong of right to the said most serene lady and princess Elizabeth and no other is therefore allowed to call, write, name or entitle himself or have himself called, written, named or entitled King or Queen of England or Ireland nor to use or arrogate to himself the signs and arms (commonly called armories) of the kingdoms of England or Ireland, it is therefore decided, concluded and agreed that the most Christian King [Francis] and Queen Mary . . . shall henceforth abstain from using or bearing the said title and arms of the kingdom of England or Ireland. . . .

Since it seems good to Almighty God, in whose hand are the hearts of kings, to incline the minds of the said most Christian King and Queen Mary fully to show mercy and grace to their nobility and people of their realm of Scotland, and in turn the said nobility and people have of their own free will professed, acknowledged and promised their obedience and loyalty henceforth towards their said most Christian king and queen, for the better nourishing, cherishing and continuance thereof the said most Christian king and queen by their said representatives have given assent to certain prayers of the said nobility and the supplications of the people presented to them tendering to the honour of the said king and queen, the common weal of the said kingdom and the preservation of their obedience. . . .

Foedera, xv, 593-7.

Concessions to the Scots

1. Upon the complaint made by the nobility and people of this country against the number of soldiers kept up here in time

of peace, supplicating the lords deputies of the King and Queen to afford some remedy therein for the relief of the country; the said deputies having considered the said request to be just and reasonable, have consented, agreed and appointed in the name of the King and Queen, that hereafter their Majesties shall not introduce into this kingdom any soldiers out of France, or any other nation whatsoever, unless in the event of a foreign army's attempting to invade and possess this kingdom, in which case the king and queen shall make provision by and with the counsel and advice of the three estates of this nation. And as for the French soldiers that are just now in the town of Leith, they shall be sent back into France at the same time that the English naval and land armies together with the Scottish army shall remove in such form as shall be more amply devised. . . .

IV. Concerning the petition relating to the assembling of the States, the lords deputies have agreed, consented and appointed that the States of the kingdom may assemble in order to hold a Parliament on the 10th day of July now running; and that on the said day the Parliament shall be adjourned and continued according to custom from the said 10th day of July until the 1st day of August next. . . . And this assembly shall be as valid in all respects as if it had been called and appointed by the express commandment of the king and queen. . . .

V. Concerning the article relating to peace and war, the lords deputies have consented, granted and appointed that neither the king nor the queen shall order peace or war within Scotland but by the advice and consent of the three estates. . . .

VI. Touching the petition presented to the lords deputies relative to the political government and the affairs of state within this kingdom, the said lords have consented, accorded and agreed that the three estates shall make choice of twenty-four able and sufficient persons of note of this realm; out of which number the queen shall select seven, and the states five, for to serve as an ordinary council of state during her majesty's absence, for administration of the government. . . . It is specially declared that the concession of this article shall in nowise prejudge the king and queen's rights for hereafter, nor the rights of this crown. . . .

VII. Concerning the petition presented to the lords deputies respecting the offices of the crown, they have consented, agreed and appointed that hereafter the king and queen shall not employ any stranger in the management of justice, civil or criminal, nor yet in the offices of chancellor, keeper of the seals, treasurer, comptroller, and such like offices; but shall employ therein the native subjects of the kingdom. *Item,* that their majesties shall not put the offices of treasurer and comptroller into the hands of any clergyman, or other person who is not capable to enjoy a state office. . . .

VIII. The lords deputies have agreed that in the ensuing parliament the states shall form, make and establish an act of oblivion, which shall be confirmed by their majesties the king and queen, for sopiting and burying the memory of all bearing of arms, and such things of that nature as have happened since the 6th day of March 1558[/9]. . . .

IX. It is agreed and concluded that the estates shall be summoned to the ensuing Parliament according to custom: and it shall be lawful for all those to be present at that meeting who are in use to be present, without being frightened or constrained by any person. . . .

XIII. It is agreed and concluded that if any bishops, abbots or other ecclesiastical persons shall make complaint that they have received any harm either in their persons or goods, these complaints shall be taken into consideration by the Estates in Parliament, and such reparation shall be appointed as to the said estates shall appear to be reasonable. And in the meantime it shall not be lawful for any person to give them any disturbance in the enjoyment of their goods nor to do them any wrong, injury or violence. . . .

XVII. Whereas on the part of the nobles and people of Scotland there have been presented certain articles concerning religion and certain other points in which the lords deputies would by no means meddle, as being of such importance that they judged them proper to be remitted to the King and Queen; Therefore the said nobles of Scotland have engaged that in the ensuing Convention of Estates some persons of quality shall be chosen for to repair to their majesties and remonstrate to them the state of their affairs, particularly those last mentioned, and such others as could not be decided by the lords deputies and to understand their intention and pleasure concerning what remonstrances shall be made to them on the part of this kingdom of Scotland.

Keith, *History of Affairs of Church and State in Scotland* (Spottiswoode Soc.), i, 298-306.

1560   ACTS OF
'REFORMATION PARLIAMENT'

The withdrawal of the French and English left the Scots free to settle their own affairs, and in August 1560 a parliament met which passed acts in accordance with the reformers' programme. It was far from clear, however, if this parliament and its legislation were legal in terms of the 'Concessions' of July. Besides, Queen Mary never approved these acts, which did not become the law of the land until they were passed afresh after the deposition of Mary and the accession of James VI in 1567.

The thre estaitis then being present understanding that the jurisdictioun and autoritie of the bischope of Rome callit the paip usit within this realme in tymes bipast has bene verray hurtful and prejudiciall to our soveranis autoritie and commone weill of this realme Thairfoir hes statute and ordanit that the bischope of Rome haif na jurisdictioun nor autoritie within this realme in tymes cuming And that nane of oure saidis soveranis subjectis of this realme sute or desire in ony tyme heireftir title or rycht be the said bischope of Rome or his sait to ony thing within this realme under the panis of barratrye, that is to say proscriptioun banischement and nevir to bruke honour office nor dignitie within this realme. And the controvenaris heirof to be callit befoir the Justice or his deputis or befoir the lordis of sessioun and punist thairfoir conforme to the lawis of this realme And the furnissaris of thame with fynance of money and purchessaris of thair title of rycht or manteanaris or defendaris of thame sall incur the same panis. And that na bischop nor uther prelat of this realme use ony jurisdictioun in tymes to cum be the said bischop of Romeis autoritie under the pane foirsaid.

Forsamekle as thair hes bene divers and sindrie actis of

parliament maid in King James the first secund thrid ferd and
fyftis tymes kingis of Scotland for the tyme and als in our
soverane Ladeis tyme not aggreing with Goddis holie word,
And be thame divers personis tuke occasioun of mantenance
of idolatrie and superstitioun in the kirk of God and repressing
of sic personis as wer professouris of the said word, quhair-
throw divers innocentis did suffir: for eschewing of sic in
tyme cuming The thre estaitis of parliament hes annullit and
declarit all sik actis maid in tymes bipast not aggreing with
Goddis word and now contrair to the confessioun of oure
fayth according to the said word publist in this parliament to
be of nane avale force nor effect And decernis the saidis actis
and every ane of thame to have na effect nor strenth in tyme
tocum Bot the samyn to be abolishit and extinct for evir insa-
fer as ony of the saidis actis ar repugnant and contrarie to the
confessioun and word of God foirsaidis ratifiit and apprevit
be the saidis estaitis in this present parliament.

Forsamekle as almichtie God be his maist trew and blissit
word hes declarit the reverence and honour quhilk suld be
gevin to him and be his sone Jesus Christ hes declarit the
trew use of the sacramentis willing the same to be usit
according to his will and word Be the quhilk it is notoure
and perfitlie knawin that the sacramentis of baptisme and of
the body and blude of Jesus Chryst hes bene in all tymes
bipast corruptit be the papistical kirk and be thair usurpit
ministeris And presentlie notwithstanding the reformatioun
already maid according to Goddis word yit nottheless thair
is sum of the same papis kirk that stubburnlie perseveris in
thair wickit idolatrie, sayand mess and baptizand conforme to
the papis kirk, prophanand thairthrow the sacramentis foirsaidis in quiet and secreit places, regardand thairthrow nather
God nor his holie word: Thairfoir it is statute and ordanit in
this present parliament that na maner of persone or personis
in ony tymes cuming administrat ony of the sacramentis
foirsaidis secreitlie or in ony uther maner of way bot thai that
ar admittit and havand power to that effect and that na
maner of person nor personis say messe nor yit heir messe
nor be present thairat under the pane of confiscatioun of all
thair gudis movable and unmovable and puneissing of thair
bodeis at the discretioun of the magistrat within quhais
jurisdictioun sik personis happynnis to be apprehendit for
the first falt, Banissing of the realme for the secund falt And

justifying to the deid for the thrid falt: And ordanis all schireffis stewartis baillies and thair deputis provestis and baillies of burrowis and utheris jugeis quhatsumever within this realme to tak diligent sute and inquisitioun within thair boundis quhair ony sik usurpit ministerie is usit messe saying or thai that beis present at the doing thairof ratifyand and apprevand the samyn, and tak and apprehend thame to the effect that the panis abovewrittin may be execute upoun thame.

A.P.S., ii, 534-5.

1560-61   FIRST BOOK OF DISCIPLINE

A 'Book of Reformation' had been commissioned by the provisional government on 29 April 1560 and completed by 20 May, but there are reasons for believing that the Book of Discipline as it is preserved in Knox's History *of the* Reformation *was a much expanded version which did not take its final form until January 1561. The document, even in its final shape, consisted of recommendations made by a committee of ministers to 'the lords' — that is, the protestant nobles and lairds who were in control of the administration for the time being — and it must not be mistaken for legislation which was carried into effect. The extracts below are from Dickinson's edition of Knox's* History, *with references to the pages in vol. ii.*

[The Kalendar]

Keeping of holy days of certain Saints commanded by man, such as be all those that the Papists have invented, as the Feasts (as they term them) of Apostles, Martyrs, Virgins, of Christmas, Circumcision, Epiphany, Purification, and other fond feasts of our Lady . . . we judge them utterly to be abolished from this Realm (281).

[Church Buildings]

As we require Christ Jesus to be truly preached, and his holy Sacraments to be rightly ministered; so can we not cease to require idolatry, with all monuments and places of the same, as abbeys, monasteries, friaries, nunneries, chapels, chantries, cathedral kirks, canonries, colleges, other than presently are parish Kirks or Schools, to be utterly suppressed . . . (283).

Lest that the word of God, and ministration of the Sacraments, by unseemliness of the place come in contempt, of necessity it is that the churches and places where the people ought publicly to convene be with expedition repaired in doors, windows, thatch, and with such preparations within, as appertaineth as well to the majesty of the word of God as unto the ease and commodity of the people.[1] . . . Every Church must have doors, close windows of glass, thatch or slate able to withhold rain, a bell to convocate the people together, a pulpit, a basin for baptism, and tables for the ministration of the Lord's Supper . . . (320-1).

[Admission of Ministers]

It appertaineth to the people, and to every several congregation, to elect their Minister. . . . For altogether this is to be avoided, that any man be violently intruded or thrust in upon any congregation. But this liberty with all care must be reserved to every several kirk, to have their votes and suffrages in election of their Ministers (284-5).

The admission of Ministers to their offices must consist in consent of the people and Kirk whereto they shall be appointed, and in approbation of the learned Ministers appointed for their examination. . . .[2] Other ceremony than the public approbation of the people, and declaration of the chief minister, that the person there presented is appointed to serve

1 'Agreed on' [by the lords] in margin.
2 This is very vague. The following extracts from the proceedings of the general assembly are more explicit:
That the examination of all these who have not been examined already shall be in the presence of the superintendent, and of the best reformed kirk within his bounds nearest the place where the minister is to be established; providing always that the judgement of the best learned being present be sought in the examination and admission, and that he who shall be so admitted shall not be removed, according to the order of the Book of Discipline (*B.U.K.*, i, 15). Touching persons to be nominat to kirks, that nane be admitted without the nomination of the people, and due examination and admission of the superintendent; and who have been otherwayes intrused since the yeir 1558, to make supplication for their provision according to the foresaid act (Ibid., 16).

that Kirk, we cannot approve; for albeit the Apostles used the imposition of hands, yet seeing the miracle is ceased, the using of the ceremony we judge is not necessary (286).

[Readers and Exhorters]

To the kirks where no ministers can be had presently, must be appointed the most apt men that distinctly can read the Common Prayers[3] and the Scriptures, to exercise both themselves and the kirk, till they grow to greater perfection; and in process of time he that is but a Reader may attain to the further degree, and by consent of the kirk and discreet ministers, may be permitted to minister the sacraments; but not before that he be able somewhat to persuade by wholesome doctrine, besides his reading, and be admitted to the ministry as before is said. . . . If from Reading he begin to Exhort, and explain the Scriptures, then ought his stipend to be augmented; till finally he come to the honour of a Minister (287, 290).

[The Care of the Poor]

Every several kirk must provide for the poor within the self. . . . We are not patrons for stubborn and idle beggars who, running from place to place, make a craft of their begging, whom the Civil Magistrate ought to punish; but for the widow and fatherless, the aged, impotent, or lamed, who neither can nor may travail for their sustentation, we say that God commandeth his people to be careful. And therefore, for such, as also for persons of honesty fallen in[to] decay and penury, ought such provision be made that [of] our abundance should their indigence be relieved. How this most conveniently and most easily may be done in every city and

3 In earlier documents issued by the reformers, 'the Common Prayers' had meant the English Book of Common Prayer, and that book was widely used in Scotland in 1560. But already copies of the Book of Common Order (which Knox had used in Geneva) were finding their way to Scotland, and the meaning of the phrase here must remain indeterminate. By acts of 1562 and 1564 the general assembly prescribed the use of the Book of Common Order (*B.U.K.*, i, 30, 54).

other parts of this Realm, God shall show you wisdom and the means, so that your minds be godly thereto inclined. All must not be suffered to beg that gladly so would do; neither yet must beggars remain where they choose; but the stout and strong beggar must be compelled to work, and every person that may not work must be compelled to repair to the place where he or she was born (unless of long continuance they have remained in one place), and there reasonable provision must be made for their sustentation, as the church shall appoint (290-1).

[Superintendents]

To him that travelleth from place to place, whom we call Superintendents, who remain, as it were, a month or less in one place, for the establishing of the kirk, and for the same purpose changing to another place, must further consideration be had. And, therefore, to such we think six chalders [of] bear, nine chalders [of] meal, three chalders [of] oats for his horse, 500 merks [of] money . . . be payed . . . yearly (289).

Because we have appointed a larger stipend to those that shall be Superintendents than to the rest of the Ministers, we have thought good to signify unto your Honours such reasons as moved us to make difference betwix preachers at this time. . . .[4] We consider that if the Ministers whom God hath endued with his [singular] graces amongst us should be appointed to several and certain places, there to make their continual residence, that then the greatest part of this Realm should be destitute of all doctrine. . . . And therefore we have thought it a thing most expedient for this time[5] that, from the whole number of godly and learned [men], now presently in this Realm, be selected twelve or ten (for in so many Provinces have we divided the whole),[6] to whom

4 I.e., when, in view of the shortage of ministers, it might have seemed preferable to appoint each to a parochial charge.

5 But not inexpedient at other times. E.g., *Register of the Kirk Session of St. Andrews* (S.H.S.), i, 75: Wythowt the cayr [of] superintendentis, neyther can the kyrk be suddenlie erected, neyther can th[ei] be retened in disciplin and unite of doctrin; . . . o[f] Crist Jesus and of his apostolis we have command and exempill to appoynt me [n] to sic chergis. Cf. p. 137 below.

6 At another point in the Book of Discipline, where the dioceses are described in detail, they number only ten. The discrepancy is one of the indications that even in its final form the document had not been thoroughly revised.

charge and commandment shall be given to plant and erect churches, to set order and appoint ministers . . . to the countries that shall be appointed to their care where none are now. . . (291).

These men must not be suffered to live as your idle Bishops have done heretofore; neither must they remain where gladly they would. But they must be preachers themselves, and such as may make no long residence in any one place till their churches be planted and provided of Ministers, or at the least of Readers. . . . In visitation . . . they shall not only preach, but also examine the life, diligence, and behaviour of the Ministers; as also the order of their churches, [and] the manners of the people. They must further consider how the poor be provided; how the youth be instructed . . . (292-3).

After that the Church be established, and three years be passed, we require that no man be called to the office of a Superintendent who hath not two years, at the least, given declaration of his faithful labours in the ministry of some church (295).[7]

[Education]

Seeing that God hath determined that his Church here in earth shall be taught not by angels but by men . . . of necessity it is that your Honours be most careful for the virtuous education and godly upbringing of the youth of this Realm. . . . Of necessity therefore we judge it, that every several church have a Schoolmaster appointed, such a one as is able, at least, to teach Grammar, and the Latin tongue, if the town be of any reputation. If it be upland [i.e. rural] where the people convene to doctrine but once in the week, then must either the Reader or the Minister there appointed, take care over the children and youth of the parish, to

7 The acts of the general assembly throw more light on the superintendents' functions:

It was ordained, that if ministers be disobedient to superintendents in anything belonging to edification, they must be subject to correction. . . .

It is concluded be the haill Ministers assemblit, that all Ministers salbe subject to ther Superintendents in all lawfull admonitiouns, as is prescryvit alsweill in the Booke of Discipline as in the electioun of Superintendents. . . .

The Superintendents take count what bookes every Minister hes in store in the tyme of their visitation, and how the said Minister, and every ane of them, does profite from tyme to tyme in reiding and studying the samein (B.U.K. i, 14-15).

instruct them in their first rudiments, and especially in the Catechism, as we have it now translated in the Book of our Common Order, called the Order of Geneva. And further, we think it expedient that in every notable town, and especially in the town of the Superintendent, [there] be erected a College, in which the Arts, at least Logic and Rhetoric, together with the Tongues, be read by sufficient Masters . . . (295-6).

The Grammar Schools and of the Tongues being erected as we have said, next we think it necessary there be three Universities in this whole Realm, established in the towns accustomed. The first in Saint Andrews, the second in Glasgow, and the third in Aberdeen. . . (297).

[The Rents and Patrimony of the Kirk]

These two sorts of men, that is to say, the Ministers and the Poor, together with the Schools, when order shall be taken thereanent, must be sustained upon the charges of the Church. And therefore provision must be made, how and of whom such sums must be lifted. But before we enter in this head, we must crave of your Honours, in the name of the Eternal God and of his Son Christ Jesus, that ye have respect to your poor brethren, the labourers and manurers of the ground; who by these cruel beasts, the Papists, have been so oppressed that their life to them has been dolorous and bitter. . . . Ye must have compassion upon your brethren, appointing them to pay so reasonable teinds, that they may feel some benefit of Christ Jesus now preached unto them (302-3).

Neither do we judge it to proceed from justice that one man shall possess the teinds of another; but we think it a thing most reasonable, that every man have the use of his own teinds, provided that he answer to the Deacons and Treasurers of the Church of that which justly shall be appointed unto him. We require Deacons and Treasurers rather to receive the rents, nor the Ministers themselves, because that of the teinds must not only the Ministers be sustained, but also the Poor and Schools. And therefore we think it most expedient that common Treasurers, to wit, the Deacons, be appointed from year to year, to receive the whole rents appertaining to the Church . . . (303).

The sums able to sustain these forenamed persons [i.e., ministers, teachers and the poor] and to furnish all things appertaining to the preservation of good order and policy within the Church, must be lifted off the teinds. . . . We think that all things doted to hospitality, all annual rents, both in burgh and [to] land, pertaining to Priests, Chantries, Colleges, Chaplainries, and to Friars of all Orders, to the Sisters of the Seans,[8] and to all others of that Order, and such others within this Realm, be received still to the use of the Church or Churches within the towns or parishes where they were doted. Furthermore to the upholding of the Universities and sustentation of the Superintendents, the whole revenue of the temporality of the Bishops', Deans', and Archdeans' lands, and all rents of lands pertaining to the Cathedral Churches whatsoever. And further, merchants and rich craftsmen in free burghs, who have nothing to do with the manuring of the ground, must make some provision in their cities, towns, or dwelling places, for to support the need of the Church (304).

[The Kirk Session]

Men of best knowledge in God's word, of cleanest life, men faithful, and of most honest conversation that can be found in the Church, must be nominated to be in election. . . . The election of Elders and Deacons ought to be used every year once . . . lest that by long continuance of such officers, men presume upon the liberty of the Church. It hurts not that one man be retained in office more years than one, so that he be appointed yearly, by common and free election; provided always, that the Deacons, treasurers, be not compelled to receive the office again for the space of three years . . . (309-10).

The Elders being elected, must be admonished of their office, which is to assist the Minister in all public affairs of the Church; to wit, in judging and decerning causes; in giving of admonition to the licentious liver; [and] in having respect

8 I.e., the Convent of St Katharine of Sienna, which gave its name to the district of Sciennes in Edinburgh.

to the manners and conversation of all men within their charge. . . .

Yea, the Seniors ought to take heed to the life, manners, diligence and study of their Ministers. If he be worthy of admonition, they must admonish him; of correction, they must correct him. And if he be worthy of deposition, they, with the consent of the Church and Superintendent, may depose him . . . (310).

[Public and Family Worship]

Baptism may be ministered whensoever the Word is preached; but we think it more expedient, that it be ministered upon the Sunday, or upon the day of prayers, only after the sermon. . . . Four times in the year we think sufficient to the administration of the Lord's Table[9] . . . the first Sunday of March . . . the first Sunday of June . . . the first Sunday of September . . . and the first Sunday of December . . . ; we study to suppress superstition. . . . We think that none are apt to be admitted to that Mystery who cannot formally say the Lord's Prayer, the Articles of the Belief, and declare the Sum of the Law.

Further, we think it a thing most expedient and necessary, that every Church have a Bible in English, and that the people be commanded to convene to hear the plain reading or interpretation of the Scripture. . . .

Every Master of household must be commanded either to instruct, or else cause [to] be instructed, his children, servants, and family, in the principles of the Christian religion. . . . Men, women and children would be exhorted to exercise themselves in the Psalms, that when the Church conveneth, and does sing, they may be the more able together with common heart and voice to praise God.

In private houses we think it expedient, that the most grave and discreet person use the Common Prayers at morn and at night, for the comfort and instruction of others (313-4).

[*The Book of Discipline was ultimately subscribed, on 27 January 1560/61, by a number of the Lords, who promised* 'to set the same forward at the uttermost of our powers': *with, however, the following reservation* – 'Providing that

9 In 1562 the general assembly ordained the Communion to be ministered four times yearly in burghs and twice yearly in rural areas (*B.U.K.*, i, 30).

the Bishops, Abbots, Priors, and other prelates and beneficed men, which else have adjoined them to us, bruik the revenues of their benefices during their lifetimes, they sustaining and upholding the Ministry and Ministers, as is herein specified, for preaching of the Word, and ministering of the Sacraments of God' (324).]

1561 PROCLAMATION
CONCERNING STATE OF RELIGION

After Mary's return to Scotland, in August 1561, the constitutional position of the reformed church depended not on the acts of 1560 but on a royal proclamation. It should, however, be added that acts of council in 1562 making financial provision for the reformed church and acts of parliament of 1563 conferring on ministers the right to manses and glebes did imply official recognition, with the royal assent, of the reformed church.

Forsamekle as the Quenis Majestie hes understand the grete inconventis [*sic*] that [may] cum throwch the division presently standing in this realme for the differens in materis of religioun, that hir Majestie is maist desirous to see pacifiit be any gude ordour to the honour of God and tranquillite of hir realme, and menys to tak the samyn be the avyse of hir Estatis sa sone as convenientlie may be; and that hir Majesteis godly resolution thairin may be greitlie hinderit in cais ony tumult or seditioun be rasit amangis the liegis, gif ony suddane alteratioun or novatioun be preissit or attemptit befoir that the ordour may be establissed. Thairfore, for eschewing of the saidis inconvenientis, hir Majestie ordanis lettres to be direct to charge all and sindrie liegis, be oppin proclamatioun at the mercat croce of Edinburgh, and utheris places neidfull, that they, and every ane of thame, contene thame selffis in quietnes, keip peax and civile societie amangis thame selffis; and in the meyntyme, quhill the States of hir realme may be assemblit, and that hir Majestie have takin a finall ordour be thair avise and publict consent, − quhilk hir Majestie hopis

salbe to the contentment of the haill, — that nane of thame
tak upoun hand, privatlie or oppinlie, to mak ony alteratioun
or innovatioun of the state of religioun, or attempt ony thing
aganis the forme quhilk hir Majestie fand publict and universalie standing at hir Majesteis arrivall in this hir realme, under
the pane of deid: with certificatioun that gif ony subject of
the realme sall cum in the contrair heirof, he salbe estemit
and haldin a seditious persoun and raser of tumult; and the
said payne sal be execute upoun him with all rigour, to the
exemple of utheris. Attour, hir Majestie, be the avyse of the
Lordis of hir Secrete Counsell, commandis and chargeis all
hir liegis, that nane of thame tak upoun hand to molest or
trouble ony of hir domestic servandis or personis quhatsumevir cumit furth of France, in hir Graces cumpany, at this
tyme, in word, ded, or countenance, for ony caus quhatsumevir, other within hir palice or outwith, or mak ony
[devisioun or?] invasioun upoun ony of thame under quhatsumevir cullour or pretence, under the said pane of deid;
albeit hir Majestie be sufficientlie persuadit that hir gude and
loving subjectis wald do the samyn for the reverence thay
beir to hir persoun and authorite, nochtwithstanding that na
sic commandment war publist.

R.P.C., i, 266-7.

1561 ABSTRACTS OF
ECCLESIASTICAL RENTALS

*An arrangement made in February 1561/2, whereby the
existing possessors of benefices were to retain two-thirds of
their revenues, while the remaining third was to be uplifted
by the crown, partly for its own use and partly to pay
stipends to the clergy of the reformed church, necessitated a
survey of ecclesiastical wealth, recorded in Books of
Assumption. The first Account of the Collector of Thirds,
from which the following figures are taken, relates to the
revenues of the year 1561. The figures given, it must be
emphasised, are thirds of the total income under each head.*

Bishopric of Aberdeen

Money	£551. 5s. 7d.[1]
Wheat	1 chalder 2 bolls 2 firlots 2 2/3 pecks
Bere	11 c. 13 b. 2 f. 2 2/3 p.
Meal	8 c. 1 b. 2 f.
Oats	2 c. 11 b. 2 f. 2 p.
Marts[2]	15 5/6
Muttons	47
Capons	262
Poultry	476
Geese	18 1/3
Swine	5 2/3
Moorfowls	76

Abbey of Dunfermline

Money	£837. 16s. 11d.
Wheat	9 c. 9 b. 1 1/3 p.
Bere	34 c. 5 b. 2 1/3 p.[3]
Meal	5 c.
White oats	20 c. 7 b. 2 f.
Horse corn	29 c. 1 b. 1 f. 2 2/3 p.[4]
Capons	124 1/3
Poultry	255
Cheese	50 stones[5]
Butter	11 1/3 stones
Salt	3 c. 13 1/3 b.
Lime	6 c. 10 2/3 b.

Accounts of the Collectors of Thirds
(Scot. Hist. Soc.)

1 This figure was amended in subsequent years to £275. 12s. 9½d., on the ground that the 1561 figure had included certain revenues no longer received by the bishop and had been based partly on 'owir hie prices of salmond'.

2 Salted carcases of cattle.

3 Reduced after 1562 to 21 c. 15 b. 3 f. 1 p. on the ground that it had been 'wrang charged in baith the yeiris' (i.e., 1561 and 1562).

4 Horse corn was evidently an inferior kind of oats, possibly identical with the 'blak aittis' mentioned elsewhere. The figure was reduced to 16 c. 2 f. from 1563.

5 The cheese, butter, salt and lime do not appear in 1561 and 1562, but are added in later years.

1572 ARRANGEMENTS FOR
SUCCESSION TO BISHOPRICS

It had been decided in 1567 that, in general, benefices should be filled by the nominees of the lawful patrons, subject to examination by the superintendents, but no attempt had been made to apply this practice to the greater benefices, including the bishoprics. The question became acute when the arch-bishopric of St. Andrews fell vacant by the death of John Hamilton in 1571. The government of the Regent, Mar, appointed John Douglas, rector of the university of St. Andrews, to the vacant see, without consulting the church, and this action raised a storm of protest, expressed by John Erskine of Dun, superintendent of Angus. At a convention held at Leith in January 1571/2 a compromise was reached.

Erskine of Dun to the Regent Mar

. . . So by the kirk spiritual offices are distributed, and men admitted and receaved thereto. And the administratioun of the power is committed by the kirk to bishops or superinten-dents. Wherefore, to the bishops and superintendents pert-eaneth the examinatioun and admissioun of men to offices and benefices of spirituall cure, whatsoever benefice it be, als weill bishopricks, abbaceis and pryoreis, as the inferior benefices. That this perteaneth, by the Scriptures of God, to bishops and superintendents is manifest. . . . We have expressed plainlie by Scriptures that to the office of a bishop perteaneth examinatioun and admissioun to spirituall cure and office, and also to oversee them who are admitted, that they walke uprightlie and exerce their office faithfullie and purelie. To tak this power from the bishop or superintendent is to take away the office of a bishop, that no bishop be in the kirk; which were to alter and abolishe the order which God hath appointed in his kirk. . . . A greater offence or contempt of God and his kirk can no prince doe, than to sett up by his authoritie men in spiritual offices, as to creat bishops and pastors of the kirk; for so to doe is to conclude no kirk of God to be; for the kirk can not be, without it have the owne proper jurisdictioun and libertie, with the ministratioun of suche offices as God hath appointed. In speeking [of] this tuiching the libertie of the kirk, I meane not the hurt of the

137

king or others in their patronages, but that they have their
privileges of presentatioun according to the lawes; providing
alwise that the examinatioun and admissioun perteane onlie
to the kirk, of all benefices having cure of soules. . . .

Calderwood, *History of the Church of Scotland*, iii, 157-9.

Acts of the Convention of Leith

It is thocht, in consideratioun of the present state, that the
names and titillis of archebischoppis and bischoppis are not
to be alterit or innovat, nor yit the boundes of the dioceis
confoundit; bot to stand and continew in tyme cuming as
thay did befoir the reformatioun of religioun: at leist to the
kingis majesties majoritie, or consent of parliament.

That personis promovit to archebischoprikkis and bischoprikkis be, safar as may be, indewed with the qualiteis spec-
ifeit in the Epistlis of Paule to Timothe and Tytus.

That thair be a certane assembly or cheptoure of learnit
ministeris annext to every metrapolitan or cathedrall seatt.

To all archebischoprikkis and bischoprikkis vacand, or
that sall happin to vaik heirefter, personis qualifeit to be
nominat within the space of yeir and day eftir the vacance;
and the personis nominat to be xxx yeirs of age at the leist.

The deane, or, failyeing the deane, the nixt in dignitie of
the cheptoure, during the tyme of the vacance salbe vicar
generall and use the jurisdictioun *in spiritualibus* as the
bischop mycht have usit.

All bischoppis and archebischoppis to be admittit heirefter sall exerce na farther jurisdictioun in spirituall functioun
nor the superintendentis hes and presently exerces, quhill
the same be agreit upoun.

And that all archebischoppes and bischoppis be subject to
the kirk and generall assembly thairof *in spiritualibus* as thay
ar to the king *in temporalibus,* and haif the advise of the best
learnit of the cheptoure, to the nowmer of sex at the leist, in
the admissioun of sic as sall have spirituall functioun in the
kirk. As alsua, that it be lauchfull to als mony utheris of the
cheptoure as plesis to be present at the said admissioun and
to voit thairanent.

B.U.K., i, 209.

138

The principal novelty of this act was that it permitted the levying of a stent or assessment for the poor.

[After reference to previous acts, which had not been put to due execution:] It is thocht expedient and ordanit alsweill for the utter suppressing of the saidis strang and ydill beggaris, sa outragious ennemeis to the commoun weill, as for the cheritabill releving of the aigit and impotent puyr people, . . . that all personis . . . to be takin wandering and misordering thame selffis contrary to the effect and meaning of thir presentis salbe apprehendit . . . and . . . committit in ward in the commoun presoun, stokkis or irnis . . . quhill thay be put to the knawlege of ane assyise . . . and gif thay happin to be convicted to be adjugeit to be scurgeit and burnt throw the girssill of the rycht eare with ane het irne of the compasse of ane inche about . . . quhilk punisement anys ressavit he sall not suffer agane the lyke for the space of lx dayis thaireftir, bot gif at the end of the same lx dayis he be found to have fallin agane in his ydill and vagabound trade of lyff, than being apprehendit of new he salbe adjugeit and suffer the panis of death as a theif. . . .

All ydill personis gaying about in ony cuntre of this realme using subtile, crafty and unlauchfull playis, as juglerie, fast and lowis and sic utheris, the ydill people calling thame selffis egiptianis or ony uther that fenyeis thame to have knawlege in physnomie, palmestre or utheris abused sciencis quhairby thay perswade the people that they can tell thair weardis, deathis and fortunes and sic uther fantasticall ymaginationis, and all personis being haill and stark in body and abill to wirk allegeing to have bene hereit in the sowthland brint in the lait troubles about Edinburgh and Leith . . . and all menstrallis, sangstaris and taill tellaris not avowit in speciall service be sum of the lordis of parliament or greit barronis or be the heid burrowis and cities for thair commoun menstrallis . . . all vagaboundis scollaris of the universiteis of Sanctandrois, Glasgow and Abirdene not licencit be the rector and dene of faculte of the universitie to ask almous . . . salbe takin, adjugeit, demed and puneist as strang beggaris and vagaboundis. . . .

And sen cheritie wald that the puyr, aigit and impotent
personis sould be als necessarlie providit for as the vagaboundis
and strang beggaris ar repressit and that the aigit, impotent and
puyr people sould have ludgeing and abyding places throuch-
out the realme to settill thame selffis intill, . . . the eldaris
and deaconis in everie citie, burgh and gude toun and the
heidismen of ilk parochyn to landwart sall . . . tak inquisitioun
of all aigit, puyr, impotent and decayed personis borne within that parochyn or quhilkis wer dwelling and had thair maist
commoun resort in the said paroche the last sevin yeris bipast
quhilkis of necessitie mon leif be almous, and . . . mak a
register buke . . . and . . . considdir quhat thair neidfull
sustentatioun will extend to in the owlk and than be thair
gude discretionis taxt and stent the haill inhabitantis within
the parochyn according to the estimatioun of thair substance
without exceptioun of personis to sic oulklie charge and con-
tributioun as salbe thocht sufficient to sustene the saidis
puyr people . . . and at the end of the yeir that alsua the
taxatioun and stent roll be alwayis maid of new for the alteratioun that may be throw deith or the incres or diminutioun
of mennis gudis and substance.

And that the eldaris in citeis, burrowis and gude townis
and heidismen of the parochynnis to landwart sall gif a test-
imoniall to sic puyr folk as thay find not borne in thair awin
parochyn sending or directing thame to the nixt parochyn
and sa frome parochyn to parochyn quhill thay be at the
place quhair thay were borne or had thair maist commoun
resort and residence during the last sevin yeris.

A.P.S., iii, 86-8.

1578   A 'BOND OF FRIENDSHIP'

*Illustrations have already been given of bonds between
greater men and lesser men.*[1] *Other bonds were made between
equals, for political, religious or sometimes criminal purposes.
They are usually thought of, rightly, as having furnished*

1 See p. 97 above.

obstacles or problems to governments anxious to extend their authority and a respect for the law, but the following example shows that a bond, if faithfully carried out, might make a useful contribution to local stability.

Be it kend till all men be thir present letres We, Hew Erll of Eglintoun Lord Montgomerie, Williame Erll of Glencarne Lord Killmawars, Robert Lord Boid, Sir Mathow Campbell of Lowdoun knycht shereff of Air, Johnne Wallace of Cragie for him selff, Hew Maister of Eglintoun, James Maister of Glencarne, Thomas Maister of Boid, Hew Campbell of Tarringane, our eldest sones and apparent airis, and the said Johnne Wallace of Cragie taking the burding apoun him for Johne Wallace his sone and appering air, quha salbe comprehendit herin and subscrive thir presentis at his majoritie, Seing diverse querrelles and contraverseis arrysing alsweill amangis our freindis as uthers our nychtbouris, tending to the truble and brek of the cuntre, For repressing quhairof and for the zeall and ernist affectioun we bear to peax and commone quietnes and that we may be the mair able frelie and without impediment to awaitt apoun the Kingis Majesties service as it sall pleis his hienes to employe us, As alswa for confirming and gud interteinement of the ald bandis amitie and kindnes amangis our houssis, To be bundin and oblist and be thir presentis apoun our fayth and honouris the halie evangeill tuicheit solempnatlie bindis and oblissis us to tak trew faythfull afald[2] and plane partt all togiddir and ilkane with utheris alsweill be way of law as deid, persutt as defence, be our selffis our landis houssis guddis freindis servandis dependaris and all that we may move, in all and quhatsumevir actionis causis querrellis contraverseis and debettis movit or to be movit be or aganis us or ony ane of us our servandis or freindis propirlie depending apoun us aganis quhatsumevir persoun or personis (the Kingis Majestie and his hienes auctoritie allanerlie except), and that all actionis caussis and querrellis movit or to be movit be or aganis us ony ane of us or our foirsaidis salbe ane and comone as we and ilkane of us haid speciale and like enteres thairintill; That all our castellis houssis strenthis pertening to us or ony ane of us salbe readie and patent to us and ilkane of us as the cause and occasioun sall require; That we sall meit and convene als oft as salbe

2 loyal.

141

requisit, sall give uthir our trew faythfull best advise and
counsall in all effaris, sall keip utheris counsallis and secreteis,
nocht reveill nor bewray the samin, and sall nocht wranguslie
nor unkindlie tak utheris guddis landis offices rowmes takkis
steiddingis or possessiones, fee corrupt or accept utheris
servandis feallaris[3] or dependaris, procuir knaw or suffir the
harme skayth or dishonnour of ony of us, bot sall resist and
stop the samin to our uttirmest and sall give als haistie
knawlege thairof as salbe possible to quhomesumevir of us it
sall concerne, and sall speik nor do na thing directlie nor
indirectlie that may be prejudiciall dishonorabill or offensive
to uthir in ony soirt; And give it salhappin as God forbid ony
different[4] slauchtir blude or uther inconvenent to fall outt
amangis ony of us our freindis servandis or dependaris the
samin of quhatsumevir wecht or qualitie it be of salbe submittit to the decisioun and jugement of the remanent of us
subscriveris of this band, quha salhave full powar and
auctoritie to juge decyde and decerne thairintill, quhais sentence and decreit bayth the pairteis sall byde att fullfill and
observe without reclamatioun or appelatioun and salbe als
valide and effectuall in all respectis and have als full executioun as the samin haid bene gevin and pronuncit eftir
cognitioun in the cause be the Lords of Sessioun, Justice
Generale of Scotland or ony uthir Juge ordiner within this
realme; And will and grauntis that this band be als valide and
sufficient submissioun in all respectis as give the said different
slauchtir blude or inconvenient efter committing thairof war
speacialie submittit to the saidis persones subscriveris heirof
be bayth the pairteis be blank or uthirwayis quhilk also we
promise to do as we salbe requirit; And in the meyntyme for
the bettir quietnes We and everie ane of us faythfullie and
be our aythis promisis bindis and oblissis us that quhasaevir
of us or our foirsaidis salhappin to be offendit be uthir of
us or thair foirsaidis we nor thay sall nawayis take revenge
thairof be way of deid quhill we have first desyrit the pairtie
offendent to repair and amend the samin give[5] it be ane of
our selffis or cause the samin be repairit and amendit give
it be ane of our freindis servandis and dependaris and quhill

3 employees.
4 dispute.
5 if.

142

we have signifeit and gevin knawlege thairof to the remanent
subscriveris of this band that thai may cognosce and decerne
thairintill as said is; And give it salhappin as God forbid ony
of us to be willfull obstinat or stubburne and haveing offendit
to refuise to repair and amend our offence at the sycht of the
remanent subscriveris heirof and to cause our freindis
servandis and dependaris do the lyk in thair estaitt and degre,
Or being offendit to refuise mesour and reasoun at the sycht
of the remanent subscriveris heirof, To be bundin and oblist
and be thir presentis letres bindis and oblissis us to tak ane
efald[6] trew and plane pairtt with the ressonabill and moderat
pairtie aganis the willfull stubburne and obstinat bayth be
way of law and deid till he be constranit be law force or
freindlie dealling to cum to ressoun and conformitie: quhilk
and all the premissis We and ilkane of us hes be our aythis
apoun our fayth and honnouris faythfully and solempnantly
promisit and sworne to observe and keip undir the pane of
perjurie infamie and perpetuall defamatioun. In witnes
quhairof to thir presentis subscrivit with our handis our
seillis ar affixt At Striveling [13 June 1578].

Abbotsford Club Miscellany, i, 44-7.

6 loyal.

1578   SECOND BOOK OF DISCIPLINE

The constitution of the reformed church had all along been
something of a patchwork. Its central organ of government
was the general assembly, but the composition of the assembly
was ill-defined and its status indeterminate. Regional admin-
istration was in the hands of bishops, superintendents and
commissioners (appointed in areas where there was neither
bishop nor superintendent). There was as yet no organ of
government intermediate between the diocese (of bishop,
superintendent or commissioner) and the parish. Besides,
there were many unsolved problems of endowment.
From 1575, after the return to Scotland from Geneva of
Andrew Melville, an energetic campaign was conducted for

definition, and the novel view emerged that all ministers were equal in both order and jurisdiction, so that the entire administration of the church must lie not with individual overseers but with gatherings of ministers and elders. The Second Book of Discipline offered logical and comprehensive answers to all outstanding problems. But the Second Book of Discipline, like the First, was not accepted by the civil power, which alone could have put it into full effect, and it must be regarded as a series of recommendations rather than as legislation.

[The Two Kingdoms]

I. 2. The kirke . . . hes a certane power grantit be God, according to the quhilk it uses a proper jurisdiction and governement, exerciseit to the confort of the haill kirk. This power ecclesiasticall is an authoritie granted be God the Father, throw the Mediator Jesus Christ, unto his kirk gatherit, and having the ground in the Word of God; to be put in execution be them, unto quhom the spirituall government of the kirk be lawfull calling is committit.

I. 4. This power and policie ecclesiasticall is different and distinct in the awin nature from that power and policie quhilk is callit the civill power, and appertenis to the civill government of the commonwelth; albeit they be both of God, and tend to one end, if they be rightlie usit, to wit, to advance the glorie of God and to have godlie and gud subjectis.

I. 5. For this power ecclesiasticall flowes immediatlie from God, and the Mediator Jesus Christ, and is spirituall, not having a temporall heid on earth, bot onlie Christ, the onlie spirituall King and Governour of his kirk.

I. 8. It is proper to kings, princes and magistrates, to be callit lordis, and dominators over their subjectis, whom they govern civilly; bot it is proper to Christ onlie to be callit Lord and Master in the spirituall government of the kirk: and all uthers that bearis office therein aucht not to usurp dominion therein, nor be callit lordis, bot onlie ministeris, disciples and servantis. For it is Christis proper office to command and rewll his kirk universall, and every particular kirk, throw his Spirit and Word, be the ministrie of men.

I. 9. Notwithstanding, as the ministeris and uthers of the ecclesiasticall estait ar subject to the magistrat civill, so aught the person of the magistrat be subject to the kirk spiritually and in ecclesiasticall government. And the exercise of both these jurisdictiones cannot stand in one person ordinarlie. The civill power is callit the Power of the Sword, and the uther the Power of the Keyes.

I. 10. The civill power sould command the spiritual to exercise and doe their office according to the Word of God: the spiritual rewlaris sould requyre the Christian magistrate to minister justice and punish vyce, and to maintaine the libertie and quietness of the kirk within their boundis.

I. 14. . . . The ministeris exerce not the civill jurisdictioun, bot teich the magistrat how it sould be exercit according to the Word.

I. 15. . . . Finally, as ministeris are subject to the judgement and punishment of the magistrat in externall things, if they offend; so aucht the magistratis to submit themselfis to the discipline of the kirk gif they transgresse in matteris of conscience and religioun.

[Offices in the Church]

II. 6. . . . There are foure ordinarie functiones or offices in the kirk of God: the office of the pastor, minister or bishop; the doctor; the presbytar or eldar; and the deacon.

II. 8. Therefore, all the ambitious titles inventit in the kingdome of Antichrist, and in his usurpit hierarchie, quhilkis ar not of ane of these foure sorts, togither with the offices depending thereupon, in ane word, aucht all utterlie to be rejectit.

III. 5. In the order of election it is to be eschewit that na person be intrusit in ony of the offices of the kirk contrar to the will of the congregation to whom they ar appointed, or without the voce of the elderschip. . . .

IV. 1. Pastors, bischops or ministers ar they wha ar appointit to particular congregationes, quhilk they rewll be the Word of God and over the quhilk they watch. In respect whairof sumetymes they ar callit pastors, becaus they feid their congregation; sumetymes *episcopi*, or bischops, because they watch over their flock; sumetymes ministers, be reason of their service and office; and sumetymes also *presbyteri*, or seniors, for the gravity in manners quhilk they aucht to have in taking cure of the spirituall government, quhilk aucht to be most deir unto them.

V. 1. Ane of the twa ordinar and perpetuall functions that travell in the Word is the office of the doctor, quha also may be callit prophet, bischop, elder, catechizar, that is, teichar of the Catechisme and rudiments of religione.

V. 6. Bot to preiche unto the people, to minister the sacraments and to celebrate mariages, perteines not to the doctor, unlesse he be utherwyse orderlie callit. . . .

VI. 2. . . . . The elderschip is a spirituall function, as is the ministrie. Eldaris anis lawfully callit to the office, and having gifts of God meit to exercise the same, may not leive it again.

VI. 5. As the pastors and doctors sould be diligent in teiching and sawing the seed of the Word, so the elders sould be cairfull in seiking the fruit of the same in the people.

[Church Courts]

VII. 2. Assemblies ar of four sortis. For aither ar they of particular kirks and congregations, ane or ma, or of a province, or of ane haill nation, or of all and divers nations professing one Jesus Christ.

VII. 3. All the ecclesiasticall assemblies have power to convene lawfully togidder for treating of things concerning the kirk, and perteining to thair charge. They have power to appoynt tymes and places to that effect; and at ane meiting to appoynt the dyet, time and place for anuther.

VII. 10. . . . When we speik of the elders of the particular congregations, we mein not that every particular parish kirk can or may have their awin particular elderschips, specially to landwart; bot we think thrie or four, mae or fewar, particular kirks, may have ane common elderschip to them all, to judge thair ecclesiasticall causes.

VII. 21. The nationall assemblie, quhilk is generall to us, is a lawfull convention of the haill kirks of the realm or nation, where it is usit and gatherit for the common affaires of the kirk; and may be callit the generall eldership of the haill kirk within the realme. Nane ar subject to repaire to this assemblie to vote bot ecclesiasticall persons, to sic a number as shall be thocht gude be the same assemblie; not excluding uther persons that will repaire to the said assemblie, to propone, heir and reason.

[Deacons]

VIII. 3. Thair office and power is to receave and to

distribute the haill ecclesiasticall gudes unto them to whom
they ar appoyntit. This they aucht to do according to
the judgement and appoyntment of the presbyteries[1] or
elderschips (of the quhilk the deacons ar not), that the patrimonie of the kirk and puir be not convertit to privat men's
usis, nor wrangfullie distributit.

[The Patrimony of the Kirk]

IX. 1. Be the patrimonie of the kirk we mein whatsumever
thing hath bene at ony time before, or shall be in tymes
coming, gevin, or be consent or universall custome of countries professing the Christian religion applyit to the publique
use and utilitie of the kirk. Swa that under this patrimonie
we comprehend all things gevin, or to be gevin, to the kirk
and service of God, as lands, biggings, possessions, annual-
rents, and all sic lyke, wherewith the kirk is dotit, aither be
donations, foundations, mortifications, or ony uther lawfull
titles, of kings, princes or ony persons inferiour to them;
togither with the continuall oblations of the faithfull. We
comprehend also all sic things as be lawis, or custome, or use
of countries, hes bene applyit to the use and utilitie of the
kirk; of the quhilk sort ar teinds, manses, gleibs, and sic lyke,
quhilks, be commoun and municipall lawis and universall
custome, ar possessit be the kirk.

IX. 2. To tak ony of this patrimonie be unlawfull meinis,
and convert it to the particular and profane use of ony person,
we hald it ane detestable sacriledge befoir God.

[The Duty of the Christian Magistrate]

X. 2. It perteinis to the office of a Christian magistrat to
assist and fortifie the godly proceidings of the kirk in all
behalfes; and namely, to sie that the publique estait and
ministrie thereof be manteinit and susteinit as it apperteins,
according to Godis Word. . . . [4] To assist and manteine the
discipline of the kirk, and punish them civilly that will not
obey the censure of the same; without confounding alwayis
the ane jurisdiction with the uther. [5] To sie that sufficient
provision be made for the ministrie, the schules and the
puir. . . . [7] To mak lawis and constitutions agreeable to
God's Word, for advancement of the kirk and policie
thereof. . . .

1 Presbytery is here used in the sense of kirk session.

[Abuses]

XI. 2. . . . The admission of men to Papisticall titles of benefices, sic as serve not, nor have na function in the Reformit Kirk of Christ, as abbottis, commendatoris, prioris, prioressis, and uther titles of abbyis, quhais places are now for the most pairt, be the just judgement of God, demolishit and purgit of idolatrie, is plaine abusion. . . .

XI. 3. Siclyke that they that of auld wer callit the chapiters and convents of abbayis, cathedrall kirks, and the lyke places, serve for nathing now, bot to set fewes and tacks, if onything be left of the kirk lands and teinds, in hurt and prejudice thairof, as daily experience teiches, and thairfoir aucht to be utterly abrogat and abolishit. Of the lyke nature ar the deanes, archdeanes, chantors, subchantors, thesaurers, chancellars, and uthers having the lyke titles flowing from the Pape and canon law onlie, wha heve na place in the reformit kirk.

XI. 5. Neither aucht sic abusers of the kirk's patrimony to have vote in parliament, nor sit in councell under the name of the kirk and kirk-men, to the hurt and prejudice of the libertie thairof, and lawes of the realm made in favouris of the reformit kirk.

[Bishops]

XI. 9. As to bischops, if the name ἐπίσκοπος be properly takin, they ar all ane with the ministers, as befoir was declairit. For it is not a name of superioritie and lordschip, bot of office and watching. Yit, because in the corruption of the kirk, this name (as uthers) hes bene abusit, and yit is lykelie to be, we cannot allow the fashion of thir new chosin bischops, neither of the chapiters that ar electors of them to sic offices as they ar chosen to.

XI. 10. Trew bischops sould addict themselves to ane particular flock, quhilk sindry of them refuses; neither sould they usurpe lordship over their brethren and over the inheritance of Christ, as these men doe.

XI. 13. It agries not with the Word of God that bischops sould be pastors of pastors, pastors of monie flocks, and yit without anie certaine flock, and without ordinar teiching. . . .

[General Assemblies]

XII. 8. The nationall assemblies of this countrey, callit commonlie the Generall Assemblies, aucht alwayes to be reteinit in their awin libertie, and have their awin place; with power to the kirk to appoynt tymes and places convenient for the same: and all men, als weill magistrats as inferiours, to be subject to the judgement of the same in ecclesiasticall causes, without any reclamation or appellation to ony judge, civill or ecclesiasticall, within the realm.

[Distribution of Revenues]

XII. 12. As for the kirk rents in generall, we desyre the order to be admittit and mentainit amangis us that may stand with the sinceritie of God's Word and practise of the purity of the kirk of Christ; to wit, that as was before spoken, the haill rent and patrimonie of the kirk, exceptand the small patronages before mentionat, may be dividit in four portions: Ane thereof to be assignit to the pastor for his intertainment and hospitalitie: An uther to the eldars, deacons, and uther officers of the kirk, sic as clerks of assemblies, takers up of the psalmes, beadels and keipers of the kirk, sa far as is necessar; joyning therewith also the doctors of schules, to help the ancient foundations where neid requires: The third portion to be bestowit upon the puir members of the faithfull, and on hospitals: The fourth, for reparation of the kirks, and uther extraordinar charges as ar profitable for the kirk; and also for the common weil, if neid requyre.

[Conclusions]

XIII. 2. Nixt, we sall becum an example and paterne of gude and godly order to uther nations, countries and kirks, professing the same religion with us. . . .

XIII. 3. Mairover, gif we have any pity or respect to the puir members of Jesus Christ, who so greatly increase and multiplie amanges us, we will not suffer them to be langer defraudit of that part of the patrimonie of the kirk quhilk justly belangs unto them: And by this order, if it be deuly put to execution, the burden of them sall be taken of us to our great confort, the streits sall be cleansed of thair cryings and murmurings; swa as we sall na mair be an skandall to uther nations, as we have hitherto bene, for not taking order with the puir amanges us, and causing the Word quhilk we profess to be evill spokin of, giving occasion of sclander to the enemies and offending the consciences of the sempil and godly.

XIII. 4. Besydes this, it sall be a great ease and commoditie to the haill common people, in relieving them of the beilding and uphalding of thair kirks, in bigging of brigges, and uther lyke publick warks. It sall be a relief to the labourers of the ground in payment of their teinds; and schortlie, in all these things, whereinto they have bene hitherto rigorously handlit be them that were falslie callit kirkemen, thair tacksmen, factours, chalmerlanes and extortionars.

Finally, to the king's Majestie and common weill of the countrey this profite shall redound: that, the uther affaires of the kirk beand sufficientlie provydit according to the distribution of the quhilk hes bene spokin, the superplus, beand collectit in the treasurie of the kirk, may be profitablie imployit and liberallie bestowit upon the extraordinar support of the effaires of the prince and commoun weill, and speciallie of that part quhilk is appoyntit for reparation of kirks.

Calderwood, iii, 529 et seq.; B.U.K., ii, 488 et seq.

1581 NEGATIVE CONFESSION

The ascendancy of Esmé Stewart, Duke of Lennox, and rumours of plots with France and Spain for the restoration of Roman Catholicism led to a kind of popish scare which found expression in a comprehensive renunciation of all things papistical. The document was to form the first part of the National Covenant in 1638.

Ane shorte and generall confessione of the true Christiane fayth and religion according to Godis worde and actis of our perliamentis subcryved by the kingis majestie and his houshold with sindrie otheris to the glorie of God and good example of all men, at Edinburgh the 28 day of Januare 1580 [1581] and 14 yeare of his Majesties Reigne.

We all and everie one of us underwritten protest, that after

long and dew examination of our owne consciences in
matteris of true and false religioun, are now throughly
resolved in the trueth by the worde and sprit of God, and
therefore we beleve with our heartis, confesse with our
mouthes, subscryve with our handis, and constantly affirme
before God and the whole world, that this onely is the true
Christiane fayth and religion pleasing God and bringing
salvation to man, quhilk is now by the mercy of God reveled
to the World by the preaching of the blessed evangell, and is
receaved, beleved and defended by manie and sindrie notable
kyrkis and realmes, but chiefly by the kyrk of Scotland, the
kingis majestie, and three estatis of this realme, as Godis
eternall trueth and onely ground of our salvation, as more
perticulerly is expressed in the confession of our fayth
stablished and publictly confirmed by sindrie actis of
perlamentis, and now of a long tyme had bene openly professed by the kingis Majestie and whole body of this realme
both in brught and land: To the quhilk confession and forme
of religion we willingly aggree in our conscience in all poyntis
as unto Godis undoubted trueth and veritie grounded onely
upon his written worde. And therefore we abhorre and detest
all contrarie religion and doctrine, but cheifly all kynd of
papistrie in generall and perticular headis even as they are
now damned and confuted by the worde of God and kyrk of
Scotland; but in speciale we detest and refuse the usurped
authoritie of that Romane Antichrist upon the scriptures of
God, upon the kyrk, the civill magistrate and conscience of
men: All his tyrannous lawes made upon indifferent thinges,
agaynst our christiane libertie; his erroneous doctrine agaynst
the sufficiencie of the written worde, the perfection of the
lawe, the office of Christ, and his blessed ewangell; his cor-
rupted doctrine concernyng originall synne, our naturall
inabilitie and rebellion to godlines, our justification by fayth
onely, our imperfect sanctification, and obedience to the
law; the nature, number and µse of the holie sacramentis; his
fyve bastard sacramentis, with all his ritis, ceremoneis, and
false doctrine added to the ministration of the true sacramentis
without the worde of God: his cruell judgement agaynst
infantis deperting without the sacrament, his absolute necessitie of baptisme, his blasphemous opinion of transsub-
stantiation, or reall presence of Christis body in the elementis,

151

and receaving of the same by the wicked, or bodeis of men; his dispensationeis with solemnet othes, perjuries, and degrees of mariage forbidden in the worde, his crueltie agaynst the innocent devorced; his divilishe mes, his blasphemous preisthead, his prophane sacrifice for the synnes of the dead and the quyck, his canonization of men, calling upon angelis, or sainctis deperted, worshiping of imagrie and croces, dedicating of kyrkis, altaris, dayis, vowes to creatures, his purgatorie, prayeris for the dead, praying or speaking in a strange language, with his processioneis and blasphemous letanie, and multitude of advocattis or mediatoreis; his manyfold ordoures, auricular confession, his despered and uncertayne repentance, his generall and doubtsome fayth, satisfactioneis of men for theyr synnes; his justification by workes, his opus operatum, workes of supererogation, meritis, perdones, peregrinationes, and stationeis; his holy water, baptisyng of bellis, cungering of spirits, crocing, saning, anoynting, conjuring, hallowing of Godis good creatures with the superstitious opinion joyned therewith; his worldlie monarchie and wicked hierarchie, his three solemnit vowes with all his shavelingis of syndrie sortes; his erroneous and bloodie decretes made at Trent, with all the subcryveris and approveris of that cruell and bloodie band conjured agaynst the kyrk of God; and fynally we detest all his vane allegories, ritis, signes and traditioneis broght in the kyrk without or agaynst the worde of God and doctrine of this true reformed kyrk, to the quhilk we joyne our selves willingly in doctrine, fayth, religion, discipline, and use of the holie sacramentis, as lyvely memberis of the same in Christ our head, promising and swearing by the great name of the Lord our God that we shall continue in the obedience of the doctrine and discipline of this kyrk and shal defend the same according to our vocation and power all the dayes of our lyves, under the panes conteyned in the law, and danger both of body and saule in the day of Godis fearfull judgement. And seing that manie are styrred up by Satan and that Romane Antichrist to promise, sweare, subcryve, and for a tyme use the holie sacramentis in the kirk deceatfully agaynst there owne conscience, mynding hereby fyrst, under the externall clok of the religion to corrupt and subvert secretly Godis true religion within the kirk, and afterward, when tyme may serve, to become open ennemeis and persecutoris of the same, under vane hope of the papis dispensation, divised agaynst the worde of God to his greater confusion and theyr dowble condemnation in the day of the Lord Jesus, we therefore, willing to tak away all susspition of hypocrisie and of syk dowble dealing with God and his kirk, protest and call the searcher of all heartis for witnes, that our myndis and heartis do fullely aggree with this our confession, promise, othe, and subscription; so that we are not moved for any worldly respect, but are perswaded onely in our conscience throught the knawledge and love of Godis true religion prented in oure heartis by the holie sprit, as we shall answer to him in the day when the secretis of all heartis shalbe disclosed. And because we perceave that the quietnes and stabilitie of our religion and kirk doth depend upon the savetie and good behaviour of the kyngis majestie as upon ane confortable instrument of Godis mercy graunted to this countrey for the mainteining of his kyrk and ministration of justice amongis us, we protest and promise solemnetly with our heartis under the same othe, hand writ, and panes, that we shall defend his persone and authoritie with our geyr, bodyes, and lyves in the defence of Christis evangell, libertie of our countrey, ministration of justice, and punishment of iniquitie, agaynst all enemeis within this realme or without, as we desyre our God to be a strong and mercyfull defender to us in the day of our death and cuming of our Lord Jesus Christ, to whome with the Father and the Holie Sprit be all honour and glorie eternally.   Amen.

Nat. MSS. Scot., iii, No. LXX.

1584 'BLACK ACTS'

An ultra-protestant reaction against the administration of Lennox took the form of a coup d'état, the Ruthven Raid, in August 1582, which involved the seizure and forcible detention of the king's person. The general assembly approved this action, and in return the new government conceded a measure

*of approval to the policy of the Second Book of Discipline,
one consequence of which was the establishment of presbyteries in a few places. When the king escaped from the
Ruthven Raiders, in June 1583, a strongly conservative
policy was adopted by an administration headed by James
Stewart, Earl of Arran, a former associate of Lennox. The
'Black Acts', passed in May 1584, amounted, in effect, to the
royal answer to the Second Book of Discipline.*

c. 2. . . . Our Soverane lord and his thrie estatis assemblit in
this present Parliament ratefeis and apprevis and perpetuallie
confirmis the royall power and auctoritie over all statis alsweill spirituall as temporall within this realme in the persoun
of the kingis majestie our soverane lord his airis and successouris. And als statutis and ordinis that his hienes, his said
airis and successouris, be thame selffis and thair counsellis,
ar and in tyme to cum salbe juges competent to all personis
his hienes subjectis of quhatsumevir estate degrie functioun
or conditioun that ever they be of, spirituall or temporall, in
all materis quhairin they or ony of thame salbe apprehendit
summound or chargeit to ansuer to sic thingis as salbe
inquirit of thame be our said soverane lord and his counsell. . . .
    c. 4. Forsamekle as in the trublous tymis during thir
xxiiij yeris bypast syndrie formis of jugementis and jurisdictionis alsweill in spirituall as temporall causis ar enterit in the
practis and custome quhairby the kingis majesties subjectis
ar oftymis convocat and assemblit togidder . . . na sic ordour
as yit being allowit of and approvit be his majestie and his
thrie estatis in Parliament. . . . And speciallie his hienes and
his estatis considering that in the saidis assembleis certane his
subjectis have takin upoun thame to justifie and auctorize
the fact perpetrate aganis his hienes persoun and estate at
Ruthven and prosecutit thairefter, quhill his majestie at
Goddis pleasour recoverit his libertie, having in thair pretendit
maner maid actis thairupoun, kepis the same in register, and
as yit semis to allow the said attemptat, althocht now publictlie condampnit be his hienes and estatis as treasounable. . . .
Oure soverane lord and his thrie estatis assemblit in this
present parliament dischargeis all jugementis and jurisdictionis
spirituall or temporall accustomat to be usit. and execute
upoun ony of his hienes subjectis quhilkis ar not approvit be
his hienes and his saidis thrie estatis convenit in Parliament:

and decernis the same to ceis in tyme cumming quhill the
ordour thairof be first sene and considerit be his [hienes and
his saidis thrie] estatis [convenit] in Parliament and be
allowit and ratefeit be thame. . . . And als it is statute and
ordinit . . . that nane of his hienes subjectis of quhatsumever qualitie estate or functioun they be of, spirituall or
temporall, presume or tak upoun hand to convocat convene
or assemble thame selffis togidder for halding of counsellis
conventionis or assembleis to treát consult and determinat in
ony mater of estate, civill or ecclesiasticall (except in the
ordinare jugementis), without his majesties speciall command-
ement, expres licence had and obtenit to that effect under the
panis ordinit be the lawis and actis of Parliament aganis sic
as unlawfullie convocatis the kingis liegeis.

c. 8. . . . It is statute and ordinit . . . That nane of his
subjectis . . . sall presume or tak upoun hand privatlie or
publictlie in sermonis, declamationis or familiar conferencis,
to utter ony fals, untrew or slanderous spechis to the disdane,
reproche, and contempt of his majestie, his counsell and
procedingis, or to the dishonour, hurt or prejudice of his
hienes, his parentis and progenitouris, or to midle in the
effairis of his hienes and his estate, present bygane and in
tyme cumming, under the panis contenit in the actis of
Parliament aganis makaris and tellaris of lesingis . . . : Attour
becaus it is understand unto his hienes and to his thrie
estatis that the buikis of the *Cronicle* and *De jure regni apud
Scotos* maid be umquhill Mr George Buchannan and imprentit
sensyne contenis syndrie offensive materis worthie to be
delete, It is thairfoir statute and ordinit that the havaris of
the saidis tua volummis in thair handis inbring and deliver the
same to my lord secretare or his deputis within fourtie dayis
efter the publicatioun heirof, To the effect that the saidis tua
volumis may be perusit and purgit of the offensive and extra-
ordinare materis specifiit thairin not meit to remane as
accordis of treuth to the posteritie . . .

c. 20. Oure soverane lord and his thrie estatis of Parliament statutis and ordinis That Patrik, Archiebischop of
Sanctandrois, and utheris the bishopis within this realme
useand and exerceand the functioun and auctoritie of
bishoppis, with sic utheris as salbe constitute the kingis
majesties Commissionaris in Ecclesiasticall causis, Sall and

may direct and put ordour to all materis and causis ecclesiasticall within thair dioceisis, viset the kirkis and state of the
ministrie within the same, Reforme the collegeis thairin,
Resave his hienes presentationis to benefices, And gif collationis thairupoun as they sall find the personis presentit
qualefeit and worthie, And mak report of sic as they find
insufficient in dew tyme, And that na presentationis to
benefices be directit in tyme cumming to ony utheris . . .

A.P.S., iii, 292-303.

1587 ACT OF ANNEXATION

*The first statute to attempt to deal comprehensively with the
ecclesiastical property followed the well-tried lines of annexation or revocation, on the argument that the king could now
recover the great part of his patrimony which had been
alienated of old to the Church. The ecclesiastical temporality
(that is, broadly, lands and their revenues) was annexed to the
crown, but the spirituality (that is, the teinds) was not so
annexed, though no steps were taken to turn it over to the
reformed church.*

Oure soverane lord and his thrie estatis of parliament per-
fitelie understanding the greitest pairt of his proper rent to
haif bene gevin and disponit of auld to abbayis, monasteries and utheris personis of clergy quhairby the crown hes
bene sa greitly hurte that thairefter his maist noble progenitouris had not sufficient meanis to beir furth the honour
of thair estait as thai had befoir, quhilk hes bred sindrie inconvenientis within this realme, and seing the causes of the
dissolutioun of the patrimonie of the crown to the kirk
efter the trewth knawin ar fund nathir necessar nor profitt-
able and that be mony occasionis throw a lang process of
tyme the derth hes sa gritlie increscit not onlie in this realme
bot in all cuntries that the princes chairges ar not able to be
uphaldin be that part of the patrimonie quhilk now restis in
his handis; and his hienes for the grite luif and favour quhilk
he beiris to his subjectis being nawayes myndit to greve

156

thame with importable taxationis specialie for his royall
supporte, it is fund maist meit and expedient that he sal have
recours to his awin patrimonie disponit of befoir . . . as ane
help maist honourable in respect of himself and leist grevous
to his people and subjectis.

And thairfoir oure said soverane lord and his saidis thrie
estaitis of parliament be the force of this present act haif
unit, annexit and incorporat and unitis, annexis and incorp-
oratis to the crown of this realme' to remane tharwith as
annext and as it wer propirtie thairof in all tyme cuming
. . ., all and sindrie landis, lordschippis, baronies, castellis,
touris, fortalices, mansionis, maner places, milnis, multuris,
woddis, schawes, parkis, fischeingis, townis, villages, burrowis
in regalitie and baronie, annuelrentis, tenementis, reversionis,
custumes greit and small, fewfermes, tennentis, tennendries
and service of frie tennentis and all and sindrie utheris com-
moditeis, proffittis and emolumentis quhatsumevir alsweill
to burgh as to land, . . . quhilkis at the day and dait of thir presentis, viz. [29 July 1587] pertenis to quhatsumevir arch-
ibischope, bischop, abbot, prior, prioresse, quhatsumevir
uther prelate, uther ecclesiasticall or beneficit persoun of
quhatsumevir estait, degrie hie or law, and at the day and
dait of thir presentis pertenis to quhatsumevir abbay, convent,
closter, quhatsumevir ordour of freris or nunis, monkis or
channonis howsoevir thai be nameit, and to quhatsumevir
college kirk foundit for chantorie and singing or to quhatsumevir prebendarie or chaiplanrie quhairevir they ly or be situate . . ., and siclike all and sindrie commoun landis bruikit
be chaptouris of cathedrall kirkis and chantorie colleges as
commoun . . ., to be in all tymes heireftir takin, haldin and
reput as it wer the propertie and patrimonie of the croun, to
remane thairwith in all tyme cuming efter the forme . . . of
the act of annexatioun maid in the tyme of . . . King James
the secund. . . .

[Exception is made of properties already erected into
temporal lordships, namely the whole or parts of the lands of
the following religious houses: Torphichen, Scone, Deer, Newbattle, Holyrood, Dunfermline, Paisley, Pluscarden and
Arbroath.]

It is alwayes understand . . . that under the said annexatioun
or ony claus heirin specifiet the teyndscheves and utheris
teyndis of quhatsumever landis within this realme pertening

157

to ony persounage or vicarage ar not nor sall not be comprehendit except quhair the teynd and stok is sett togidder[1] ...,
bot that the samin sall remane with the present possessouris. ...

Reservand alwayes and exceptand to all archibischoppis,
bischoppis, abbottis, priouris, prioresses, commendatairis and
utheris possessouris of greit benefices of the estait of prelattis
and quhilkis befoir had or hes voit in parliament thair principall castles, fortalices, houssis and mansionis with the
biggingis and yairdis thairof ... quhilkis sall remane ... for
thair residence and habitatioun. ...

Exceptand alsua furth of the said annexatioun all and
quhatsumever mansionis of personnages and vicarages annext
to parroche kirkis with four aikeris of the gleib maist ewest[2]
to the kirk and commodious for the minister serving the cuir
thairof for his better residence. ...

Exceptand in lyk maner all and sindrie landis, proffittis, tenementis, annuelrentis, teyndscheves and utheris emolumentis
and proffittis quhatsumever gevin, grantit and disponit for
intertenement of maisteris and studentis in colleges erectit
for the exercise of lerning and for grammer scuillis and for
sustentatioun of ministeris makand thair residence in burrowis
quhair thair is na uther stipend appointit to thame. ...

A.P.S., iii, 431.

1 I.e., in effect, where land and teinds were leased together in return for a
single payment.
2 nearest, or most convenient.

1587 ACT FOR
SHIRE REPRESENTATION IN PARLIAMENT

*An act of King James VI at last gave effect to an act passed
by James I in 1428.[1] As the preamble to the act of 1587
relates, the parliament of December 1585 had received a
petition that the small barons and freeholders should be
represented and had remitted the matter to the king. His
attitude was favourable, possibly out of a genuine desire to*

1 p. 80 above.

broaden the basis of parliament, but additional stimulus was
given to him by the offer of those who sought representation
to make a payment of £40,000.

Thairfore his Majestie, now efter his lauchfull and perfeit aige
of xxj yeiris compleit, sittand in plane parliament, Declaris
and decernis the said act maid be king James the first to tak
full effect and executioun, and ratefeis and apprevis the same
be thir presentis, and for the bettir executioun thairof ordanis
the commissioners of all the schirefdomes of this realme
according to the nowmer prescrivit in the said act of parliament to be electit be the frehalders foirsaidis at the first heid-
court efter Michaelmes yeirlie, or failyeing thairof at ony
uther tyme quhen the saidis frehalders plesis convene to that
effect, or that his Majestie sall require thame thairto, Quhilkis
conventionis his Majestie declaris and decernis to be lauchfull.
And the saidis commissioners being chosin as said is for ilk
schircfdome, Thair names to be notefeit yeirlie in write to the
directoure of the chancellarie be the commissioners of the
yeir preceding: And thairefter quhen ony parliament or generall conventioun is to be haldin, that the saidis commissioners
be warnit at the first be virtew of preceptis furth of the chancellarie, or be his hienes missive lettres or chargeis, And in all
tymes thairefter be preceptis of the chancellarie as salbe
direct to the utheris estaittis. And that all frehalders be taxt
for the expensis of the Commissioners of the schires passing to
parliamentis or generall counsellis. . . . And that the saidis
Commissioners . . . salbe equall in nowmer with the commissioners of burrowis on the articles and have voit in parliamentis and generall counsellis in tyme cuming. And that his
Majesties missives befoir generall counsellis salbe directit to
the saidis commissioners, or certane of the maist ewest[2] of
thame, as to the commissioners of burrowis in tyme cuming.
And that the lordis of counsell and sessioun sall yeirlie direct
lettres at the instance of the saidis commissioners for convening of the frehalders to cheis the Commissioners for the nixt
yeir and making of taxationis to the effect abonewrittin: And
that the comperance of the saidis commissioners of the schires
in parliamentis or generall counsellis sall releif the haill remanent small baronis and frehalders of the schires of thair sutes
and presence aucht in the saidis parliamentis. . . .

2 nearest, or most convenient.   *A.P.S.*, iii, 509, c. 120.

1592 ACT AUTHORISING
PRESBYTERIAN GOVERNMENT

Episcopal administration, though reaffirmed by the 'Black Acts' in 1584 and not yet formally abrogated, had been eroded stage by stage as presbyteries multiplied and became increasingly effective from 1586 onwards. In 1592 the government of the church by general assemblies, synods, presbyteries and kirk sessions was formally authorised.

Oure soverane lord and estaittis of this present parliament, following the lovable and gude example of thair predicessouris, hes ratifiet and apprevit and be the tennour of this present act ratifies and apprevis all liberties, privileges, immunities and freedomes quhatsumevir gevin and grantit be his hienes, his regentis in his name or ony of his predicessouris, to the trew and haly kirk presentlie establishit within this realme. . . .

And siclyk ratifies and apprevis the general assemblies appoyntit be the said kirk, and declairis that it salbe lauchfull to the kirk and ministrie everilk yeir at the leist and ofter *pro re nata* as occasioun and necessitie sall require to hald and keip generall assemblies providing that the kingis majestie or his commissioner with thame to be appoyntit be his hienes be present at ilk generall assemblie [and] befoir the dissolving thairof nominat and appoint tyme and place quhen and quhair the nixt general assemblie salbe haldin. And in cais nather his majestie nor his said commissioner beis present for the tyme in that toun quhair the said generall assemblie beis haldin, than and in that cais it salbe lesum to the said generall assemblie be thame selffis to nominat and appoynt tyme and place quhair the nixt generall assemblie of the kirk salbe keipit and haldin as they haif bene in use to do thir tymes bypast.

And als ratifies and apprevis the sinodall and provinciall assemblies to be haldin be the said kirk and ministrie twyis ilk yeir as thay haif bene and ar presentlie in use to do within every province of this realme. And ratifeis and apprevis the presbiteries and particulare sessionis appointit be the said kirk with the haill jurisdictioun and discipline of the same kirk aggreit upoun be his majestie in conference had be his hienes with certain of the ministrie convenit to that effect. . . .

Item the kingis majestie and estaittis foirsaidis declairis
that the secund act of the parliament haldin at Edinburgh the
xxii day of May, the yeir of God [1584]¹ sall na wayes be
prejudiciall nor dirogat any thing to the privilege that God hes
gevin to the spirituall office beraris in the kirk concerning
headis of religioun, materis of heresie, excommunicatioun,
collatioun or deprivatioun of ministeris or ony sic essentiall
censouris speciall groundit and havand warrand of the Word
of God. Item . . . annullis the xx act of the same parliament
[at Edinburgh 1584]² . . . and thairfoir ordanis all presentationis to benefices to be direct to the particular presbiteries in all
all tyme cuming, with full power to thame to giff collationis
thairupoun and to put ordour to all materis and caussis
ecclesiasticall within thair boundis. . . .

A.P.S., iii, 541-2.

1 p. 152 above.
2 p. 155 above.

1592   A BOND OF MANRENT¹

Be it kend till all men be thir present lettres, me schir Umphrie
Colquhoune of Luss, knycht, to becum man servand and
dependar to ane nobill and potent lord George erlle of
Huntlie, lord Gordoun and Baidyenocht, etc., that I, and all
that I may mak, of kin, freindis, servandis, suriuance², vassellis,
and dependaris sall at all timis heireftir, witht our haill forces,
serve, concur, and assist with the said nobill lorde, in all and
quhatsumeuir his actionis and caussis, contra quhatsumeuir
persoun or persones, clan or clannis, within this realm, for
quhatsumeuir causs he hes to do, in deidlie feidis, bypast,
present, and to cum, and sall tak trew, plaine and eafald ³
pairt with, and sall entir in bluid witht his aduersar pairtie,
and be reddy baith to perseu and defend, and wair⁴ our lyffis
and heritages in his lordschipis adois, as we salbe employit,
aganis quhatsumeuir persones within this realme, the authorite

1 See p. 97 above.   4 expend.
2 presumably a mis-reading for 'surname'.
3 loyal.

only exceptit, etc., in witnes quhairof, I have subscriuit this
present band of seruice, witht my awin hand, at Blacknes, the
sextein day of Marche, the yeir of God M.V^c four scoir alevin
yeris, befor thir witness, Aulay Makcaulay of Artingaipill,
Gorg Gordoun of Govlis, Thomas Gordoun of Drumbulg.

Wmphra Colquhone of Luss, knycht

Spalding Club Miscellany, iv, 247.

1598-1618   INVENTORIES OF GOODS

*Possibly the source which, above all others, can be used to
present an all-round picture of Scottish economic and social
life, from the sixteenth century onwards, is the inventories of
the 'goods, gear, debts and sums of money' of persons
deceased, contained in vast numbers in the Records of
Testaments. One sample is given below in full and abstracts
of others follow, selected to show the possessions and the
economic relationships of Scots in town and country. It
should be said that the outstanding impression made on anyone who reads the original volumes is the overwhelming pre-
ponderance of agrarian interests in the Scottish economy.
Testament after testament, on page after page, list cattle and
sheep, wheat, bere and oats, even among the possessions of
town-dwellers, and it is indeed a somewhat tedious task to
find testaments which relate only to what we should consider to be urban interests.[1] It must be kept in mind that the
sums of money mentioned are — like all sums of money
mentioned in this book except where otherwise specified — in
Scots currency, which by 1600 had fallen to the level of one-
twelfth of sterling, at which level it remained.*

---

1 Particulars of some outstanding testaments of wealthy merchants are given
in G. Donaldson, *Scotland: James V to James VII*, 251-2.

The inventarie and testament dative of the guidis and geir of umquhile Patrik Wauch in Glenboy within the parochin of Methie and scherefdome of Forfar, quha decessit intestat the first day of November the yeir of God 1592 yeiris, faithfullie maid and gevin up be James Wauche, his son, for himself and in name of Thomas, Jhon, Katheren, Marioun and Agnes Wauchis, laufull bairnis to the defunct and executoris datives decernit to him be decreit of this auditorie[2] upon the fourt day of Marche 1597 yeiris.

In the first, aucht oxin, price of the pece £8, summa £64; thrie ky, price of the pece 10 merkis, summa £20; ane auld mear price £10; fyve yowis, price of the pece 30s., summa £7. 10s.; fyve hogis, price of the pece 20s., summa £5; ten bollis victuall, quherof fyve bollis beir, price of the boll £4, summa £20, fyve bollis aittis, price of the boll 50s., summa £12. 10s. Item in utensill and domicill with his abulyement[3] estimeit to ten merkis.

Summa of the inventarie £153. 2s. 4d.

Na dettis awand to the deid.

Dettis awand be the deid to utheris. In the first to Leonard Leslie, Abbot of Couper, for the few maill of the landis occupeit be the defunct the said yeir, 10 merkis 10s.; to William Blair of Balgillo, takkisman of the teindschavis of the saidis landis occupeit be the defunct, for the teind dewitie therof the said yeir, 25 merkis; to Ewine Bane, servand, for his fee and bountay of the terme preceding the defunctis deces, £4; to Elspot Richie, servand woman, for hir fee and bountay of the said terme, £4.

Summa of the dettis foirsaidis £32.

Summa of the fre geir, dettis deducit, £121. 3s. 4d. To be dividit in thrie partis becaus the relict levis, ilk part is £40. 7s. 9d

Commissariot of St. Andrews, Record of Testaments, 4 March 1597/8.

(ii)
Inventory of Cristal Thomesone, gardener, burgess of Canongate, who died on 8 October 1597.

In the barnyard, 1 stack of bere estimated to 12 bolls, @ £8 a boll; 3 stacks of oats estimated to 24 bolls, @ £5 a boll;

2 The commissary court.
3 clothing.

certain beans and pease upon the heads of the said 3 stacks, estimated to 7 bolls, @ 10 merks a boll; a 'rouk'[4] of pease estimated to 5 bolls, @ 10 merks a boll; ready money, £30; furnishing, utensils and clothing, £30. Total, £366.

Debts due to the defunct: by James Murray in Wester Dudingstoun and William Patersoun, merchant, burgess of Edinburgh, conform to a bond, 400 merks with 24 merks as interest; by Andrew Chalmeris, burgess of Canongate, conform to a bond, 200 merks; [and others]. Total, £573. 5s.

Debts due by the defunct: to Jonet Porteous, £20; to Andrew Chalmers, of yard mail,[5] £20; to William Fentoun, tailor, £11; to John Achesoun, of yard mail, £24. 3s.; to John Thomsone, maltman, for ale, £12; to John Watsoun, baxter in Edinburgh, £4. 12s. 8d.; to John Congiltoun for the price of 8 thraves of bere straw, 4 merks; to James Bannatyne of Brochtoun, for the ferm and teind of the lands of Discheflatt and Medowflatt for crop and year 1597, 42 bolls of bere @ 10 merks a boll. Total, £280.

Edinburgh Tests., 6 Feb. 1598/9.

(iii)
Inventory of William Dalyell, merchant, burgess
of Glasgow, who died in April 1593.

A quarter of the barque called the *Grace of God,* with her furniture, estimated at £200; in a cellar, 137 bolls of 'gret salt',[6] £205. 10s.; 6 'pockis of waid' [bags of woad, a dye], £180; 41 beaver skins, £200; furnishing, utensils and clothing, £26. 13s. 4d. Total, £895. 10s.

Ibid., 19 Feb. 1598/9.

(iv)
Inventory of John Bissert, merchant, burgess
of Glasgow, who died in June 1617.

200 ells of round[7] cloth at the bleaching, £160; 140 ells of linen, with him in England, £105; 120 ells of linen, £144; 60 ells of linen, £90; 139 ells of round linen, £92. 13s. 4d.; 60 ells of round linen, £42; bought by him in England before his

4 rick or stack.
5 rent paid for a yard or garden.
6 coarse salt.
7 coarse.

decease:- a web of broad black English cloth, containing 30 ells, £180, and two sticks[8] of indigo frieze, each containing 40 ells, £144; 'in the buith of Glasgow of small waris', £26. 13s. 4d.; furnishing, utensils and clothing, £66. 13s. 4d. Total, £1231.

Debts to the defunct include sums due by John Ritchie, cooper in Ireland, £120, and by James Hammiltoun, merchant, for 'merchand waris', £400.

Glasgow Tests., 4 Dec. 1617.

(v)
Inventory of Andrew Tran, provost of Irvine, who died on 4 December 1617.

In the barque called the *Guid Fortoune* of Irvine, certain merchandise which at the time of his departing for France he appointed his spouse to buy and load the barque with, together with his part of the said barque, £400; 10 bolls of corn in his barn, @ £4 a boll; 4 bolls of bere @ £7.6s. a boll; sown on the ground, 3 bolls of wheat, 'estimat to the ferd corne',[9] £22; furnishings, utensils and clothing, £300. Total, £796, 7s. 8d.

Debts to the defunct include several sums due for house mail and booth mail, for wine, iron, salt and other merchandise.

Ibid., 18 Apr. 1618.

8   rolls.

9   I.e., valued on the expectation of a fourfold increase at the harvest, and the estimate in an inventory would certainly not be above the average yield.

1600   JAMES VI TO SIR WALTER DUNDAS

This letter is one of many illustrations of the poverty of the crown in this period. The king's guests at the entertainment on the occassion of the baptism of Prince Charles were expected to send provisions and were invited to partake of their 'awne guid cheir'.

Richt traist freind we greit you hertlie wele. The solempnitie
of the Baptisme of our dearest sone being appointit at
Halyruidhous upoun the xxiij day of December instant,
quhairat sum princis of France strangearis with the speciallis
of our nobilitie being invyted to be present: Necessar it is that
great provisioun, guid cheir, and sic uther thingis necessar for
decoratioun thairof be provydit: Quhilkis can not be had without the help of sum of our loving subjectis quhairof accomp-
ting you ane of the speciallis, We have thocht gude to
requeist you effectuusly to propyne us with vennysoun, wyld
meit, brissell foulis,[1] caponis, with sic uther provisioun as is
maist seasonabil for that tyme, and earand[2] to be send in to
Halyruidhous upoun the xx day of the said moneth of
December instant. And heirwithall to inveit you to be present
at that solempnitie to tak pairt of your awne guid cheir; As ye
tender our honnour and the honnour of the cuntrey. Swa we
commit you to God from Linlychtqw this vj of December
1600.

JAMES R.

Walter MacLeod (ed.), *Royal Letters etc. from the Family Papers of Dundas of Dundas*, No. 33.

1 meaning uncertain, possibly turkeys.
2 in advance.

1605 INSTRUCTIONS TO BORDER COMMISSION

His accession to the English throne in 1603 enabled James VI to tackle the problem of the Borders on an Anglo-Scottish basis and in 1605 a conjoint commission of five Scottish and five English 'justices' was appointed.

That thay have ane speciall cair and regaird for removing of
deidlie feidis[1] within the saidis boundis and for preventing of
sic occasionis as may ather renew bigane feidis or mak new
inimiteis to aryse within the cuntrey, and utherwayis with all
haist possibill to suppres, sa fer as in thame lyis, that

1 feuds.

unnaturall and barbarous custome.

That they caus delyverie to be maid of all personis fugitive fra the one cuntrey to the uther, or that utherwayis ar suspect guiltie, and that to the ordinar officer and minister that sall demand thame to justice.

That thay caus extract the names of all outlawis, rebellis, fugitives and outlawis, and utheris unanswerable to the lawis, and tak ordour how that ather thay may be maid furth-cummand to justice, or then the cuntrey be voydit of thame.

That thay inquyre for the registeris and nottes maid be the Lieutennantis clerkis on ather syde of all souerteis found for any personis to be ansuerable to justice, that accordinglie thay may demand thair entrie from thair cautioner, and that thairby also thay may understand the Lieutennantis pro-cedingis.

That lykwayis all actis of cautioun and generall bandis that hes bene gevin be any duelling within these boundis may be considerit of, and the pairteis band to be burdynit to mak thair men ansuerable according thairto.

That speciall cair be had for expelling furth of the saidis boundis of all idle vagaboundis quhais meanis to leif and sustene thameselffis being unknawne caryis ane presumptioun of thair unlawfull purchase for thair mantenance.

That all these in quhome thair can be expectit na houpe of amendement and ar thocht incorrigible may be removit furth of that cuntrey to some uther place, quhair the change of air will mak in thame ane exchange of thair maneris.

That the armour quhilk hes servit the brokin people within these boundis in thair lewd actionis may be takin frome thame, and that nane of thame quhais bipast behaviour makis thame suspect be permitted to have horses for any uther use or of better valew then ordinarie wark horses for the lauboring of the ground.

That thay exact ane particular accompt of the commissioneris that salbe apointit for administratioun of justice and causing of executioun to be done upoun the offendouris, and that thay sett doun the formes how the saidis commissioneris sall pro-ceid in the justice courtis to be haldin be thame, and uther-wayis baith be thair authoritie and advyse assist thame as thair salbe occasioun.

R.P.C., vii, 703.

The act of 1592 in favour of presbyterian government had not produced a complete presbyterian system throughout the whole country, and the continued existence of individual commissioners as overseers facilitated the revival of an episcopal system. Besides, it had been agreed that the king could nominate ministers to vacant bishoprics so that they could sit and vote in parliament. By 1606, considerable progress had been made towards the restoration of episcopal government, and the logical step was taken of restoring to the bishops the properties of which they had been deprived by the act of annexation of 1587.

Oure soverane lord, now in his absens furth of his kingdome of Scotland, ernestlie desyring sa to provyde for the just and politique government of that estait as his faithfull subjectis thairof may perfytlie knaw that absens breidis nocht in his royall mind oblivioun of thair gude bot that he is daylie mair and mair cairfull of sic thingis as may tend maist to the honour, proffitt and perpetuall stabilitie and quietnes of the said kingdome, quhairin understanding religioun and justice to be sa necessar fundamentis and pillaris as by thame the authoritie of the princes and quietnes of the peopill in all tymes bypast hes cheiflie bene establischit and mantenit quhill of lait in his majesteis young yeiris and unsetlit estaitt the ancient and fundamentall policie consisting in the mantenance of the thrie estaittis of parliament hes bene greatumlie imparit and almost subvertit, specialie by the indirect abolischeing of the estait of bischoppis by the Act of Annexatioun . . ., quhairby albeit it wes nather menit by his majestie nor by his estaittis that the said estait of bischoppis consisting of benefices of cure and being ane necessar estait of the parliament suld onywayes be suppressit, yit his majestie by experience of the subsequent tyme hes cleirlie sene that the dismembering and abstracting frome thame of thair levingis hes brocht thame in sic contempt and povertie that they ar nocht hable to furneis necessaris to thair privat familie, mekill less to beir the charges of thair wonted rank in parliament and generall counsaillis . . . : Thairfoir his majestie with express advyse

and consent of the saidis haill estaittis of parliament, being
cairfull to repone, restoir and redintegrat the said estait of
bischoppis to thair ancient and accustomed honour, digniteis,
prerogatives, privilegis, levingis, landis, teyndis, rentis, thriddis
and estaitt, as the samyn wes in the reformit kirk maist
ample and frie at ony tyme befoir the act of annexatioun
foirsaid, be the tennour heirof retreittis, rescindis, reduces,
cassis, abrogattis and annullis the foirsaid act of annexatioun....

A.P.S., iv, 281-2.

1609   ACT ESTABLISHING
JUSTICES OF THE PEACE

*Several acts, from 1579 onwards, had revealed a tendency to
commit to 'justices', appointed by the king, powers to
suppress disorder and to take action to prevent outbreaks of
violence. The act of 1609, from which the establishment of
the office of justice of the peace in Scotland is usually dated,
laid its main emphasis on prevention, but the new office had
a long struggle against the competition of older judicatures.
Consequently the act is significant mainly for the indications
it gives of Jacobean concepts of government and of the
problems facing an administration set on securing respect
for law and order.*

Forsamekle as . . . [the] brutall custome of deadlie feadis[1]
. . . wes become sa frequent in this realme as the subjectis of
greatest rank and qualitie upoun everie nauchtie occasioun of
base and unworthie controverseis of neighbourheid for turves,
foldykis,[2] furris[3] or marches of landis, foolishe wordis or
drunken discordis betwene thair meanest servandis and
dependeris and ony uther in the countrey did so readelie
imbrace the protectioun of thair injust and unnecessarie
querrellis as did mony tymes involve thameselffis and thair
haill freindschip in maist bludie and mortall trubles whilk

1 feuds.
2 dykes to enclose stock.
3 furrows.

they did prosecute with sic malice and crueltie as . . . did
distract the kingdome in opposite factiounis and mony tymes
furnessit mater of maist pernicious seditious and civill warris,
. . . yit the corruptioun wes sa universall that the greatest part
prevailing aganis the best that cruel barbaritie hath baith
continuance and daylie incresce untill his majestie bending
the excellent wisdome and rare graces of his royall mynd
(wheirwith God hes indewit him mair abundantlie than any
king that evir did regne in this iland) aganis that godles un-
natural and bestlie custome did devyse and establishe a maist
godlie just and prudent law and ordinance[4] for the course to
be observed for removeing upoun equitable and just con-
ditiounes the deadlie feadis whilk then stude in great number
betwene the maist powerfull subjectis in this kingdome and
thair kinsmen assisteris and partakeris in the executioun
wheirof God haveing miraculouslie assistit his majesteis maist
halie and just intentioun eftir exceding great cair and panis
tane by his majestie in tryell of all the originall caussis of the
saidis disordis . . . his majesteis admirable constancie hes sa
ouercome all difficulteis that the haill knawin feadis within
the kingdome being now removed . . . his majesteis haill
subjectis findis sic joy and happines in the sweit fruittis of his
wisdome and providence expressed in that caise that they
earnestlie wische that his majestie wha hes sa cairfullie
exterminat that abhominable pest of deadlie feedis may in
his singular wisdome find meanis for evir to prevent the reviveing of that monster: wheirin his majestie considering that
nathing gaif sa great grouth and strenth to that bipast barbaritie as the slouth of magistratis in nocht suppressing the
first seidis of these dissentionis whilk being small and weak
in the beginning . . . were then easilie to be satlit gif diligence
and authoritie had bene joynit for repressing thairof . . . his
majestie and estaittis foirsaidis ratefeis and appreves the former
act maid by his hienes for abolischeing of deadlie feedis in
everie heid, clause and article thairof and forther statutis and
ordanis that in everie schyre within this kingdome thair sall
be yeirlie appointit by his majestie some godlie, wyse and
vertuous gentilmen of good qualitie, moyen and reporte,
making residence within the same, in sic number as the

4 The Act 'anent removeing and extinguischeing of deidlie feidis' passed by a
Convention of Estates in 1598 (A.P.S., iv, 158, c. 1) and ratified by Parliament in
1600 (A.P.S., iv, 233, c. 31).

boundis of the schire sall require, to be commissionaris for
keiping his majesties peace, to quhome his majestie with
advyse of the lordis of his privie counsell shall give power and
commissioun to oversie, trye and prevent all sic occasionis as
may breid truble and violence amongis his majesteis subjectis
or forceable contempt of his majesteis authoritie and breache
of his peace, and to command all persones in quhome they
sall sie manifest intentioun to mak truble or disordour ather
by gathering togidder of idill and disordourlie persones or by
publict bearing or wearing of pistolettis or uther forbiddin
weaponis and sic uther ryottous and swaggering behaviour to
bind themselffis and find cautioun under competent panis to
observe his majesteis peace and for thair comperance befoir
his majesteis justice or lordis of privie counsaill to undirly sic
ordour as sall be foundin convenient for punishing of thair
transgressionis or staying of trublis and enormiteis, and gif
neid sall be to require the duetefull and obedient subjectis of
the schyre to concur with them in preventing all sic con-
temptis and violences or for taking and warding of the wilfull
and dissobedient authouris, committeris and fostereris of these
crymes and disordouris . . ., ordaning alsua the saidis commissionaris to gif true advertesment and informatioun to the
lordis of his majesteis privie counsaill, justice generall and his
deputtis his majesteis thesaurar and other magistratis and
officeris quhome it efferis off the names of sic faithfull and
unsuspect witnessis and assyssouris to be summonit in all
crymes and disordouris whilkes salhappin to fall furth within
the saidis shyres as salbe knawin to be maist meit and hable
for tryell and probatioun of the samin and for eschewing that
sic as ar ather aged, seiklie or unhable to travell or ignorant
of the factis to be tryit be nocht unjustlie vexit or unnecessarlie
drawin frome thair awin houssis and affaris for materis whereof they ar nocht hable to gif ony light.

A.P.S., iv, 434.

1609 STATUTES OF IONA

*On 23 August 1609 Andrew Knox, Bishop of the Isles, as
the king's commissioner, met several of the leading chiefs of*

the Isles to draw up a code of statutes. On the following day the chiefs who are named in the preamble to the statutes, along with two or three others, signed a bond undertaking to continue in the profession of the 'true religion', to obey the king as supreme in all causes, both spiritual and temporal, and to observe the laws and acts of parliament of the kingdom.

The Court of the South and North Illis of Scotland haldin at Icolmekill be ane Reverend Father in God, Andro, Bischop of the Illis, haveand speciall pouer and commissioun to that effect of his Majestie and Counsell. . . . The quhilk day in presence of the said reverend father the speciall barronis and gentilmen of the saidis Yllis undirwritten, viz. Angus McDonald of Dunnoveg, Hector McCleane of Dowart, Donald Gorme McDonald of Slait, Rorie McCloyd of Hareis, Donald McAllane VçEane of Ilanterane, Lauchlane McCleane of Coill, Rorie McKynnoun of that Ilk, Lauchlane McClane of Lochbowie, Lauchlane and Allane McCleanis brether german to the said Hectour McClane of Dowart, Gillespie McQuirie of Ullowa, Donald McFie in Collonsaye, togidder with the maist pairt of thair haill speciall freindis, dependairis and tennentis. . . .

[I] Thay haif all aggreit in ane voice, lyk as it is presentlie concludit and inactit, that the ministeris alswele plantit as to be plantit within the parrochynis of the saidis Illandis salbe reverentlie obeyit, thair stipendis dewtifullie payit thame, the ruynous kirkis with reasounable diligence repairit, the sabothis solemplie keipit, adultereis, fornicationis, incest, and sic uther vyle sklanderis seveirlie punist, mariageis contractit for certane yeiris simpliciter dischairgit and the committaris thairof haldin, repute and punist as fornicatouris, and that conforme to the lovable Actis of Parliament of this realme and disciplein of the Reformit Kirk. . . .

[II] The quhilk day the foirsaidis personis, considering and haveing found be experience the grite burdyne and chairges that thair haill cuntreymen, and speciallie thair tennentis and labourairis of the ground, hes sustenit be furnissing of meit, drink, amd intertenyment to straingeris, passingeris and utheris idill men without ony calling or vocatioun to win thair leiving, hes, for releif of passingeris and straingairis, ordanit certane oistlairis to be set doun in the maist convenient placeis within every Ile, and that be every ane of the foirnamit speciall men within thair awne boundis as thay sall best devyse; quhilkis oistlairis sall haif furnitoure sufficient of meit and drink to be sauld for reasonable expensis.

[III] And also thay consent and assentis, for releif of thair said intollerable burdyn, that na man be sufferit to remaine or haif residence within ony of thair boundis of the saidis Iles without ane speciall revenew and rent to leive upoun, or at the leist ane sufficient calling and craft quhairby to be sustenit. And, to the intent that na man be chairgeable to the cuntrey be halding in houshold of ma gentilmen nor his proper rent may sustene, it is thairfore aggreit and inactit, with uniforme consent of the foirsaidis personis, barronis and gentilmen within-nameit, that thay and ilkane of thame sall sustene and interteny the particular number of gentilmen in houshald undirwritten, − to wit, the said Angus McDonald six gentilmen, the said Hectour McCleane of Dowart aucht gentilmen, the saidis Donald Gorme McDonald, Rorie Mc-Cloyde, and Donald McCawne VcEane, ilkane of thame sex gentilmen, the saidis Lauchlane McCleane of Coill and Rorie McKynnoun ilkane of thame thrie gentilmen, the said Lauchlane McCleane, bruther to the said Hectour, thrie servandis; and the saidis gentilmen to be sustenit and inter-teneit be the foirnamit personis ilkane for thair awne pairtis as is above rehersit, upoun thair awne expensis and chairges, without ony supplie of thair cuntreyis. . . .

[IV] Thay haif all aggreit in ane voice . . . that quhatsum-cvir personc or personis, strangearis or inborne within the boundis of the saidis Yllis, salhappin to be found soirning, craveing meit, drink or ony uther geir fra the tennentis and inhabitantis thairof be way of conyie[1] as thay terme it, except for reasonable and sufficient payment fra the oistlairis to be appointit as is foirsaid, thay salbe repute and haldin as thevis and intollerable oppressouris, callit and persewit thair-fore before the judge competent as for thift and oppressioun. . .

[V] The quhilk day, it being foundin and tryit be appeir-ance that ane of the speciall causis of the grite povertie of the saidis Ilis, and of the grite crueltie and inhumane bar-baritie quhilk hes bene practisit be sindrie of the inhabitantis

1 This term is clearly related to *conveth* (p. 25 above), and this alleged levy the successor of ancient rights to exact maintenance.

of the samyn upoun utheris thair naturall freindis and
nychtbouris, hes been thair extraordinair drinking of strong
wynis and acquavitie brocht in amangis thame, pairtlie be
merchandis of the maneland and pairtlie be sum trafficquaris
indwellaris amangis thame selffis, ffor remeid quhairof it is
inactit . . . that no persone nor personis indwellairis within
the boundis of the saids haill Iles bring in to sell for money
ather wyne or acquavitie, undir the pane of tinsale of the
samyn. . . . And forder, gif it salhappin ony merchand on the
mainland to bring ather wyne or acquavitie to the saidis Iles
or ony of thame, it is lykwyse inactit that quhatsumevir
persone or personis indwellairis thairof that salhappin to buy
ony of the samyn fra the said merchand sall pay for the first
fault fourty pundis money, the secund fault ane hundreth
pundis, and the thrid fault the tinsale of his haill rowmes,
possessiounis, and moveable goodis . . . without prejudice
alwyse to ony persone within the saidis Illis to brew acquavitie and uthir drink to serve thair awne housis, and to the
saidis speciall barronis and substantious gentilmen to send
to the Lawland and thair to buy wyne and acquavitie to
serve thair awne housis. . . .

[VI] It is inactit that everie gentilman or yeaman within
the said Ilandis, or ony of thame, haveing childreine maill
or famell, and being in goodis worth thriescore ky, sall put at
the leist thair eldest sone, or haveing no childrene maill thair
eldest dochter, to the scuillis on the Lawland, and interteny
and bring thame up thair quhill thay may be found able
sufficientlie to speik, reid, and wryte Inglische. . . .

[VII] Considdering ane lovable Act of Parliament of this
realme be the quhilk . . . it is expreslie inhibite, forbiddin
and dischairgit that ony subject within this his Majesteis
kingdome beir hagbutis or pistolletis out of thair awne
housis and dwelling places, or schuit thairwith at deiris,
hairis, or foullis . . . ; quhilk Act of Parliament, in respect of
the monstrous deidlie feidis heirtofoir intertenyit within the
saidis Yllis, hes nawyse bene observit and keipit amangis
thame as yit, to the grite hurte of the maist pairt of the inhabitantis thairof; for remeid quhairof it is inactit . . . that
na persone nor personis within the boundis of the saidis Iles
beir hagbutis nor pistolletis furth of thair awne housis and
dwelling places, nathir schuit thairwith at deiris, hairis, foullis,

nor na uther maner of way, in tyme cuming, undir the panes
contenit in the said Act. . . .

[VIII] It is lykwyse inactit . . . that na vagabound, baird,
nor profest pleisant pretending libertie to baird and flattir, be
ressavit within the boundis of the saidis Yllis be ony of the
saidis speciall barronis and gentilmen or ony utheris inhabitantis thairof, or interteneit, be thame or ony of thame in ony
soirt; but, incais ony vagaboundis, bairdis, juglouris, or suche
lyke be apprehendit be thame or ony of thame, he to be tane
and put in suir fe[n]sment and keiping in the stokis, and thairefter to be debarit furth of the cuntrey with all guidlie
expeditioun. . . .

[IX] It is aggreit unto, concludit, and inactit, seing the
principall of every clan man be ansuerable for the remanent
of the samyn, his kin, freindis, and dependairis, that, gif ony
persone or personis of quhatsumevir clan, degrie or rank,
within the boundis of the saidis Yllis, salhappin to contravein
the actis, lawis and constitutionis within-written or ony of
thame, or dissobey thair schiref or superiour foirsaid, that
then and in that caice thir presentis salbe ane sufficient
warrand to the barroun and speciall man within quhais boundis
the contravenair makes his speciall residence, to command
him to waird, and in caice of disobedience to tak and apprehend the persone or personis disobeyairis, and eftir dew tryall
of thair contraventioun in maner foirsaid to sease upoun thair
movable guidis and geir, and to be ansuerable for the samyn
to be brocht in to his Majesteis use, and to produce lykwyse
the malefactouris before the judge competent quhill his
Majestie tak forder ordour thairanent. Lykeas it is specialie
provydit that na cheif of ony clan, superiour of ony landis,
or principall of ony familie, recept or mantene ony male-
factour fugitive and dissobedient to his awne naturall kyndlie
cheif and superiour.

R.P.C., ix, 26-30.

1610   ACTS OF
GENERAL ASSEMBLY AT GLASGOW

A constitution which acknowledged the place of the bishops in administration but which also provided for the co-operation of ministers with the bishops and for the subordination of the bishops to the general assembly, came before the assembly in 1610. As a result of a policy which the king had pursued for some years, this assembly contained adequate representation of the more conservative north, where Melville's principles had not proved congenial, and the episcopal constitution was approved.

Item, it is thought expedient that the Bischops salbe Moderatours in every Diocesian Synod, and the Synods salbe haldin twyse in the yeir of the kirks of every Dyocie, viz. in Apryle and October. . . .

Item, that no sentence of excommunicatioun, or absolutioun therfra, be pronouncit against or in favours of any person without the knowledge and approbation of the Bischop of the Dyocie, quho must be ansuerable to his Majestie for all formall and unpartial proceidings therin. . . .

Item, that all presentatiouns be direct heirafter to the Bischop; and upon any presentatioun givin, or utherwayes sute made be any to be admittit to the Ministrie, the Bischop is to requyre the Ministers of these bounds quher he is to serve, to certifie by thair testificat unto him of the partie suter his conversatioun past, and abilitie, and qualificatioun for the functioun: and upon the returne of thair testificat, the Bischop is to take farther tryall; and finding him qualified, and being assisted be such of the Ministrie of the bounds quher he is to serve, as he will assume to himselfe, he is then to perfyte the haill act of ordinatioun.

Item, in depositioun of Ministers, the Bischop associating to himselfe the Ministrie of these bounds quher the delinquent served, he is then to take tryall of his fault, and, upon just cause found, to depryve him. . . .

Item, the visitatioun of ilk dyocie is to be done be the Bischop himselfe . . . And quhatever Minister, without just cause and laufull excuse made, sall absent himselfe from the visitation of the Diocesan Assembly, he salbe suspendit from his office and benefice, and, if he amend not, he salbe deprivit. . . .

Item, the Bischops salbe subject, in all things concerning thair lyfe, conversatioun, office, and benefice, to the censures of the Generall Assemblie; and being found culpable, with his Majesties advyce and consent, to be deprivit.

B.U.K., iii, 1096-7.

1611 ABOLITION OF
NORSE LAW IN ORKNEY AND SHETLAND

The implication of the treaties of 1468 and 1469,[1] by which the crown rights in the islands had merely been pledged to the Scottish crown, was that the Norse law and institutions should be preserved, and so late as 1567 the Scottish parliament had ruled that the islands should be subject to their own laws.[2] The Stewart Earls of Orkney – Robert (an illegitimate son of James V) and his son, Patrick – had exploited the situation in their own interest, and this was made the reason or pretext for the following act.

Forsamekle as the kingis majestie and his predicessouris of famous memorie with the consent and auctoritie of thair esteatis of parliament hes statute and ordanit that all and sindrie the subjectis of this kingdome sould lieve and be governit under the lawis and statutis of this realme allanarlie and be no law of foreyne cuntreyis, as in the actis maid thairanent at lenth is contenit, nochtwithstanding it is of treuthe that some personis beiring power of magistracie within the boundis of Orknay and Yetland hes thir divers yeiris bigane maist unlauchfullie tane upoun thame for thair awne privat gayne and commoditie to judge the inhabitantis of the saidis cuntreyis be foreyne lawis, making choise some-tymes of foreyne lawis and sometymes of the proper lawis of this kingdome as thay find mater of gayne and commoditie,

1 pp. 85-7 above.
2 *A.P.S.*, iii, 41, c. 48.

in heich contempt of our soverane lord and to the grite hurte
and prejudice of his majesteis subjectis: Thairfoir the lordis
of secreit counsaile hes dischargeit and be the tennour heirof
dischargeis the saidis foreyne lawis, ordaning the same to be
no forder usit within the saidis cuntreyis of Orknay and Yetland at ony tyme heirefter, and that letters of publicatioun
be direct heirupoun commanding and inhibiting all and
sindrie personis beiring office of magistracie and judicatorie
within the same that nane of thame presome nor tak upoun
hand at ony tyme heirefter to judge or censure the inhabitantis within the saidis boundis be foreyne lawis nor to pro-
ceid in ony actioun or caus criminal or civile according to
foreyne lawis, bot to use the proper lawis of this kingdome to
his majesteis subjectis in all thair actionis and caussis as thay
and ilk ane of thame will answer upoun the contrarie at thair
heichest perrell.

MS. Registrum Secreti Concilii, Acta, 1610-12, fo. 53 (cf. *R.P.C.,* ix, 181-2).

1616 EDUCATION ACT

*This act was the first piece of educational legislation after
the reformation, but many parish schools had already been
established and it may be that the real purpose of this act was
merely to encourage their extension in the Highlands.*

Forsamekle as, the kingis Majestie haveing a speciall care and
regaird that the trew religioun be advanceit and establisheit
in all the pairtis of this kingdome, and that all his Majesties
subjectis, especiallie the youth, be exercised and trayned up
in civilitie, godlines, knawledge and learning, that the vulgar
Inglishe toung be universallie plantit, and the Irishe language,[1]
whilk is one of the cheif and principall causis of the con-
tinewance of barbaritie and incivilitie amongis the inhabitantis of the Ilis and Heylandis, may be abolisheit and
removit; and quhairas thair is no meane more powerfull to
further this his Majesties princelie regaird and purpois than

1 The usual Lowland term for Gaelic.

the establisheing of scooles in the particular parrocheis of this
kingdome whair the youthe may be taught at the least to
write and reid, and be catechiesed and instructed in the
groundis of religioun; thairfore the kingis Majestie, with
advise of the Lordis of his Secreit Counsall, hes thocht it
necessar and expedient that in everie parroche of this kingdome whair convenient meanes may be had for interteyning
a scoole, that a scoole salbe establisheit, and a fitt persone
appointit to teache the same, upoun the expensis of the
parrochinnaris according to the quantitie and qualitie of the
parroche, at the sight and be the advise of the bischop of the
diocie in his visitatioun. . . .

R.P.C., x, 671-2.

1617   REGISTER OF SASINES

*It had long been a well established practice that a charter of
lands should be accompanied by a precept in which the
granter ordered his bailie to give 'actual, real and corporal
possession' of the subjects to the grantee or his representative,
by handing over earth and stone or some other token. This
giving of sasine was recorded by a notary public in an
instrument, which constituted the evidence of the trans-
ference of the property. Notaries entered the substance of
such instruments in their protocol books, which were therefore useful evidence should the instrument itself be lost or
destroyed. On several occasions throughout the sixteenth
century attempts were made to create machinery for preserving evidence of conveyances, for example by making it
compulsory to record sasines in the registers of the sheriff
courts or by making notaries transmit their protocol books
to the Clerk Register, but evidently none of those attempts
was successful. In 1599 an official Register of Sasines under
the control of the Secretary was instituted, but was discon-
tinued ten years later. The advantages of such a register were
so manifest that in 1617 the Register of Sasines was revived,
now under the authority of the Clerk Register, and this time*

179

the arrangement proved permanent.

In order to illustrate the procedure, a typical instrument is printed below, followed by the statute which finally established the Register of Sasines.

(i) An Instrument of Sasine, 1491.

In the name of God Amen. By this present public instrument be it clearly known to all that in the year of the Lord's incarnation 1491, on the 20th day of the month of June, the ninth indiction,[1] in the seventh year of the pontificate of our most holy father and lord in Christ, the Lord Innocent VIII, Pope by divine providence, in presence of me, notary public, and witnesses underwritten, personally compeared an honourable man, John Grant of Freuchy, and presented to a prudent man, John Ogilvie of Milton of Keith, bailie for this purpose of a noble and powerful lord, George, Earl of Huntly and Lord of Badenoch, a certain letter written on parchment, under the seals of the said earl and of a noble lord, Alexander, Lord of Gordon, his eldest son, of red wax impressed on white: which he reverently received from his hands and handed over to be read by me, notary public underwritten, as follows:-

George, Earl of Huntly and Lord of Badenoch, to our beloved James Grant in Balnadalocht [and three others], our bailies herefor specially appointed, greeting. Whereas we have given and granted to our beloved John Grant of Freuchy, with the consent and assent of our beloved first-born son, Alexander, Lord of Gordon, all and whole our lands of Corroo and Tullochgorm, with the pertinents, lying in our lordship of Badenoch within the sheriffdom of Inverness, as is more fully contained in our charter made thereon heritably to the said John Grant: wherefore we charge and command you and each of you, conjunctly and severally, that, immediately on sight of the presents, you or one of you give state, sasine and possession of the said lands of Corroo and Tullochgorm, with the pertinents, to the said John Grant or his certain attorney, bearer of the presents, in heritage, according to the force, form and tenor of our charter made thereon, which he has, and that you or one of you enter the same John into real, actual and corporal possession of the said

---

1 I.e., the ninth year in a cycle of fifteen.

180

lands of Corroo and Tullochgorm with the pertinents: for the doing of which we commit to you and each of you, conjunctly and severally, our full and irrevocable power by the tenor of the presents. And in token of this sasine given by you or one of you, you are to append to the presents the seal of the person giving sasine on the third tag after our seals, to remain in the possession of the said John for ever. Given under our seal and the seal of our said first-born, in token of his consent and assent, at Huntly on 14th June 1491, before these witnesses. . . .

Which letter I read in a loud and audible voice and explained in the vulgar tongue. And when it had been read and explained, the same John Ogilvie, bailie aforesaid, by the authority of his office, took up earth and stone and, by giving the same to the said John Grant, present and accepting, gave, presented and handed over state, sasine and possession of the said lands . . . heritably, according to the force, form and tenor of the precept committed to him; and he entered the said John Grant in the chief house of the said lands, and, turning all others out, shut him in and invested him. Upon which all and sundry the said John Grant asked of me, notary public, that a public instrument or public instruments, one or more, be made to him. These things were done on the ground of the said lands at ten hours before noon or thereby, the year, day, month, indiction and pontificate aforesaid, in the presence of prudent men, John Grant Paterson [etc.]

And I, Thomas Cowe, priest of the diocese of Aberdeen, notary public by imperial and royal authority [testify that I was personally present, saw and heard what was done, made a note thereon and drew up the present instrument at the request of the parties.]

(ii) Act establishing the Register of Sasines, 1617.

His Majestie with advyis and consent of the estaittis of Parliament statutes and ordanis That thair salbe ane publick Register in the whiche all reversiounes regressis[2] bandis[3] and writtis for making of reversiounes or regressis, assignatiounes thairto, dischargis of the same, renunciatiounes of wodsettis[4] and grantis off redemptioun and siclyik all instrumentis of

2 When land was disponed under reversion, the disponer had regress.
3 bonds.
4 wadsets, equivalent to mortgages or reversions.

181

seasing salbe registrat within thriescore dayes efter the date
of the same: It is alwayis declared that it sall not be necessar
to registrat anye bandis and wreatis for making of reversiounes or regressis unles seasing pas in favoures off the
pairties makeris of the saidis bandis or writtis, In the whiche
cace it is ordaned that the samen salbe registrat within thriescore dayes efter the date of the seasing. The extract off the
whiche Register sall mak faith in all caces except where the
writtis so registrated ar offered to be improvin.[5] [The royal
burghs, which had their own registers of sasines, kept by the
town clerks, are excluded from the provisions of the act.] And
to the effect the said register may presentlie and in all tyme
cuming be the moir faithfullie keipit, Thairfore our said
soverane Lord with advyis and consent foirsaid statutes and
ordanis the same registeris and registratiounes foirsaidis to be
insert thairin to appertene and belang to the present Clerk of
Register and his deputtis to be appoynted be him to that
effect and decernis and ordanis the same Registeris to be
annexed and incorporated with the said office. [The Clerk
Register to appoint deputies to] receave fra the pairties thair
evidentis and to registrat the same within the space of fourtie
aucht houres nixt efter the recept thairoff and to engrose
the haill bodie of the write in the register . . . and within the
same space sall delyver to the presentar of the samen the
evidentis markit be him with the day moneth and yeir of the
registratioun and in what leaff of the booke the same is registrat, and sall tak allanérlie for his paynis tuentie sex schill-
ingis aucht pennyes money of this realme as for the price of
ilk leafe of his register . . . And the saidis Registeris efter the
filling of the same to be repoirted[6] to the said Clerk of
Register to remayne with him and his deputtis and be patent
to all oure soverane Lordis liegis and extractis thairoff to be
gevin be him and his deputtis . . . to all salhave adoe with the
same whiche sall mak als gryit faithe as the principallis except
incace of improbatioun[7] [Registers to be kept in seventeen
places for seventeen districts] And the saidis evidentis to be
registrat in the particular bookes appoynted for the landis
within the boundis [of the particular district] or, in the
optioun of the pairtie, in the bookes of Register or sessioun
keiped be the said Clerk of Register him selff or his deputtis . . .
in Edinburgh. . . .   *A.P.S.*, iv, 545, c. 16.

5 proved false.   6 handed over.   7 proof of falsity.

1618   SIR GEORGE BRUCE'S
MINE AT CULROSS

*Sir George Bruce's under-water coal-mine, which was regarded
as one of the wonders of Scotland, indicates the development of the coal industry of the Forth area and the energetic
way in which enterprising lairds exploited the resources of
of their estates. It is also one of many illustrations of
the vigorous ingenuity of the period, which often issued in
projects and inventions much less practicable than this one.*

The mine hath two ways into it, the one by sea and the other
by land; but a man may goe into it by land, and returne the
same way if he please, and so he may enter into it by sea,
and by sea he may come forth of it: but I for varieties sake
went in by sea, and out by land. Now men may object, how
can a man goe into a mine, the entrance of it being into the
sea, but that the sea will follow him and so drown the mine?
To which objection thus I answer, That at low water, the sea
being ebd away, and a great part of the sand bare; upon this
same sand (being mixed with rockes and cragges) did the
master of this great worke build a round circular frame of
stone, very thicke, strong and joined together with glutinous
and bitumous matter, so high withall, that the sea at the
highest flood, or the greatest rage of storme or tempest, can
neither dissolve the stones so well compacted in the building,
or yet overflowe the height of it. Within this round frame (at
all adventures) hee did set workmen to digge with mattockes,
pick-axes, and other instruments fit for such purposes. They
did dig forty foot downe right, into and through a rocke. At
last they found that which they expected, which was sea-
cole: . . . so that in the space of eight and twenty, or nine
and twenty yeeres, they have digged more then an English
mile under the sea, that when men are at worke belowe, an
hundred of the greatest shippes in Britaine may saile over
their heads. Besides, the mine is most artificially cut like an
arch or a vault, all that great length, with many nookes and
by-wayes; and it is so made, that a man may walke upright
in the most places, both in and out. Many poor people are
there set on work, which otherwise through the want of
employment would perish. . . .

The sea at certaine places doth leake, or soake into the mine, which, by the industry of Sir George Bruce, is all conveyed to one well neere the land, where he hath a device like a horse-mill, that with three horses and a great chaine of iron, going downeward many fadomes, with thirty-sixe buckets fastened to the chaine; of the which eighteene goe downe still to be filled, and eighteene ascend up to be emptied, which doe emptie themselves (without any man's labour) into a trough that conveyes the water into the sea againe. . . .

Besides he doth make every weeke ninety or a hundred tunnes of salt, which doth serve most part of Scotland; some he sends into England, and very much into Germany.

Hume Brown, Early Travellers in Scotland, 116-17.

1618   FIVE ARTICLES OF PERTH

The articles relating to the worship of the church, approved by the general assembly at Perth in August 1618, were ratified by the privy council, and in the subsequent proclamation, dated 21 October, they were summarised as follows.

An act ordaining that everie minister sall have the commemoration of the inestimable benefites received from God by and through our Lord and Saviour Jesus Christ his Birth, Passion, Resurrection, Ascension and sending doun of the Holie Ghost, upon the days appointed for that use;[1] and that they sall make choice of severall and pertinent texts of Scripture, and frame their doctrine and exhortation thereto, and rebuke all superstitious observation and licentious profanation of the said dayes:

An act anent the administration of baptisme in privat houses when the necessitie sall require:

An act anent the catechizing of young children of eight yeers of age, and presenting them to the bishop to lay hands upon them, and blesse them, with prayer for increase of their

1 That is, Christmas, Good Friday, Easter, Ascension Day and Whitsunday.

knowledge and continuance of God's heavenlie graces with them:

An act anent the administration and giving of the Holie Communion in private houses to sicke and infirme persons:

An act that the blessed sacrament of the Holie Communior of the bodie and blood of our Lord and Saviour Jesus Christ be celebrate to the people humblie and reverentlie kneeling upon their knees.

Calderwood, vii, 337-9; A.P.S., iv, 596-7.

1625-33   THE ACT OF REVOCATION

Charles I's plan for a comprehensive and permanent settlement of the ecclesiastical property once again, like his father's act of 1587, used the familiar device of the revocation or annexation. A revocation was issued by the privy council in July 1625, and in fuller form in October following — before the king completed his twenty-fifth year in November. The proceedings which followed were long and complex, and their nature can best be demonstrated by a series of extracts which illustrate the principles lying behind them.

The general scope and purpose of the revocation

Howsoever we haif maid our revocatioun after the maner that our praedicessouris had formarlie done, we doe certifie and declair by these praesentis that we doe intend to mak no benefite thairof by extending it ony further then onlie aganis the erectionis and other dispositionis whatsomevir of landis, teyndis, patronageis, benefices, formarlie belonging to the Churche and since annexed tô the Crowne, and of other landis and patronages whiche onywayes sould justlie belong to the Churche or Crowne, and aganis dispositionis of lands and benefices mortified and divoted to pious uses, and of regalities and heretable offices. . . .

It is more for the publict goode then for our awne benefite that we ar moved to seik the annulling of all suche grantis

abone named whiche ar derogatorie to oure crowne and
praerogative royall. And though we might laughfullie doe
this without ony respect at all to the harme that may arrise
thairby to the praesent possessouris who haif unjustlie
acquired the same, yit, being loathe that ony of our good
subjectis who will within the tyme praefixt accept of reasoun
sould haif caus by our meanis to suffer or complayne, and to
the effect that all suche as will voluntarlie surrender ony right
they haif of the nature foirsaid betuix and the first day of
Januar nixt ensueing the date heirof may haif some reasounable compositioun for the samine, we haif appoyntit commissionaris to treate with thame thairupoun, who hathe
power from us bothe to treate and aggree with thame, and to
dispose of suche teyndis as ar recovered for our use (the
churches being planted and schooles and the poore provydit
for) to the heretouris of the ground from whence the teyndis
ar drawne at such a rate as they sall think expedient, as by
the commissioun gevin for that purpois may appeare.

(1626) *R.P.C.*, 2nd ser., i, 352.

Wee, for freeing of our said subjects from their preposterous
feares causleslie conceived upon our late revocation, and from
the unnecessarie charges which they might perhaps sustaine
either by repairing unto our person or by our persueing of
our right and title to the premises by due course of law, have
nominat and appoynted . . . the persons after-mentioned . . .
with full power to them . . . or any twelve of them . . . to
treate, deale, compone, transact, and aggrie with such person
or persons as shall at any time heerafter before the expiration
of this our commission bee contented to treate, aggrie and
modifie suche reasonable satisfaction for the said erections
and temporalities of benefices [etc.] unlawfullie acquired or
possessed by any of them and yet fitting to be secured unto
the present possessours of the said propertie upon reasonable
conditions, as said is; and concerning what composition shall
be given by the said proprietars and possessours unto us for
securing their titles of such of the premises as are fitte for
them to hold in all time coming; . . . and with power to our
saide commissionars . . . to make sufficient provision for
those churches whereof the teynds shall be resigned or disponed as aforesaid, if the saide churches bee not already
sufficiently provided, and for provyding of their ministers

186

with sufficient locall stipendes and fies, and to treat, conclude and aggree upon such pious use, and for establishing
of such schooles in the remote places of our said kingdome as
shall bee by them . . . thought expedient.

(1627) *R.P.C.*, 2nd ser., i, 510-12

The annexation of the monastic temporality

. . . Attoure his Majestie with consent forsaid declares the
richt and title of superioritie of all and sundrie lands, baronies,
mylnes, wodes, fishings, towers, fortalices, manour places and
whole pertinents thairof perteining to quhatsumever abbacies,
pryories, pryoressis, preceptories and quhatsumever uther
benefices of quhatsumever estate degrie title name or des-
ignatione the same be of, erected in temporall lordschipes,
baronies or livings befor or eftir the generall act of annexatione of kirklands maid in the moneth of Julii 1587 yeirs,
togither with the whole few maills, few fermes and other
rents and dewties of the saids superiorities, to be annexed
and to remaine with the crowne for ever; reserving to such
lords and titulars of erectiones and each one of thame who
have subscryved the generall surrander the few maills and few
fermes of thair said superiorities ay and quhyle they receave
payment and satisfactione of the soume of ane thousand
merkes usuall money of Scotland for each chalder of few
ferme victuall overhead and for each hundreth merks of few
maills and for each hundreth marks worth of all uther constant rent of the saids superiorities not consisting in victuall
or money and not being naked service of vassalles, according
to the tennor of his Majesties generall determinatione and
according to the conditiones thairin exprest; and reserving
to thame and to all uthers titulars of erectione thair propertie and propper lands, to be holdin of his Majestie and
his successors in few ferme for payment of the few ferme
dewties and other dewties contenit in the old infeftments
maid to thame, thair predicessors and authors befor the said
act of annexatione. . . .

(1633) *A.P.S.*, v, 27.

Teinds and stipends

His Majestie with consent of the thrie estates by these presents statuites, ordaines and declares that thair sall be no

teind scheaves or other teinds personage or viccarage led and
drawin within the kingdome bot that each heretor and
lyfrentar of lands sall have the leiding and drawing of thair
awin teind, the same being first trewlie and lawfullie valued,
and they paying thairfor the pryce eftir specifiet in caice they
be willing to buy the same, or otherwayes paying thairfor
the rate of teind eftirspecifiet: . . . Thairfor his Majestie . . .
haith grantit . . . commissione to the persones eftir following
. . . to prosecute and fallow furth the valuatione of quhatsumever teinds . . . which ar as yett unvalued . . . ; to appoint,
modifie and sett downe a constant and locall stipend and
maintenance to ilk minister to be payit out of the teinds of
ilk parochine . . . ; to divide ample and spatious parochines . . .
or to unite divers kirks in whole or in pairt to others . . . ; to
appoint and provyde for such other pious uses in each parochin as the estate thairof may bear; and siclyk with power to
the saids commissioners as said is to tak order that everie heretor and lyfrentar of lands sall have the leiding of thair awin
teinds parsonages and viccarages thairof, they paying the
pryce contenit in the act abonespecifiet in caice they be
willing to buy the same frome the titular having power to sell
or otherwayes paying the rate of teind exprest in the forsaid
act . . . ; to discusse and determine all questiones which may
arise betuixt the titulars and heretors anent the pryce of
teinds . . . ; and generallie with power to the saidis commissioners to decide and determine in all other pointes which may
concerne the leading and drawing of teinds, the selling and
buying of the same, or payment of the rate thairof contenit
in the actes of parliament abonespecifiet or sett downe in his
Majesties generall determinatione. . . .

(1633) *A.P.S.*, v, 34-8.

1633 THE KING'S PREROGATIVE
AND APPAREL OF CHURCHMEN

*One of the acts passed by the parliament of 1633, when
Charles I was in Edinburgh for his coronation, combined an
acknowledgement of the royal prerogative, in the terms of an*

act of 1606, with an acknowledgement of the king's power, in extension of an act of 1609, to prescribe the apparel of the clergy. Charles made use of this act to insist that the Scottish clergy should wear the same garments as were at that time worn by the clergy of the Church of England.

Our soverane Lord, with advyse, consent and assent of the whole estaites acknowledging his Majesties soveraigne authoritie, princelie power, royall prerogative and priviledge of his crowne over all estaites, persones and causes quhatsumevir within this kingdome, ratifies and approves the act of parliament maid in the yeir 1606 anent the kings royall prerogative, and perpetuallie confirmes the same for his hienes, his airs and successors, als amplie, absolutelie and frielie in all respectis as ever any of his Majesties royall progenitors did possess and exercise the same; and withall remembring that in the act of parliament maid in the yeir 1609 anent the apparell of judges, magistrats and kirkmen it was agried that quhat order soever his Majesties father of blissed memorie sould prescryve for the apparell of kirkmen and sent in writte to his clerke of register sould be a sufficient warrand for inserting the samen in the bookes of parliament to have the strength of ane act thairof, have all consented that the same power sall remaine with the persone of oure soverane lord and his successors that now is. . . .

A.P.S., v, 20-1.

The ordour appoyinted by his Majestie for the Apparrell off churchemen in Scotland, to be insert in the buiks off parliament conforme to the act off the late parliament maid thairanent.

It is our pleasure that all the lords Archbischops and Bischops within that our Kyngdome off Scotland sall in all publick places weare gownes with standing capes (such as they used at oure leite being there) and cassocks, And the inferiour clergie especiallie after they have taiken the degree off doctours or bachelours in divinitie or be preachours in any toune sall weare the same habite for faschioun bot for worth according to thair meanes, And no tippets unles they be doctours; And furder our pleasoure is that the lords Archbischops and Bischops sall in all churches where they come in tyme of divine service or sermoun be in whytes, that is in a rochett and sleeves as they weare at the tyme off our coronatioun, And especiallie whensoever they administer the holy communioun or preach. And they sall lykewayes provide thame selffis a chymer (that is a sattyn or taffetie gowne without lyning or sleeves) to be worne over thair whytes at the tyme of thair consecratioun. And we will that all Archbischops and Bischops aforesaid that are off our Privie Counsaill or off our Sessioun sall come and sitt there in there whytes and mayntayne the gravitie off thair places. And for all inferiour clergymen we will that they preach in thair black gounes; bot when they reade dyvine service, christen, burye or administer the sacrament off the lords supper, they sall weare there surplies, And if they be doctours there tippets over thame. And als weill Archbischops and Bischops as other ministers when they administer the holy communioun in our Chappell Royall or any cathedrall church within that our kyngdome sall weare capes[1] And not onely they bot all inferiour preests and ministers sall at tymes and places befoir mentioned use thair squarr cappes especiallie in all our universities. Gevin att Whytehall the 15 off October 1633. *Et sic subscribitur* C.R.

Seeled with the Court Signett
A.P.S., v, 21.

1 copes.

1633 EDUCATION ACT

This act of parliament ratified the act of council of 1616 (p. 178 above), with an important addition:

That the Bischops in thair severall visitatiounes sall have power with consent of the heritors and most pairt of the parischioners and, if the heritor being lawfullie wairnit refuissis to appear, then with consent of the most pairt of the parischioners, to set downe and[1] stent upon everie plough [land] or husband land according to the worth for maintenance and

1 *rectius* ane.

establisching of the saids schooles. And if any persone sall
find himselff greived it sall be lawfull to him to have recourse
to the lords of secreit counsall for redres of any prejudice he
may or doeth susteine; And ordaines letters to be direct for
chairging of the possessors for the tyme to answere and obey
the schoolmaisters of the dewties that sall be appointed in
maner forsaid.

A.P.S., v, 21, c. 5.

1634 'BALMERINO' SUPPLICATION

*Many of the acts passed by the parliament of 1633 had been
unpopular, but its proceedings had shown that opposition
could not make itself felt while the king, and his agents the
bishops, in effect controlled the conduct of business. The
critics of the king's policies therefore decided to approach
him by way of a supplication. This also proved futile: not
only did the king indicate that he did not approve of such
an approach, but Lord Balmerino, through whose hands the
supplication had passed, was tried for treason. The supplication
shows the profound uneasiness which existed about the king's
manipulation of parliament, and, in its combination of secular
and ecclesiastical grievances, it anticipates the National
Covenant.*

To the king's most excellent majesty, the humble
supplication of a great number of the nobility and
other commissioners in the late parliament.

Humbly sheweth, That the notes which your majesty put
upon the names of a number of your supplicants in voting
about these acts which did imply a secret power to innovate
the order and government long continued in the Reformed
Church of Scotland, and your majesty's refusing to receive
from some of your supplicants their reasons for dissenting
from the said acts, before your majesty and in your hearing
in parliament, to [*rectius* do] breed a fear of our becoming
obnoxious unto your majesty's dislike if your highness should

191

still remain unacquainted with the reasons of our opinions delivered concerning the said acts: seeing your supplicants are confident . . . that no want of affection to your majesty's service, but a careful endeavour to conserve unto your majesty the hearty affections of a great many of your good subjects that are tender in these points of novation covertly thrust upon this church, did induce our wishes and voices to appear in opposition to the said acts; . . .

First, we humbly beseech your majesty to consider that though these acts as they are conceived and may concern your majesty's prerogatives and the liberties of the church had never been moved or concluded (as they are), your majesty would have suffered no prejudice in your benefit, honour nor power; . . . that in deliberation about matters of importance, either in councils or parliaments, opinions do often differ, and they that have been of contrary mind to a resolution carried by the plurality of votes have never hither-to been censured by a prince of so much justice and goodness as your majesty.

We do also most humbly beseech your majesty to believe that all your supplicants do, in most submissive manner, acknowledge your royal prerogative in as ample manner as is contained in the Article 1606 made thereanent, and with-al do consider that the long experience and incomparable knowledge your royal father had in matters of government, as well in church as in commonwealth, is the very cause expressed in the act 1609 for giving power to his majesty to prescribe apparel to kirk-men, with their own consent. And since in all the time of his life and government for the space of 16 years thereafter he did forbear to make any change upon their former habits, we are bold to presume that in his great wisdom he thought fit that the apparel used in time of divine service ever since the Reformation of religion till his death, and to this day, should be continued, as decent in the church and most agreeable to the minds of his good subjects in this nation.

We do also beseech your majesty to consider, That under the act intitled, 'A ratification of the liberty of the church', the acts ratifying the assembly of Perth in parliament 1621 were declared to be comprehended; that most part of us being then in parliament did oppose the same; that experience

hath shewed how much these articles of Perth have troubled
the peace of this church and occasioned innumerable evils
and distractions in it; that there is now a general fear of
some novations intended in essential points of religion; and
that this apprehension is much increased by the reports of
allowance given in England for printing books of popery
and Arminianism, and the restraint of answers made to them;
and by preaching Arminianism in this country without
censure. . . .

That the minds of most of your good people being in this
perplexity, your supplicants have great reason to suspect a
snare in the subtle junction of the act 1609, concerning
apparel, with that of 1606, anent your royal prerogative;
which by a sophistical artifice should oblige us either to vote
undutifully in the sacred point of prerogative or unconscion-
ably in church novations, which blessed King James would
never have confounded. . . .

We do therefore dis-assent from the foresaid acts, as
importing a servitude upon this church unpractised before,
and giving ground for introduction of other new indefinite
devices.

We do further offer unto your majesty's consideration,
That albeit our just and heavy grievances allowed of in the
late convention of estates 1625, and 1630, to have been represented to your majesty, in hopes of refreshment to the
country's sufferings, have been altogether slighted in this
your first parliament; albeit your majesty denying your
nobility their freedom by authority to meet with the Lords
of the Articles, may seem against the constitution of a free
parliament . . . which before the parliament held in anno
1609 did always elect and chuse the Lords of the Articles
from among them of their own rank and quality,[1] there
having been no parliamentary bishops from the reformation
of religion till then,[2] nor were they such as now do cull and
single out such noblemen either popishly affected in religion
or of little experience in our laws, as having had their breeding
abroad, and so none of the ablest to be upon our Articles,
but fittest only for the clergy's mystical ends; whereas the
former practice was such as seemeth most agreeable to reason,

1 This is a very dubious assertion, for the evidence is that the method of
election had varied a good deal.

2 This is quite untrue: bishops had always sat in parliament.

193

and what every estate should do, that so they may communicate their minds with the rest of their body; . . . albeit the meeting of the gentry, and happily[3] of the burrows too, in a joint purpose to have represented . . . things worthy your majesty's consideration, were in your majesty's name interrupted; . . . yet have we all as one man consented to all your majesty's demands, and more, even to have taxations multiplied. . . .

Therefore we are confident that your majesty finding such a harmony in our affections to your service in preserving our religion and liberties, will be unwilling . . . to introduce upon the doctrine or discipline of this your Mother-Church anything not compatible with your majesty's honour, your good people's consciences, or that hath been rejected by acts and public practice of this Reformed Church.

Cobbett, *State Trials*, iii, 603-7; also, with variants, in Row, *History of the Kirk of Scotland* (Wodrow Soc.), 376-81.

3 I.e., haply.

1638 NATIONAL COVENANT

The Confession of Faith of the Kirk of Scotland, subscribed at first by the King's Majesty and his household in the year of God 1580 [1581]; thereafter by persons of all ranks in the year 1581, by ordinance of the lords of the secret council and acts of the general assembly; subscribed again by all sorts of persons in the year 1590, by a new ordinance of council, at the desire of the general assembly; with a general band for the maintenance of the true religion and the king's person, and now subscribed in the year 1638 by us noblemen, barons, gentlemen, burgesses, ministers and commons under subscribing; together with our resolution and promises for the causes after specified, to maintain the said true religion, and the King's Majesty, according to the confession aforesaid and acts of parliament: the tenor whereof here followeth: [Here follows the Negative Confession of 1581].[1]

1 pp. 150-3 above.

Like as many Acts of Parliament not onely in general do abrogate, annull, and rescind all Lawes, Statutes, Acts, Constitutions, Canons, civil or municipall, with all other Ordinances and practique penalties whatsoever, made in prejudice of the true Religion and Professours thereof; Or, of the true Kirk-discipline, jurisdiction, and freedome thereof; Or in favours of Idolatry and Superstition; Or of the Papisticall Kirk; As Act 3. Act 13. Parl. 1. Act 23. Parl. 11 Act 114. Parl. 12. of King James the sixt, That Papistry and Superstition may be utterly suppressed according to the intention of the Acts of Parliament repeated in the 5 Act Parl. 20. K. James 6. And to that end they ordaine all Papists and Priests to be punished by manifold Civill and Ecclesiastical pains, as adversaries to Gods true Religion, preached and by Law established within this Realme, Act 24. Parl. 11. K. James 6. as common enemies to all Christian government, Act 18. Parl. 16. K. James 6. as rebellers and gainstanders of our Soveraigne Lords Authority, Act 47. Parl. 3. K. James 6. and as Idolators. Act 104. Parl. 7. K. James 6. but also in particular (by and attour the Confession of Faith) do abolish and condemne the Popes Authority and Jurisdiction out of this Land, and ordaine the maintainers thereof to be punished, Act 2. Parl. 1. Act 51. Parl. 3. Act 106. Parl. 7. Act 114. Parl. 12. K. James 6. do condemne the Popes erronious doctrine, or any other erronious doctrine repugnant to any of the Articles of the true and Christian religion publickly preached, and by law established in this Realme: And ordaines the spreaders and makers of Books or Libels, or Letters, or writs of that nature to be punished, Act 46. Parl. 3. Act 106. Parl. 7. Act 24. Parl. 11. K. James 6. do condemne all Baptisme conforme to the Popes Kirk and the Idolatry of the Masse, and ordaines all sayers, willfull hearers, and concealers of the Masse, the maintainers and resetters of the Priests, Jesuites, traffiquing Papists, to be punished without any exception or restriction, Act 5. Parl. 1. Act 120. Parl. 12. Act 164. Parl. 13. Act 193. Parl. 14. Act 1. Parl. 19. Act 5. Parl. 20. K. James 6. do condemne all erroneous bookes and writtes containing erroneous doctrine against the Religion presently professed, or containing superstitious Rites and Ceremonies Papisticall, whereby the people are greatly abused, and ordaines the home-bringers of them to be punished, Act 25. Parl. 11. K. James 6.

do condemne the monuments and dregs of by-gone Idolatry; as going to the Crosses, observing the Feastivall dayes of Saints, and such other superstitious and Papisticall Rites, to the dishonour of God, contempt of true Religion, and fostering of great errour among the people, and ordaines the users of them to be punished for the second fault as Idolaters, Act 104. Parl. 7. K. James 6.

Like as many Acts of Parliament are conceaved for maintenance of Gods true and Christian Religion, and the purity thereof in Doctrine and Sacraments of the true Church of God, the liberty & freedom thereof, in her National, Synodal Assemblies, Presbyteries, Sessions, Policy, Discipline and Jurisdiction thereof, as that purity of Religion and liberty of the Church was used, professed, exercised, preached and confessed according to the reformation of Religion in this Realm. As for instance, The 99 Act Parl. 7. Act 23. Parl. 11. Act 114. Parl. 12. Act 160. Parl. 13. of King James 6. Ratified by the 4 Act of King Charles. So that the 6 Act Parl. 1. and 68 Act Parl. 6. of King James 6. in the Yeare of God 1579 declares the Ministers of the blessed Evangel, whom God of his mercy had raised up, or hereafter should raise, agreeing with them that then lived in Doctrin, and Administration of the Sacraments, and the People that professed Christ, as he was then offered in the Evangel, and doth communicate with the Holy Sacraments, (as in the reformed Kirks of this Realm they were publickly administrat) according to the Confession of Faith, to be the true and Holy Kirk of Christ Jesus within this Realm, and decerns and declares all and sundry, who either gainsayes the Word of the Evangel, received and approved, as the heads of the Confession of Faith, professed in Parliament, in the yeare of God 1560, specified also in the first Parliament of King James 6. and ratified in this present Parliament, more particularly do specify, or that refuses the administration of the Holy Sacraments, as they were then ministrated, to be no members of the said Kirk within this Realme, and true Religion, presently professed, so long as they keep themselves so divided from the society of Christs body: And the subsequent Act 69 Parl. 6. of K. James 6. declares, That there is none other Face of Kirk, nor other Face of Religion, then was presently at that time, by the Favour of God established within this

Realme, which therefore is ever stiled, Gods true Religion, Christs true Religion, the true and Christian Religion, and a perfect Religion, Which by manifold acts of Parliament, all within this realme are bound to profess, to subscribe the articles thereof, the Confession of Faith, to recant all doctrine & errours, repugnant to any of the said Articles, Act 4 & 9 Parl. 1. Act 45, 46, 47, Parl. 3. Act 71 Parl. 6. Act 106 Parl. 7. Act 24 Parl. 11. Act 123 Parl. 12. Act 194 and 197 Parl. 14. of K. James 6. And all Magistrats, Sherifs, &c. on the one parte are ordained to search, apprehend, and punish all contraveeners; For instance, Act 5 Parl. 1. Act 104 Parl. 7. Act 25 Parl. 11. K. James 6. And that notwithstanding of the Kings Majesty's licences on the contrary, which are discharged & declared to be of no force in so farre as they tend in any wayes, to the prejudice & hinder of the execution of the Acts of Parliament against Papists & adversaries of true Religion, Act 106 Parl. 7. K. James 6. On the other part in the Act 47 Parl. 3. K. James 6. It is declared and ordained, seeing the cause of Gods true Religion, and his highnes Authority are so joyned, as the hurt of the one is common to both: and that none shal be reputed as loyall and faithfull subjects to our Soveraigne Lord, or his Authority, but be punishable as rebellers and gainstanders of the same, who shall not give their Confession, and make their profession of the said true Religion, and that they who after defection shall give the Confession of their Faith of new, they shall promise to continue therein in time comming, to maintaine our Soveraigne Lords Authority, and at the uttermost of their power to fortify, assist, and maintaine the true Preachers and Professors of Christs Evangel, against whatsoever enemies and gainestanders of the same; and namely against all such of whatsoever nation, estate, or degree they be of that have joyned, and bound themselves, or have assisted, or assists to set forward, and execute the cruell decrees of Trent, contrary to the Preachers and true Professors of the Word of God, which is repeated word by word in the Articles of Pacification at Perth the 23 of Februar. 1572, approved by Parliament the last of Aprile 1573. Ratified in Parliament 1587, and related, Act 123 Parl. 12. of K. James 6. with this addition, that they are bound to resist all treasonable uproars and hostilities raised against the true Religion, the Kings Majesty, and the true Professors.

Like as all Lieges are bound to maintaine the Kings
Majesty's Royal Person and Authority, the Authority of
Parliaments, without the which neither any lawes or lawful
judicatories can be established, Act 130, Act 131 Parl. 8. K.
James. 6 and the subjects Liberties, who ought onely to live
and be governed by the Kings lawes, the common lawes of
this Realme allanerly, Act 48 Parl. 3. K. James the first; Act 79
Parl. 6.K. James the 4. repeated in the Act 131 Parl. 8. K. James
6. Which, if they be innovated or prejudged, the commission
anent the union of the two Kingdoms of Scotland and England,
which is the sole Act of the 17. Parl. of K. James 6. declares such
confusion would ensue, as this Realme could be no more a
free Monarchy, because by the fundamentall lawes, ancient
priviledges, offices and liberties, of this Kingdome, not onely
the Princely Authority of his Majesty's Royal discent hath
been these many ages maintained, but also the peoples security
of their Lands, livings, rights, offices, liberties, and dignities
preserved, and therefore for the preservation of the said true
Religion, Lawes, and Liberties of this Kingdome, it is statute
by the 8 Act Parl. 1, repeated in the 99 Act Parl. 7, Ratified
in the 23 Act Parl. 11. and 114 Act Parl. 12. of K. James 6.
and 4 Act of K. Charles, That all Kings and Princes at their
Coronation and reception of their Princely Authority, shall
make their faithfull promise by their solemne oath in the
presence of the Eternal God, that, enduring the whole time
of their lives, they shall serve the same Eternal God to the
uttermost of their power, according as he hath required in his
most Holy Word, contained in the old and new Testament.
And according to the same Word shall maintain the true
Religion of Christ Jesus, the preaching of his Holy Word, the
due and right ministration of the Sacraments now receaved
and preached within this Realme (according to the Confession
of Faith immediately preceeding) and shall abolish and gain-
stand all false Religion contrary to the same, and shall rule
the people committed to their charge, according to the will
and command of God, revealed in his foresaid Word, and
according to the laudable Lawes and Constitutions received
in this Realme, no wayes repugnant to the said will of the
Eternall God; and shall procure, to the uttermost of their
power, to the Kirk of God, and whole Christian people, true
and perfite peace in all time coming: and that they shall be

careful to root out of their Empire all Hereticks, and enemies to the true worship of God, who shall be convicted by the true Kirk of God, of the foresaid crimes, which was also observed by his Majesty, at his Coronation in Edinburgh 1633, as may be seene in the order of the Coronation.

In obedience to the Commandment of God, conforme to the practice of the godly in former times, and according to the laudable example of our Worthy and Religious Progenitors, & of many yet living amongst us, which was warranted also by act of Councill, commanding a general band to be made and subscribed by his Majesty's subjects, of all ranks, for two causes: One was, For defending the true Religion, as it was then reformed, and is expressed in the Confession of Faith abovewritten, and a former large Confession established by sundry acts of lawfull generall assemblies, & of Parliament, unto which it hath relation, set down in publick Catechismes, and which had been for many years with a blessing from Heaven preached, and professed in this Kirk and Kingdome, as Gods undoubted truth, grounded only upon his written Word. The other cause was, for maintaining the Kings Majesty, His Person, and Estate: the true worship of God and the Kings authority, being so straitly joined, as that they had the same Friends, and common enemies, and did stand and fall together. And finally, being convinced in our mindes, and confessing with our mouthes, that the present and succeeding generations in this Land, are bound to keep the foresaid nationall Oath & Subscription inviolable, Wee Noblemen, Barons, Gentlemen, Burgesses, Ministers & Commons under subscribing, considering divers times before & especially at this time, the danger of the true reformed Religion, of the Kings honour, and of the publick peace of the Kingdome: By the manifold innovations and evills generally conteined, and particularly mentioned in our late supplications, complaints, and protestations, Do hereby professe, and before God, his Angels, and the World solemnly declare, That, with our whole hearts we agree & resolve, all the dayes of our life, constantly to adhere unto, and to defend the foresaid true Religion, and (forbearing the practice of all novations, already introduced in the matters of the worship of God, or approbation of the corruptions of the publicke Government of the Kirk, or civil places and power of Kirk-men, till they be tryed & allowed in free assemblies, and in Parliaments) to labour by all meanes lawful to recover the purity and liberty of the Gospel, as it was stablished and professed before the foresaid Novations: and because, after due examination, we plainely perceave, and undoubtedly believe, that the Innovations and evils contained in our Supplications, Complaints, and Protestations have no warrant of the Word of God, are contrary to the Articles of the Foresaid Confessions, to the intention and meaning of the blessed reformers of Religion in this Land, to the above written Acts of Parliament, & do sensibly tend to the re-establishing of the Popish Religion and Tyranny, and to the subversion and ruine of the true Reformed Religion, and of our Liberties, Lawes and Estates, We also declare, that the Foresaid Confessions are to be interpreted, and ought to be understood of the Foresaid novations and evils, no lesse then if every one of them had been expressed in the Foresaid confessions, and that we are obliged to detest & abhorre them amongst other particular heads of Papistry abjured therein. And therefore from the knowledge and consciences of our duety to God, to our King and Countrey, without any worldly respect or inducement, so farre as humane infirmity will suffer, wishing a further measure of the grace of God for this effect, We promise, and sweare by the Great Name of the Lord our God, to continue in the Profession and Obedience of the Foresaid Religion: That we shall defend the same, and resist all these contrary errours and corruptions, according to our vocation, and to the uttermost of that power that God hath put in our hands, all the dayes of our life: and in like manner with the same heart, we declare before God and Men, That we have no intention nor desire to attempt any thing that may turne to the dishonour of God, or to the diminution of the Kings greatnesse and authority: But on the contrary, we promise and sweare, that we shall, to the uttermost of our power, with our meanes and lives, stand to the defence of our dread Soveraigne, the Kings Majesty, his Person, and Authority, in the defence and preservation of the foresaid true Religion, Liberties and Lawes of the Kingdome: As also to the mutual defence and assistance every one of us of another in the same cause of maintaining the true Religion and his Majesty's Authority, with our best counsel, our bodies, meanes, and whole power, against all sorts of persons whatsoever. So that whatsoever shall be done to the least of us for that cause, shall be taken as done to us all in general, and to every one of us in particular. And that we shall neither directly nor indirectly suffer ourselves to be divided or withdrawn by whatsoever suggestion, allurement, or terrour from this blessed & loyall Conjunction, nor shall cast in any let or impediment, that may stay or hinder any such resolution as by common consent shall be found to conduce for so good ends. But on the contrary, shall by all lawful meanes labour to further and promove the same, and if any such dangerous & divisive motion be made to us by Word or Writ, We, and every one of us, shall either suppresse it, or if need be shall incontinent make the same known, that it may be timeously obviated: neither do we fear the foul aspersions of rebellion, combination, or what else our adversaries from their craft and malice would put upon us, seing what we do is so well warranted, and ariseth from an unfeined desire to maintaine the true worship of God, the Majesty of our King, and peace of the Kingdome, for the common happinesse of our selves, and the posterity. And because we cannot look for a blessing from God upon our proceedings, except with our Profession and Subscription we joine such a life & conversation, as beseemeth Christians, who have renewed their Covenant with God; We, therefore, faithfully promise, for our selves, our followers, and all other under us, both in publick, in our particular families, and personal carriage, to endeavour to keep our selves within the bounds of Christian liberty, and to be good examples to others of all Godlinesse, Sobernesse, and Righteousnesse, and of every duety we owe to God and Man, And that this our Union and Conjunction may be observed without violation, we call the living God, the Searcher of our Hearts to witness, who knoweth this to be our sincere Desire, and unfained Resolution, as we shall answere to Jesus Christ, in the great day, and under the pain of Gods everlasting wrath, and of infamy, and losse of all honour and respect in this World, Most humbly beseeching the Lord to strengthen us by his holy Spirit for this end, and to blesse our desires and proceedings with a happy successe, that Religion and Righteousnesse may flourish in the Land, to the glory of God, the honour of our King, and peace and comfort of us all.

Nat. MSS. Scot., iii, No. xcvii.[2]

2 Many copies of the Covenant exist, with minor verbal variants.

The Covenant had been discreetly vague about the 'novations' and 'corruptions' which it condemned, it had professed loyalty to the king and it gave no warrant for the rejection of features of church order which had been approved by parliaments. As time passed, it became evident that the extreme wing of the opposition was disposed to go further than the Covenant, and, in particular, to attack episcopal government. However, even when the general assembly met at Glasgow in November, there was still a great deal of uncertainty and it was not generally believed that the re-formed church had ever in the past condemned episcopacy. The decisive stroke, therefore, was the production of the older registers of the assembly, with their acts against episcopacy, and the Glasgow assembly now deposed the bishops and renounced episcopal government. It was obvious that the Prayer Book of 1637 and the Canons of 1636 would be condemned, for neither of them had been authorised by assembly or parliament; and after clearing the ground by rejecting as 'unfree' the assemblies which had accepted King James's innovations, the assembly went on to condemn the Courts of High Commission and the Five Articles of Perth.

Production of the old registers

This day I produced for my first act the registers of the Kirk, and can never sufficiently admire and adore the goodnes, wysdome and providence of God in praeserving them and bringing them to our hands at sutch a tyme — magnified be His naime! — as this was a solid fondation to us, without the quhilk we wald haive seimed to haive buildet upon sand. . . . In the great committe, quhair my L. Argyle was sitting in the Tolbooth, I cleired al thair mynds that Episcopacie was condemned in this churche. I drew it up in a lairge treatise by Gods assistance, as lykwayes anent the articles; in the Assemblee I scheu al the warrants and read the verry acts themselves out of the registers and aunsuered al objections; and quhairas, both in the morning we heard of some wald publikly disput for Episcopacie and many scores came to the

house resolut to voyte for it, yet the Lord maid the Acts so
to convince thair mynds that every mans mouth acknou-
ledgit that they had bein abjured and removed; and, quhen I
was reading the roll and heard no word bot 'Abjured and
Removed,' I was struken with admiration . . . and yit my ears
sounds ever with thes words, 'Abjured and Removed.'

Johnston of Wariston's *Diary (Scot. Hist. Soc.)*, 401-3.

Condemnation of the last six general assemblies

. . . The Assembly with the universall consent of all, after
the serious examination of the reasons against every one of
these six pretended Assemblies apart, being often urged by
the Moderatour to informe themselves throughly, that without doubting, and with a full perswasion of minde, they might
give their voices, declared all these six Assemblies, of
Linlithgow 1606 and 1608, Glasgow 1610, Aberdeen 1616,
St. Andrews 1617, Perth 1618, and every one of them, to
have been from the beginning unfree, unlawfull, and null
Assemblies, and never to have had, nor hereafter to have, any
ecclesiasticall authoritie, and their conclusions to have been,
and to bee, of no force, vigour, nor efficacie: Prohibited all
defence and observance of them, and ordained the reasons of
their nullitie to be insert in the Books of the Assembly. . . .

Condemnation of the Prayer Book, Canons and
High Commission

The Assembly having diligently considered the Book of
Common Prayer, lately obtruded upon the reformed kirk
within this realme, both in respect of the manner of the
introducing thereof, and in respect of the matter which it
containeth, findeth that it hath been devised and brought in
by the pretended prelats, without direction from the kirk,
and pressed upon ministers without warrand from the kirk,
to be universally received as the only forme of divine service
under all highest paines, both civill and ecclesiasticall, and the
book it self, beside the popish frame and forms in divine
worship, to containe many popish errours and ceremonies,
and the seeds of manifold and grosse superstition and idolatrie. The Assembly, therefore, all in one voice, hath rejected
and condemned and by these presents doth reject and

condemne the said book, not only as illegally introduced, but also as repugnant to the doctrine, discipline and order of this reformed kirk, to the Confession of Faith, constitutions of Generall Assemblies, and Acts of Parliament establishing the true religion: and doth prohibite the use and practise thereof: and ordaines presbyteries to proceed with the censure of the kirk against all such as shall transgresse.

The Assembly also, taking to their consideration the Book of Cannons, and the manner how it hath been introduced, findeth that it hath been devised by the pretended prelats, without warrand or direction from the Generall Assembly: and to establish a tyrannicall power in the persons of the pretended bishops, over the worship of God, mens consciences, liberties and goods, and to overthrow the whole discipline and government of the generall and synodall assemblies, presbyteries and sessions formerly established in our kirk. Therefore the Assembly all in one voice hath rejected and condemned . . . the said book, as contrare to the Confession of our Faith, and repugnant to the established government, the Book of Discipline, and the acts and constitutions of our Kirk. . . .

The Generall Assembly, after due tryall, having found that the Court of High Commission hath been erected without the consent or procurement of the Kirk, or consent of the Estates in Parliament, that it subverteth the jurisdiction and ordinarie judicatories and assemblies of the kirk, sessions, presbyteries, provinciall and nationall assemblies, that it is not regulate by lawes civill or ecclesiasticall, but at the discretion and arbitrement of the Commissioners; that it giveth to ecclesiasticall persons the power of both the swords, and to persons meerly civill the power of the keys and Kirk censures: Therefore the Assembly all in one voice hath disallowed and condemned . . . the said court as unlawfull in it selfe, and prejudiciall to the liberties of Christs Kirk and Kingdome, the Kings honour in maintaining the established lawes and judicatories of the Kirk. . . .

Condemnation of episcopacy

. . . All the members of the Assembly being many times desired and required to propone their doubts and scruples, and every one being heard to the full, and after much agitation as fully satisfied; the Moderatour at last exhorting every one to declare his minde, did put the matter to voicing in these terms: — 'Whether according to the confession of faith, as it was professed in the year 1580, 1581, and 1590, there be any other Bishop, but a Pastour of a particular flock, having no preheminence nor power over his brethren, and whether by that Confession, as it was then professed, all other episcopacie is abjured, and ought to bee removed out of this Kirk?' The whole Assembly most unanimously, without contradiction of any one (and with the hesitation of one allanerly) professing full perswasion of minde, did voice that all episcopacie different from that of a Pastour over a particular flock, was abjured in this Kirk, and to be removed out of it. And therefore prohibites under ecclesiasticall censure any to usurpe, accept, defend, or obey the pretended authoritie thereof in time coming.

Condemnation of the Five Articles of Perth

The Assembly remembring the uniformity of worship which was in this Kirk, before the Articles of Perth, the great rent which entered at that time, and hath continued since, with the lamentable effects that it hath produced, both against Pastours and professours. . . . The matter was put to voicing, in these words: 'Whether the five articles of Perth, by the confession of Faith, as it was meaned and professed in the year 1580, 1581, 1590, 1591 ought to be removed out of this Kirk?' The whole Assembly all in one consent, one onely excepted, did voice that the five articles above specified were abjured by this Kirk, in that Confession, and so ought to be removed out of it: And therefore prohibiteth and dischargeth all disputing for them, or observing of them, or any of them, in all time comming, and ordains Presbyteries to proceed with the censures of the Kirk against all transgressours.

Act against civil places of churchmen

The Assembly most unanimously in one voice, with the hesitation of two allanerly, declared, that as on the one part the Kirk and the Ministers thereof are oblidged to give their advise and good counsell in matters concerning the Kirk or the Conscience of any whatsomever, to his Majestie, to the Parlament, to the Councell, or to any member thereof, for their resolutions from the Word of God; So on the other part, that it is both inexpedient, and unlawful in this Kirk, for Pastors separate unto the Gospel to brook civil places, and offices, as to be Justices of Peace; sit and decerne in Councell, Session, or Exchecker; to ryde or vote in Parliament, to be Judges or Assessors in any Civill Judicatorie.

Peterkin, Records of the Kirk of Scotland, 24-40; Acts of the General Assembly (Church Law Soc.), 5-30.

1640-41 CONSTITUTIONAL CHANGES

The desire for a 'free parliament', in the sense of one not managed by the king and his nominees, had been both implicit and explicit in the Supplication of 1634 and in the National Covenant. After their successes against the king, the revolutionary party passed measures to ensure parliamentary independence and also to subject the executive and the judiciary to the control of the estates.

(i) The Triennial Act, 1640.

The estates of parliament . . . have statute and ordeant that everie thrie yeir once at least a full and frie parliament shall be holdine (and oftner as his majestie shall be pleased to call them) within the boundis of this kingdome in the most commodious place and convenient tyme to be thought upon, appoynted and affixed by his majestie and his commissioner for the tyme and the estatis of parliament befor the ending and closing of everie parliament and to be the last act thairof. . . .

A.P.S., v, 268.

(ii) Act anent the Committee of the Articles, 1640.

The estates of parliament . . . have statute and declaired that according to the libertie of all frie judicatories anent thair owne preparatorie committies all subsequent parliamentis may, according to the importance of effaires for the tyme, either choose or not choose severall committies for articles as they shall thinke expedient; and that any subsequent

parliamentes, makeing electioun of committies for articles to
prepair materis for them, shall proceed in maner followeing,
to wit that these of the noblemen shall be named and
choosine by the noblemen themselves out of thair nomber,
and by the barrones commissioneris of shyres by themselves
out of ther nomber, and the burgess commissioneris of
burrous by themselves out of there nomber, the names of
the which persones so named and choosine out of everie
estate (not exceeding for every committie the nomber pre-
scryveit by the act of parliament 1587[1]) being openlie red
and mad knowne to the whole estatis sitting in plaine
parliament, the said estates . . . by ane act shall authoreize
the said persones with power to treat reason or consult
upoun the expediencie of such articles allenerlie as shall be
commited and recommendit unto them be the estates, and
to set doune such reasones and motives as they can devyse
wherby to enforce either the passing or rejecting of the
samene in parliament, to be reported with the said articles to
the remanent of the said estates assembled in parliament that
they may deliberat and advyse therupon.

A.P.S., v, 290-1.

(iii) Act anent the appointment of officers of state, councillors and lords of session, 1641.

His majestie with advyse and consent of the estates of
parliament declaires for himselffe and his successoures that
he will nominat and make choise of such able and qualified
persones to fill these places as shall be fittest for his service
and may give most contentment to the estates of parliament,
which nominatione and choise his majestie will make with the
advyse and approbatione of the saides estates of parliament
dureing there sitting and if any of the saidis places shall
happine to vaike and must be provydit in the intervall
betuixt parliamentes his majestie will choose and nominat
officeres of state and counselloures with the advyse and
approbatione of the counsell, all that nomber being warned
upoun fyftene dayes calling to meit theranent and most
pairt of the whole consenting, and in lyke maner the session-
eris with the advyse and approbatione of the most pairt of
that house; which electiones mad in the intervall shall be

1 Eight from each estate.

allowed or disallowed in the next ensueing parliament as the kingis majestie and the parliament shall thinke expedient. And the officeres of state, counsellouris and lordis of sessione so nominat and chosine by his majestie and the parliament or allowed by his majestie and them shall be provided *ad vitam vel culpam,* and they all shall be lyable to the censure of the kingis majestie and parliament.

A.P.S., v, 354-5.

1643 SOLEMN LEAGUE AND COVENANT

After the outbreak of the English civil war in 1642, the Scots found themselves wooed by both the king and the English parliament. With some hesitation, they undertook to assist the parliamentary party, but, instead of entering into a mere military and political alliance, they insisted on a religious bond. Although the first clause of the Solemn League was in truth guarded on the precise nature of the conformity in which the three kingdoms should join, the Scots were in no doubt that they had embarked on a crusade for the imposition of their own presbyterian system on England and Ireland.

We Noblemen, Barons, Knights, Gentlemen, Citizens, Burgesses, Ministers of the Gospel, and Commons of all sorts in the Kingdoms of Scotland, England and Ireland, . . . have now . . . resolved and determined to enter into a mutuall and solemn League and Covenant: Wherein we all subscribe, and each one of us for himself, with our hands lifted up to the most high God, do Swear
 1. That we shall sincerely, really and constantly, through the grace of God, endeavour in our several places and callings, the preservation of the Reformed Religion in the Church of Scotland, in Doctrine, Worship, Discipline and Government, against our common Enemies; The Reformation of Religion in the Kingdoms of England and Ireland, in Doctrine, Worship, Discipline and Government, according to the Word of God, and the example of the best Reformed Churches; And shall

endeavour to bring the Churches of God in the three Kingdoms, to the nearest conjunction and uniformity in Religion, Confession of Faith, Form of Church-government, Directory for Worship and Catechizing; That we and our Posterity after us, may, as Brethren, live in Faith and Love, and the Lord may delight to dwell in the midst of us.

2. That we shall in like manner, without respect of persons, endeavour the Extirpation of Popery, Prelacy . . . , Superstition, Heresy, Schism, Prophanesse, and whatsoever shall be found to be contrary to sound Doctrine and the power of Godliness; Lest we partake in other mens sins, and thereby be in danger to receive of their plagues; And that the Lord may be one, and his Name one in the three Kingdoms.

3. We shall with the same sincerity, reality and constancy, in our severall vocations, endeavour with our estates and lives mutually to preserve the Rights and Priviledges of the Parliaments, and the Liberties of the Kingdoms; And to preserve and defend the Kings Majesty's Person and Authority, in the preservation and defence of the true Religion, and Liberties of the Kingdoms; That the world may bear witnesse with our consciences of our Loyalty, and that we have no thoughts or intentions to diminish his Majesty's just power and greatnesse.

4. We shall also with all faithfulnesse endeavour the discovery of all such as have been, or shall be Incendiaries, Malignants, or evil instruments, by hindering the Reformation of Religion, dividing the King from his people, or one of the Kingdoms from another, or making any faction, or parties amongst the people contrary to this League and Covenant, That they may be brought to publick triall. . . .

5. And whereas the happinesse of a blessed Peace between these Kingdoms, denied in former times to our Progenitors, is by the good Providence of God granted unto us, and hath been lately concluded, and settled by both Parliaments, We shall each one of us, according to our place and interest, endeavour that they may remain conjoyned in a firme Peace and Union to all Posterity. . . .

6. We shall also according to our places and callings in this Common cause of Religion, Liberty, and Peace of the Kingdoms, assist and defend all those that enter into this League and Covenant, in the maintaining and pursuing thereof; And shall not suffer our selves directly or indirectly by whatsoever

combination, perswasion or terrour, to be divided and withdrawn from this blessed Union and conjunction, whither to make defection to the contrary part, or to give our selves to a detestable indifferency or neutrality in this cause, which so much concerneth the Glory of God, the good of the Kingdoms, and honour of the King; But shall all the dayes of our lives zealously and constantly continue therein, against all opposition, and promote the same according to our power, against all Lets and Impediments whatsoever; And, what we are not able our selves to suppresse or overcome, we shall reveale and make known, that it may be timely prevented or removed: All which we shall do as in the sight of God. . . .

A.P.S., vi, pt. i, 41; several printed versions with minor variants; cf. S.R. Gardiner, *Constitutional Documents*, 267-71.

1643   THE WESTMINSTER FORM OF CHURCH GOVERNMENT

The ecclesiastical side of the Anglo-Scottish alliance took shape in the productions of the Westminster Assembly of Divines — a Confession of Faith, a Larger and a Shorter Catechism, the Directory of Public Worship and a Form of Church Government. These documents, though produced in England, proved to have little appeal there in the long run, but they were adopted by the Scottish General Assembly and have ever since continued to be the standards of the Scottish presbyterian churches.

The Form of Presbyterial Church-Government and of Ordination of Ministers; agreed upon by the Assembly of Divines at Westminster, with the assistance of Commissioners from the Church of Scotland, as a part of the Covenanted Uniformity in Religion betwixt the Churches of Christ in the Kingdoms of Scotland, England and Ireland.

Of the Officers of the Church

The officers which Christ hath appointed for the edification of his church and the perfecting of the saints, are some extraordinary, as apostles, evangelists and prophets, which are ceased; others ordinary and perpetual, as pastors, teachers and other church-governors, and deacons.

Pastors

The pastor is an ordinary and perpetual officer in the church. . . .

Teacher or Doctor

The scripture doth hold out the name and title of teacher, as well as of the pastor: who is also a minister of the word, as well as the pastor, and hath power of administration of the sacraments. . . . A teacher or doctor is of most excellent use in schools and universities. . . .

Other Church-Governors

As there were in the Jewish church elders of the people joined with the priests and Levites in the government of the church; so Christ, who hath instituted government and governors ecclesiastical in the church, hath furnished some in His church, beside the ministers of the Word, with gifts for government, and with commission to execute the same when called thereunto, who are to join with the minister in the government of the church. Which officers reformed churches commonly call Elders.

Deacons

The scripture doth hold out deacons as distinct officers in the church: whose office is perpetual. To whose office it belongs not to preach the Word, or administer the sacraments, but to take special care in distributing to the necessities of the poor. . . .

Of the Officers of a particular Congregation

For officers in a single congregation, there ought to be one at the least, both to labour in the Word and doctrine and to rule. It is also requisite that there should be others to join in government. And likewise it is requisite that there be others to take special care for the relief of the poor. The number of each of which is to be proportioned according to the condition of the congregation.

These officers are to meet together at convenient and set times for the well ordering of the affairs of that congregation, each according to his office. It is most expedient that in these meetings one whose office is to labour in the Word and doctrine do moderate in their proceedings. . . .

Of Church-Government, and the several sorts of Assemblies for the same

Christ hath instituted a government and governors ecclesiastical in the church: to that purpose, the Apostles did immediately receive the keys from the hand of Jesus Christ, and did use and exercise them in all the churches of the world upon all occasions. And Christ hath since continually furnished some in His church with gifts of government, and with commission to execute the same when called thereunto.

It is lawful, and agreeable to the Word of God, that the church be governed by several sorts of assemblies, which are congregational, classical and synodical. . . .

Of Congregational Assemblies

The ruling officers of a particular congregation have power, authoritatively, to call before them any member of the congregation, as they shall see just occasion; to enquire into the knowledge and spiritual estate of the several members of the congregation; to admonish and rebuke.

Of Classical Assemblies

The scripture doth hold out a presbytery in a church. A presbytery consisteth of ministers of the Word and such other public officers as are agreeable to and warranted by the Word of God to be church-governors, to join with the ministers in the government of the church. The scripture doth hold forth that many particular congregations may be under one presbyterial government. . . .

Of Synodical Assemblies

The scripture doth hold out another sort of assemblies for the government of the church, beside classical and congregational, all which we call Synodical. . . . Synodical assemblies may lawfully be of several sorts, as provincial, national and oecumenical. It is lawful, and agreeable to the Word of God, that there be a subordination of congregational, classical, provincial and national assemblies, for the government of the church. . . .

Form of Church Government (approved by the General Assembly on 10 February 1645 and printed in numerous editions of the *Confessions of Faith*).

1646   EDUCATION ACT

The abolition of episcopal government had nullified the Education Act of 1633 (p. 190 above), but in 1646 powers were given to presbyteries similar to those previously vested in the bishops, in more explicit and better defined terms. This act of 1646 was rescinded in 1661 by the Act Rescissory (p. 225 below), but the act of 1633 thereupon became once more operative.

The Estates of parliament considdering how prejudiciall the want of schooles in manie congregations hathe bene and how beneficiall the founding therof in everie congregation wilbe to this kirk and kingdome Doe thairfore statute and ordane that there be a School founded and a Scholemaster appointed in everie paroche (not alreadie provyded) by advyse of the presbitrie. And to this purpose that the heritouris in everie congregation meet amongst themselfis and provyde a commodious hous for the schole and modifie a stipend to the schole master whiche sall not be under ane hundereth merkis nor above tua hundereth merkis to be payit yeirlie at tuo termes. And to this effect that they set doune a stent upon everie ones rent of stock and teind in the paroche proportionallie to the worth therof for mantenance of the schoole and payment of the scholemasteris stipend; whiche stipend is declarit to be dew to the scholemasteris and clerkis of kirk sessionis.[1] And if the heritouris sall not conveene, or being

1 These two offices were commonly held by the same individual.

conveened sall not aggrie amongst themselfis, than and in that
case the presbitrie sall nominat tuell honest men within the
boundis of the presbitrie who sall have power to establish a
schoole, modifie a stipend for the schoolmaster with the
latitude before exprest, and set doune a stent for payment
therof upon the heritouris whilk salbe alse valide and effectuall as if the samen had bene done be the heritouris
themselfis. . . .

A.P.S., vi, pt. i, 554, c. 171.

1647 ENGAGEMENT

*The operations of the English parliamentarians, with their
Scots allies, led to the defeat of the king at Naseby (1645).
When Charles subsequently surrendered to the Scots, they
handed him over to the English. It was soon seen that there
was little chance of a compromise which would have preserved some of his authority, and that, as power in England
passed from the parliament (which was in a majority presbyterian) to the army (where the independents prevailed),
there was little prospect for the fulfilment of the Solemn
League. A party in Scotland therefore decided to come to
terms with the king and offer him armed help in return for
a guarantee of presbyterianism in Scotland and an undertaking to give presbyterianism a three years' trial in England.*

His Majesty giving belief to the professions of those who have
entered into the League and Covenant, and that their intentions are real for preservation of his Majesty's person and
authority according to their allegiance, and no ways to
diminish his just power and greatness, his Majesty, so soon as
he can with freedom, honour and safety be present in a free
parliament, is content to confirm the said League and Covenant by Act of Parliament in both kingdoms, for security
of all who have taken or shall take the said Covenant, provided that none who is unwilling shall be constrained to take
it. His Majesty will likewise confirm by Act of Parliament in

England, presbyterial government, the directory for worship and assembly of divines at Westminster, for three years, so that His Majesty and his household be not hindered from using that form of Divine Service he hath formerly practised; and that a free debate and consultation be had with the Divines at Westminster, twenty of His Majesty's nomination being added unto them, and with such as shall be sent from the Church of Scotland, whereby it may be determined by His Majesty and the two Houses how the Church government, after the said three years, shall be fully established as is most agreeable to the Word of God: that an effectual course shall be taken by Act of Parliament, and all other ways needful or expedient, for suppressing the opinions and practices of Anti-Trinitarians, Anabaptists, Antinomians, Arminians, Familists, Brownists, Separatists, Independents, Libertines, and Seekers, and generally for suppressing all blasphemy, heresy, schism, and all such scandalous doctrines and practices....

And whereas after the return of the Scottish army to Scotland, the Houses of Parliament of England did resolve and appoint the army under command of Sir Thomas Fairfax to disband, and they having entered into an engagement to the contrary, His Majesty was carried away from Holdenby against his will by a party of the said army, and detained in their power until he was forced to fly from amongst them to the Isle of Wight; and since that time His Majesty and the Commissioners of the kingdom of Scotland have earnestly pressed that His Majesty might come to London in safety, honour and freedom for a personal treaty with the two Houses and the Commissioners of the Parliament of Scotland, which hath not been granted: and whereas the said army hath in a violent manner forced away divers members of both Houses from the discharge of their trust, and possessed themselves of the City of London and all the strengths and garrisons of the kingdom. . . .

And, forasmuch as His Majesty is willing to give satisfaction concerning the settling of religion and other matter in difference, as is expressed in this Agreement, the kingdom of Scotland doth oblige and engage themselves first in a peaceable way and manner to endeavour that His Majesty may come to London in safety, honour and freedom for a personal treaty with the Houses of Parliament and the Commissioners of

Scotland upon such Propositions as shall be mutually agreed on between the kingdoms, and such Propositions as His Majesty shall think fit to make; and that for this end all armies may be disbanded. And in case this shall not be granted, that Declarations shall be emitted by the kingdom of Scotland in pursuance of this Agreement, against the unjust proceedings of the two Houses of Parliament towards His Majesty and the kingdom of Scotland, wherein they shall assert the right which belongs to the Crown in the power of the militia, the Great Seal, bestowing of honours and offices of trust, choice of Privy Councillors, the right of the King's negative voice in Parliament; and that the Queen's Majesty, the Prince, and the rest of the royal issue, ought to remain where His Majesty shall think fit, in either of the kingdoms, with safety, honour and freedom. And upon the issuing of the said Declarations, that an army shall be sent from Scotland into England, for preservation and establishment of religion, for defence of His Majesty's person and authority, and restoring him to his government, to the just rights of the Crown and his full revenues, for defence of the privileges of Parliament and liberties of the subject, for making a firm union between the kingdoms, under His Majesty and his posterity, and settling a lasting peace; in pursuance whereof the kingdom of Scotland will endeavour that there may be a free and full Parliament in England, and that His Majesty may be with them in honour, safety and freedom, and that a speedy period be set to this present Parliament, and that the said army shall be upon the march before the said peaceable message and Declaration be delivered to the House; and it is further agreed that all such in the kingdoms of England or Ireland, as shall join with the kingdom of Scotland in pursuance of this Agreement, shall be protected by His Majesty in their persons and estates; and that all such His Majesty's subjects of England and Ireland as shall join with him in pursuance of this Agreement may come to the Scotch army and join with them, or else put themselves into other bodies in England and Wales for prosecution of the same ends as the King's Majesty shall judge most convenient, and under such Commanders or Generals of the English nation as His Majesty shall think fit, and that all such shall be protected by the kingdom of Scotland and their army in their persons and estates, and where any injury or wrong is done to them therein, that they shall be careful to see them fully repaired so far as is in their power to do, and likewise, where any injury or wrong is done to those that join with the kingdom of Scotland, His Majesty shall be careful for their full reparation.

That His Majesty or any by his authority or knowledge shall not make nor admit of any cessation, pacification, nor agreement for peace whatsoever, nor of any Treaty, Propositions, Bills, or any other ways for that end, with the Houses of Parliament or any army or party in England and Ireland, without the advice and consent of the kingdom of Scotland....

That His Majesty shall contribute his utmost endeavours both at home and abroad for assisting the kingdom of Scotland in carrying on this war by sea and land, and for their supply by monies, arms, ammunition, and all other things requisite, as also for guarding the coasts of Scotland with ships, and protecting all Scottish merchants in the free exercise of trade and commerce with other nations; and His Majesty is very willing and doth authorise the Scots army to possess themselves of Berwick, Carlisle, Newcastle-upon-Tyne, Tynemouth, and Hartlepool, for to be places of retreat and magazine, and when the peace of the kingdom is settled, the kingdom of Scotland shall remove their forces, and deliver back again the said towns and castles; that, according to the large Treaty, payment may be made of the remainder of the Brotherly Assistance which yet rests unpaid; and likewise of the £200,000 due upon the late Treaty made with the Houses of Parliament for the return of the Scots army, as also that payment shall be made to the kingdom of Scotland for the charge and expense of their army in this future war, together with due recompense for the losses which they shall sustain therein: that due satisfaction, according to the Treaty on that behalf between the kingdoms, shall be made to the Scottish army in Ireland, out of the land of that kingdom or otherwise.

That His Majesty, according to the intention of his father, shall endeavour a complete union of the kingdoms, so as they may be one under His Majesty and his posterity; and, if that cannot be speedily effected, that all liberties, privileges, concerning commerce, traffic, and manufactories peculiar to the subjects of either nation, shall be common to the subjects of both kingdoms without distinction; and that there be a communication of mutual capacity of all other privileges of the subject in the two kingdoms; that a competent number of ships shall be yearly assigned and appointed out of His Majesty's navy, which shall attend the coast of Scotland for a guard and freedom of trade to his subjects of that nation; that His Majesty doth declare that his successors as well as himself are obliged to the performances of the Articles and conditions of this Agreement; that His Majesty shall not be obliged to the performance of the aforesaid articles until the kingdom of Scotland shall declare for him in pursuance of this agreement, and that the whole articles and conditions aforesaid shall be finished, perfected and performed before the return of the Scots army; and that when they return into Scotland at the same time, *simul et semel,* all arms be disbanded in England.

Carisbrook, the 26th of December.

Gardiner, *Constitutional Documents of the Puritan Revolution,* 347-52.

1649   ACT OF CLASSES

The army raised by the Engagers on the king's behalf was cut to pieces at Preston in November 1648. The majority in the general assembly, and the more extreme covenanters generally, had all along denounced the Engagement, and the military defeat of the Engagers meant that power fell into the hands of the extremists. Their policy was to rely on no compromise and on no alliance and to repudiate the support of all who had deviated from the strictest interpretation of the Solemn League. The Act of Classes (23 January 1649) excluded from office of any kind those who were comprised in four classes.

The First Classe

Generall officers who led and accompanied the army into England, and all those officers that continowed in the engadgement . . . and all those persons who wer plotters, cheef actores, and pryme promotters of the late unlaufull engagement from the beginning to the end therof in parlement, committeis or otherwise; and sicklyk all these who were

cheeff actoris and pryme promotters of the horrid rebellioun
of James Grahame [Marquis of Montrose] and who since have
either accepted of charge or joyned as volunteers in the said
unlaufull engadgement or taken the oath in committeis or
subscrived the band for themselves or others for the engadgement or sat in the committees or other meetings and gave
ordour for prosequuting the said engadgement or who otherwise gave or received and execute ordoris aganst others for
prosequuting the said engadgement. . . .

The Second Classe

[Those] who not being included in the first classe have bene
formerlie classed or censured for malignancie . . . and since
have ather accepted of charge or joyned as voluntiers in the
said unlaufull engadgement; . . . and siclyk all those persons,
altho not formerlie classed and not being included in the
first classe, who wer officers which wer upon any of the
expeditions into England or Scotland for the said engagement;
and siclyk all these who concurred in petitions protestatiounes
remonstrances or letters for moving the parliament or committeis to cary on the engagement; and siclyk all these who
protested aganst the caus of the fast or the kirks declaratiounes or petitions of the presbiteries or kirk sessions aganst
the engadgement, or red, or caused read, at kirk doores the
committeis observatiounes aganst the assemblies declaratioun,
or interrupted Divyne service or magistrats and persons of
quality, or who removed at the reading of the assemblies
declaratioun; sicklyk all those who not onlie took the oath
injoyned by the last parlement for the engagement in committeis or subscryved the band or declared themselffis readie
to doe the same, bot also seduced others or protested aganes
others for not taking the oath or not subscribeing the band;
siclyk all these who injoyned and pressed others to subscryve
the band or tak the oath for carying on the engagement. . . .

The Thrid Classe

[Those] who (not being included in the first or second classes)
sat in parliament and committee of estats and took the oaths
forsaid for the engagement, or sat as clerkis in any of these or
any other judicatories and gave no publict testimony aganst
the said engagement, caried on therin by thair service, or were

any way knowne to have beene for the same in judgement manifested by thair expressions and actions; siclyk all these persons who have taken the oath forsaid or subscryvit the band for the engagement or who in committeis of warre or other meetings, Toun Counsall or other courtis have refuised or opposed the desyres of any petitions from shyres, presbiteries, sessions or other kirk judicatories aganst the engagement, . . . Lykas all persons who in their speeches and actions did evidence thair judgement for and affectioun to that sinfull course, or who (in such a tyme of tryall after such petitions from the shires and such declaratiounes and warnings from the Church evidenceing to all the unlaufulnes of the engagement aganst Covenant and Treaties) did not give any countenance to the cause or testimony of thair judgement and affectioun aganst such a defection and dangerous war when and where they had the opportunity to doe it with others.

The Fourth Classe

[Those] who being members of judicatories, clerkis and persons in publict trust as aforsaid are given to uncleannesse, brybery, swearing, drunkennesse, or deceiving, or are otherwise openlie profane and grosslie scandalous in thair conversatioun or who neglect the worship of God in thair families.

[Those in the first class were excluded from office for life, those in the second for ten years, those in the third for five years, and those in the fourth for one. But readmission was in every case to be preceded by satisfaction to the Kirk, which thus obtained a veto on public appointments.]

A.P.S., vi, pt. ii, 143-7.

1650 REMONSTRANCE

Charles I was executed a week after the Act of Classes was passed. The faction in power in Scotland agreed, after some negotiations, to accept Charles II as king on condition that he took the Covenants. However, the Act of Classes meant in effect that no one was allowed to fight for Charles II who had fought for Charles I, and an army in which political and ecclesiastical reliability was of more account than military experience was routed by Cromwell at Dunbar (3 September 1650). 'Resolutions' were then passed which in effect annulled the Act of Classes, but the extremists, contending that the trouble was that the Act of Classes had not been rigorously enough applied, presented their'Remonstrance to the Committee of Estates (October 1650). In the division of the presbyterians into moderate 'Resolutioners' and extreme 'Remonstrants' or 'Protesters' (whose strength lay mainly in the south-west), lay the source of much trouble not only in weakening Scotland in the face of English pressure but also in producing a lasting division which, after 1660, facilitated the revival of episcopacy.

Althoughe wee do not judge of the undertakings of the Lords people by the successe, and be not shaken by the dissipating of our armey, nor brought in question our causse, yet wee thinke ourselves, and all the people of this land, called by thesse late dispensations to searche and tray our wayes. . . .

That wiche is obvious, in the first place, amonge the sinns of the land, is our late proceidings with the King [Charles II]; quherin, that wee be not mistakin, wee shall distinguish betuix our deuty and our sinns. Wee owe and acknouledge for our deutie to usse all lawfull wayes and means for reclaming the King, and to owne his intrest according to oure vocatione, so fare as he owns and prosecuttes the causse. Bot we are convinced that it is our sinne, and the sin of the kingdome, that quhen the King had walked in the wayes of his fathers oppositione to the worke of reformation, and the soleme league and covenant . . . that after all this, commissioners should have beine warrandit to assure him of his present admissione to the exercisse of his royall power, upone his profession to joyne in the causse and covenant, not onlie without aney furder evidence of his repentance, unto the renewing of the Lord's contrawersie with his fathers housse, and without convincing evidences of the realitie of his profession and his forsaiking his former principalls and wayes; but quhen ther was pregnant presumptions, if not cleir evidences, of the contrarey. . . .

In the nixt place, the grate and mother sin of this nation wee conceave to be the backslydinge breache of covenant and engagements unto the Lord. . . . So wee humblie desyre your lordships to lay to heart:—

How unanswerable ye have walked to your soleme ingagement to purge the judicatories and armies, and to fill the places of truste and power with men of knowin good affection to the causse of God and of a blamles and Christian conversation. Have not some amongest you beine the cheiffe obstructors of the worke, by retarding conclusions, by studing to make them ineffectuall, quhen they have beine takin; by your partiall dealling, differencing men according to ther intrests, countenancing, favoring, keiping in and helping to places of power and trust suche malignant and profane persons as might be subservient to your deseinges; by your reckoning it qualificatione good aneuche if a man be free of accession to the ingagement, thoughe he were otherwayes malignant or prophaine; by your sparing of thosse in eminent places and truste in the judicatories and armies and taking no trayell of the qualifications, according to your vowis, quhill you wer doing some deutie upone them of lower degree, quherby it hath come to passe that ther remaine yet spots in your judicatories wich diminishes your crydit and authority, and occasione is given to the enimies to blaspheme the causse of God. . . .

Peterkin, *Records of the Kirk of Scotland*, 604-6.

1652-4 SCOTLAND AND THE COMMONWEALTH

The union of Scotland with the Commonwealth of England became effective through conquest in 1651. There could be no genuinely negotiated union, and when, in 1652, Scottish commissioners gave their consent to terms of union they had in truth no alternative. An act of union was not passed until 1656, but the delay had arisen through Cromwell's difficulties with his parliaments, and an ordinance of 1654 provided

*formally for Scottish representation in the parliament at
Westminster and for free trade between the two countries.*

*It had been made clear, in a Declaration issued in 1652,
that the government of the Commonwealth would protect
not only 'such ministers whose consciences oblige them to
wait upon God in the administration of spiritual ordinances
according to the order of the Scottish Churches', but also
'others who, not being satisfied in conscience to use that
form, shall serve and worship God in other Gospel way'.*[1]
*Both the Instrument of Government, which established the
Protectorate in 1653, and the Humble Petition and Advice,
which reinforced the Protector's authority in 1657, repeated
that the official policy was toleration, 'provided this liberty
be not extended to Popery or Prelacy, nor to such as, under
the profession of Christ, hold forth and practise
licentiousness'.*[2]

(i) Scottish Attitudes in 1652.

... It doth by necessary and cleir consequence establish in
the Church a vast and boundles toleracion of all sorts of
errour and heresies without any effectuall remedie for suppressing the same; notwithstanding that there bee the same
morall and perpetuall obligation upon us to suppress and
extirpate heresie no less then profanenes: Lykeas this dec-
laracion doe allow diverse wayes of worshipping God under
the name of Gospell wayes. ...

'Reasons for the dissent of Glasgow,' in Terry, *Cromwellian Union* (Scot. Hist. Soc.), 35.

... We conceive ourselves bound by the Law of God and oath
of Covenant agreeable thereto to endeavour the preservation
of the liberties of this nation and just fundamentall lawes
thereof, which we judge to be altogether infringed be the
forme of the now demanded incorporatioun which tho car-
rieing along with it a change of the whole fundamentall
frame of government and all thinges thereupon dependent is
not presented to the full and frie deliberation of the people
in their collectede bodie, but first concluded without their
advyce and knowledge and now offered in a divydit way
without a previous condiscension in what might preserve from

1 Firth, *Scotland and the Commonwealth* (Scot. Hist. Soc.), xxxvi-xxxvii;
A.P.S., vi, pt. ii, 809.
2 Gardiner, *op. cit.*, 416, 454-5.

the dangerous consequences that may follow so great a change if not carefullie guarded against. . . .

We dar not add to nor diminish from the matters of Jesus Christ, dearer to us then all thinges earthlie, which is so far from being secured by any thing offered for that effect that it is diverse wayes prejudiced and a fundation laid downe in generall and doubtsome termes of a vast tolleration. . . .

'Doubts and scruples of Lanark,' ibid., 74-5.

(ii) Ordinance for Union, 12 April 1654.

His Highness the Lord Protector of the Commonwealth of England, Scotland and Ireland, &c., taking into consideration how much it might conduce to the glory of God and the peace and welfare of the people in this whole island, that after all those late unhappy wars and differences, the people of Scotland should be united with the people of England into one Commonwealth and under one Government, and finding that in December, 1651, the Parliament then sitting did send Commissioners into Scotland to invite the people of that nation unto such a happy Union, who proceeded so far therein that the shires and boroughs of Scotland, by their Deputies convened at Dalkeith, and again at Edinburgh, did accept of the said Union, and assent thereunto; for the completing and perfecting of which Union, be it ordained, and it is ordained by his Highness the Lord Protector of the Commonwealth of England, Scotland and Ireland, and the dominions thereto belonging, by and with the advice and consent of his Council, that all the people of Scotland, and of the Isles of Orkney and Shetland, and of all the dominions and territories belonging unto Scotland, are and shall be, and are hereby incorporated into, constituted, established, declared and confirmed one Commonwealth with England; and in every Parliament to be held successively for the said Commonwealth, thirty persons shall be called from and serve for Scotland.

[The monarchy and parliament of Scotland are abolished. The St. Andrew's Cross is to be received into the Arms of the Commonwealth.]

And be it further ordained by the authority aforesaid, that all customs, excise and other imposts for goods transported from England to Scotland, and from Scotland to England, by sea or land, are and shall be so far taken off and discharged,

224

as that all goods for the future shall pass as free, and with
like privileges and with the like charges and burdens from
England to Scotland, and from Scotland to England, as goods
passing from port to port, or place to place in England; and
that all goods shall and may pass between Scotland and any
other part of this Commonwealth or the dominions thereof,
with the like privileges, freedom, charges and burdens as such
goods do or shall pass between England and the said parts
and dominions, any law, statute, usage or custom to the contrary thereof in any wise notwithstanding, and that all goods
prohibited by any law now in force in England to be transported out of England to any foreign parts, or imported,
shall be and hereby are prohibited to be transported or imported by the same law, and upon the same penalties, out of
Scotland to any foreign parts aforesaid, or from any foreign
parts into Scotland.

And be it further ordained by the authority aforesaid, that
all cesses, public impositions and taxations whatsoever, be
imposed, taxed and levied from henceforth proportionably
from the whole people of this Commonwealth so united.

[Feudal services and heritable jurisdictions are abolished.]

Gardiner, *Constitutional Documents*, 418-22; *A.P.S.*, vi, pt. ii, 816-7.

1661 ACT RESCISSORY

The preamble to this act relates that the miseries of the
previous twenty years had been the consequence of the
'neglects, contempts and invasions which . . . were, upon the
specious (but false) pretexts of reformation (the common
cloak of all rebellions), offered unto the sacred person and
royal authority' of Charles I; that, although Charles had
visited Scotland in 1641 and complied with legislation sub-
versive of the royal power, his 'unparalleled condescensions'
did not make his subjects ashamed of their 'former miscar-
riages'; and that, when the king 'had not left unto them any
pretence or shadow of any new desire', they joined in a
league with the parliament of England against him.

Thairfor the Kings Majestie and estates of Parliament doe heirby Rescind and annull the pretendit Parliaments keept in the
years 1640, 1641, 1644, 1645, 1646, 1647 and 1648 and all
acts and deids past and done in them and declare the same to
be henceforth voyd and null; and his Majestie, being unwilling
to take any advantage of the failings of his Subjects dureing
those unhappie tymes, is resolved not to retaine any remembrance thairof but that the same shall be held in everlasting
oblivion and that, all differences and animosities being for-
gotten, his good subjects may in a happie union under his
Royall Government enjoy that happines and peace which his
Majestie intends and really wisheth unto them as unto himselff, doth therfor by advice and consent of his estates of
Parliament grant his full assureance and indemnity to all
persones that acted in, or by vertew of the said pretendit
Parliaments and other meitings flowing from the same to be
unquestioned in their lives or fortunes for any deid or deids
done by them in thair said usurpation or be vertew of any pretendit Authority deryved therfrom; Excepting alwayes such as
shall be excepted in a generall act of indemnity to be past be
his Majestie in this Parliament.

A.P.S., vii, 86-87.

1662   ACT RESTORING
EPISCOPAL GOVERNMENT

Forasmuch as the ordering and disposall of the externall
government and policie of the church doth propperlie belong
unto his majestie as ane inherent right of the croun,[1] by vertew
of his royall prerogative and supremacie in causes ecclesiasticall;
and in discharge of this trust his majestie and his estates of
parliament takeing to their serious consideration that in the
beginning of, and by, the late rebellion within this kingdome
in the yeer 1637 the ancient and sacred order of bishops wes

1 This phraseology is repeated in the Act of Supremacy of 1669, which
acknowledged the king's 'supreme authority and supremacy over all persons and
in all causes ecclesiastical'.

cast off, their persons and rights wer injured and overturned and a seeming paritie[2] among the clergie factiously and violently brought in, to the great disturbance of the publict peace, the reproach of the reformed religion and violation of the excellent lawes of the realme for preserveing ane orderlie subordination in the church; and therwithall considering what disorders and exorbitancies have been in the church, what encroachments upon the prerogative and rights of the croun, what usurpations upon the authoritie of parliaments, and what prejudice the libertie of the subject hath suffered by the invasions made upon the bishops and episcopall government, which they find to be the church government most agreeable to the Word of God, most convenient and effectuall for the preservation of treuth, order and unite and most suteable to monarchie and the peace and quyet of the state: Thairfor his majestie, with advice and consent of his estates of parliament, hath thought it necessar and accordingly doth heirby redintegrat the state of bishops to their antient places and undoubted priveledges in parliament, and to all their other accustomed dignities, priveledges and jurisdictions; and doth heirby restore them to the exercise of their episcopall function, presidencie in the church, power of ordination, inflicting of censures and all other acts of church discipline, which they are to performe with advice and assistance of such of the clergie as they shall find to be of knoun loyaltie and prudence; [reviving Acts of Parliament in favour of episcopal government; rescinding acts by which 'the sole and only power and jurisdiction within this church doth stand in the generall, provinciall and presbyteriall assemblies and kirk sessions,' particularly that of 1592; and restoring to the bishops the commissariot jurisdiction[3] and their temporalities].

A.P.S., vii, 372-4.

2 Pairtie *in the printed record is an obvious misreading for* paritie.
3 The right of appointing the commissaries, those judges who exercised jurisdiction in executry and matrimonial cases, had previously been restored to the bishops in 1609.

1662 ACT CONCERNING
BENEFICES AND STIPENDS

*Clergy admitted to parishes since the abolition of lay patron-
age in 1649 were required to seek presentation from the
patrons and collation[1] from the bishops. On 1 October 1662
the Council ordained that ministers who had refused to
comply with the requirement must remove by 1 November,
and, although an extension was subsequently given until
February 1663, about 270 ministers, mainly in the Protester
strongholds of the dioceses of Glasgow and Galloway, refused
to comply.*

The Kings most excellent Majestie . . . considering that
notwithstanding the right of patronages be duely setled and
established by the antient and fundamentall lawes and constitutions of this kingdome, yet diverse ministers in this
Church have and doe possesse benefices and stipends in their
respective cures, without any right or presentation to the
same from the patrons; and it being therfor most just that
lawfull and undoubted patrons of kirks be restored to the
possession of the rights of their respective advocations, donations and patronages: Therfor his Majestie, with advice and
consent of his Estates of Parliament, doth statut and ordaine
that all these ministers who entered to the cure of any
paroche in burgh or land within this kingdome in or since the
yeer 1649 (at and befor which time the patrons wer most
injuriously dispossessed of their patronages) have no right
unto nor shall receave uplift nor possesse the rents of any
benefice, modified stipend, mans or gleib for this present
cropt 1662, nor any yeer following, but their places, benefices
and kirks are *ipso iure* vacand. Yet his Majestie, to evidence
his willingnes to passe by and cover the miscariages of his
people, doth, with advice forsaid, declare that this act shall
not be prejudiciall to any of these ministers in what they
have possessed or is due to them, since their admission; and
that everie such minister who shall obtaine a presentation
from the lawfull patron and have collation from the bishop
of the dyocie wher he liveth betuixt and the tuentieth of
September nextocome, shall from thenceforth have right to,

1 The patron directed his presentation to the bishop, who thereupon conferred the benefice on the presentee.

and enjoy his Church benefice, manse and gleib as fully and
freely as if he had been lawfullie presented and admitted therto at his first entrie or as any other minister within the Kingdome doth or may doe. And for that end it is heirby ordained
that the respective patrons shall give presentations to all the
present incumbents who in due time shall make application
to them for the same. And in caice any of these Churches
shall not be thus duely provided befor the said tuentieth of
September, then the patron shall have freedome to present
another betuixt and the tuentieth day of March 1663, which
if he shall refuise or neglect, the presentation shall then fall
to the bishop *jure devoluto* according to former lawes. And
siclyk his Majestie with advice forsaid doth statute and ordeane
the Archbishops and Bishops to have the power of new
admission and collation to all such Churches and benefices as
belong to their respective sees and which have been vaiked
since the yeer 1637, and to be carefull to plant and provide
these their oune kirks conforme to this act.

A.P.S., vii, 376.

1662 ACTS AGAINST
COVENANTS AND CONVENTICLES

(i)

The Estates of Parliament takeing into their consideration the
miseries, confusions, bondage and oppressions this Kingdome
hath groaned under since the yeer 1637, with the causes and
occasions thairof, . . . and since the rise and progresse of the
late troubles did in a great measure proceid from some
treasonable and sedicious positions infused into the people,
that it wes lawfull to subjects, for reformation, to enter into
Covenants and leagues, or to take up armes against the King
or those commisionated by him and suchlyke, . . . And considering that as the present aige is not fullie freed of those
distempers, so posterity may be apt to relapse therein if
timeous remeid be not provided: Therfor the Kings Majestie

and Estates of Parliament doe declare that those positions, that it is lawfull to subjects upon pretence of reformation, or other pretence whatsoever, to enter into leagues and covenants or to tak up armes against the King; or that it is lawfull to subjects pretending his Majesties authority to tak up armes against his person or those commissionated by him, or to suspend him from the exercise of his royall government, or to put limitations upon their due obedience and alledgeance, are rebellious and treasonable; . . . and particularly that these oaths wherof the one wes commonlie called The Nationall Covenant (as it wes sworne and explained in the yeer 1638 and therefter), and the other entituled a solemn League and Covenant wer, and ar, in themselffs unlawfull oaths and wer taken by and imposed upon the subjects of this kingdome against the fundamentall lawes and liberties of the same; and that ther lyeth no obligation upon any of the subjects from the said oaths, or either of them, to endeavour any change or alteration of government either in Church or State; and therfor annulls all acts and constitutions ecclesiastick or civill approveing the said pretended Nationall Covenant or League and Covenant, or makeing any interpretations of the same or either of them.

A.P.S., vii, 377-8.

(ii)

His Majestie, considering that under the pretext of religious exercises, diverse unlawfull meitings and conventicles (the nurseries of sedition) have been keept in private families; hath thought fit, with advice [and consent of his estates conveened in this present Parliament], heirby to declare that as he doth and will give all due encouragement to the worship of God in families amongst the persons of the familie and others who shall be occasionally ther for the tyme, so he doth heirby discharge all private meitings or conventicles in houses which under the pretence of, or for, religious exercises, may tend to the prejudice of the publict worship of God in the Churches, or to the alienating the people from their lawfull pastors, and that duetie and obedience they ow to Church and State. And it is heirby ordained that none be heirafter permitted to preach in publict or in families within any dio-cesse, to teach any publict school, or to be pedagogues to the

childrene of persons of qualitie,without the licence of the
ordinary of the Diocesse [i.e., the bishop].

1663   ACT AGAINST SEPARATION AND
DISOBEDIENCE TO ECCLESIASTICAL
AUTHORITY[1]

As his Majestie doeth expect from all his good and duetifull
subjects a due acknowledgement and hearty complyance with
his Majesties Government ecclesiasticall and civill as it is now
established by law within this kingdome, and that in order
therunto they will give their cheerfull concurrence, countenance and assistance to such Ministers as by publict Authority
are or shall be admitted in their severall paroches, and attend
all the ordinary meitings of divine worship in the same; so
his Majestie doth declare that he will and doth account a
withdrawing from and not keeping and joyning in these
meitings to be seditious and of dangerous example and consequence. And therfor and for preventing the same for the
future His Majestie with advice and consent of his Estates
in Parliament doth heirby statute ordean and declare that all
and every such person or persons who shall heirafter ordinarly
and wilfully withdraw and absent themselffs from the
ordinary meitings of divine worship in their oune paroche
church on the Lord's day (whither upon the accompt of pop-
erie or other disaffection to the present government of the
church) shall therby incur the paines and penalties underwritten, viz. each nobleman, gentleman and heritor the losse
of a fourt parte of ilk yeers rent in which they shall be
accused and convicted; and every yeoman tennent or fermer
the losse of such a proportion of their frie moveables (after
the payment of their rents due to their master and landlord)
as his Majesties Councill shall think fit, not exceiding a fourt
parte thairof; and every burgesse to losse the liberty of

1 This act was known as 'The Bishops' Drag Net'.

merchandizeing, tradeing and all other liberties within burgh
and fourt parte of their moveables. . . .

A.P.S., vii, 455, c. 9.

1663, 1672. AMENDMENTS TO POOR LAW

*It was hoped that the development of manufactures would
alleviate the problem of unemployment, but, when an act of
1663 authorising manufacturers to press vagabonds into their
service proved ineffective, the erection of work-houses was
authorised in 1672. Little seems to have been achieved along
those lines, but much of this legislation remained the law
until 1845 and in the course of time a fair number of parishes
did avail themselves of the power to impose an assessment.*

(i)

[Previous acts are ratified] with this addition, that it shall be
leisum to all persons or societies who have or shall set up
any manufacturies within this kingdom, to seize upon and
apprehend the persons of any vagabonds who shall be fund
begging . . . and to imploy them for their service as they
shall see fit, the same being done with the advice of the
respective magistrats of the place wher they shall be seized
upon. . . .

Lykeas his majestie . . . ordaines the heritors of each
paroche, or as many of them as shall happen to meit upon
publict intimation made at the paroche kirk upon any sabboth
at the dissolveing of the church from the first sermon, by any
of the heritors of the paroche or by the imployers of the
poore, to make up a stent roll for mantenance of the poore
in their paroche who shall be imployed as said is, . . . the one
halff therof to be payed by the heritors either conforme to
the old extent of their lands within the paroche, or conforme
to the valuation by which they last payed assessment or
otherwayes, . . . and the other halff thairof to be layd upon
the tennents and possessors according to their means and
substance. . . .   *A.P.S.*, vii, 485-6.

[Ministers and elders are to compile lists of poor], condiscending upon their age and condition, if they be able or unable to worke, by reasoun of age, infirmity or disease, and where they wer borne, and in what paroches they have most haunted dureing the last thrie yeires preceiding the uptakeing of these lists . . . and . . . the heritors who, and the possessors of their land, are to beir the burding of the maintainance of the poor persones of each paroch, or any of them who shall meit with the saids ministers and elders, shall condiscend upon such as throwgh age and infirmity are not able to worke, and appoint them places wherin to abide, that they may be supplied by the contributions at the paroche-kirk: and if the same be not sufficient to entertaine them, that they give them a badge or ticket to aske almes at the dwelling houses of the inhabitants of their owne paroche onlie, without the bounds quhairof they are not to beg. . . .

Such of the saids poor persones as are of age and capacity to worke, be first offered to the heritors or inhabitants of each paroche, that if they will accept any of them to become their apprentices or servants they may receive them upon their obleidgment to entertaine and sett to worke the saids poor persones, and to releiff the paroch of them . . . and that the rest of the saids poor persones be sent to the correction-houses: for whose entertainment the saids heritors shall cause collect the saids contributions and appoint a quarters allowance to be sent alongs with them, with cloathes upon them to cover their nakedness and the said allowance to be payed quarterlie theraftir, by way of advance.

With power also to the saids commissioners of excise in each shire quarterlie to take ane account of the diligence of these of each paroch for performeing of the premisses. . . .

And his majestie . . . doeth impower . . . the masters of the correction-houses to put and hold the saids poor people to worke as they shall see them most capable and fitt; and incaice of their disobedience, to use all maner of severitie and correction, by wheeping or otherwise (excepting torture). . . .

It shall be lawfull to coallmasters, saltmasters and others who have manufactories in this kingdome to seize upon any vagabonds or beggars, wherevir they can find them, and to put them to worke in their coal-hewghs or other manufactories. . . .

A.P.S., viii, 89-91.

1669 ACT FOR
REPAIRING ROADS AND BRIDGES

This act, ineffective as it was, remained the foundation of highway maintenance until its piecemeal supersession by local turnpike acts, mainly from about 1750 onwards, and the 'statute labour' which it instituted continued to operate in some areas until well through the nineteenth century.

Our Soverane Lord Considering how necesser it is for the good of the people that hie ways be made and mantained for readie and easie passage travell and traffick through the Kingdom; And that the care therof which hath been layd upon the Justices of Peace hath yet for the most parte proven ineffectuall in regaird the saids Justices have not had speciall orders and warrands for that effect. For remeid whairof his Majestie with advice and consent of the Estates of Parliament, doth appoint and ordain the Shirreff of the shire and one of his deputies being always ane heretor therin and the Justices of Peace in each shyre to conveen at the heid burgh of the shire upon the first tuisday of May yeerly for ordering of highways bridges and ferries; with power to them or major parte of them that shall happen to conveen To set doun a particular list of the hie ways bridges and ferries, within thair bounds, and to divyde the paroches of the saids bounds as they ly most euest[1] to the severall high ways to be repaired, and as they may have the most equall burden; And to appoint such of their number or others oversiers of such parts & portions of the saids high ways as are most convenient & nearest to their ordinary residence; And to nominat such of their number as they sie fit to survey and give an accompt of the hie ways bridges and ferries unto the rest; with power to them to appoint meitings from tyme to tyme till the said survey list and division of the saids high ways be closed. Which persons . . . are heirby authorized and strictly required to call and conveen all tennents and coatters and their servants, within the bounds appointed for their parts of the high ways, by publict intimation at the paroch kirks upon Sabboth day immediatly after the first sermon, or any other way that they shall think fit, To have in readiness horses, carts, sleds, spades,

1 nearest, or most conveniently.

shovells, picks, mattocks, and such other instruments as shall
be required, for repairing of the saids high ways . . . With
power to them also to designe such of the saids persons, as
they find to be most skilfull, to attend and direct the rest
and to appoint them fit wages for their attendance. Provyding
that the days they are required to work doe not exceid the
number of sex days for man and horse yeerlie for the first
three yeers and four days yeerlie therafter; and that they be
only betuixt the bear seid[2] yeerlie and hay time or harvest
therafter. With power to the saids Justices or Oversiers .to
poind the readiest goods of the absents for tuentie shillings
scots money for the absence of ilk man dayly and threttie
shillings for the man & horse, without farther solemnity but
appriseing the same upon the ground of the land, and thairwith to hyre others in place of the absents . . . Which high
ways shall be tuenty foot of measure broad at least, or broader
if the same have been so of before, and shall be so repaired
that horses and carts may travell summer and winter therupon . . . And because the work of the inhabitants within the
severall bounds will not be able sufficiently to repair the
high ways and others forsaid, Thairfor his Majestie . . . doth
heirby authorize and require the wholl freeholders and heretors of the severall shires to conveen at the respective heid
burghs the first tuisday of June yeerly, and to call for ane
account from the justices of peace of what is neidfull for
reparation of high ways and others forsaid, and what charges
and expences is requisite . . . And accordingly to stent the
heretors of the said shyre . . . not exceiding ten shillings scots
upon each hundreth pund of valued rent in one yeer. . . .

A.P.S., vii, 574, c. 37.

2 The time of sowing bere.

1669 DECLARATION OF INDULGENCE

*The Declaration of Indulgence of 1669 was associated with a
phase during which the government sought to conciliate,
rather than repress, the nonconformists. A second indulgence,*

in 1672, authorised some fifty more of the 'outed' ministers to 'preach and exercise the other parts of the ministerial function' in specified parishes; and a third, in 1679, after the rebellion which was crushed at Bothwell Brig, relaxed the law in favour of house conventicles in certain areas, provided the preacher had not taken part in the rebellion.

Wheras by the act of councill and proclamation at Glasgow in the year 1662 a considerable number of ministers were at once turned out and so debarred from preaching of the gospell and exercise of the ministry, wee are gratiously pleased to authorise yow our privy councill to appoynt so many of the outed ministers as have lived peaceably and orderly in the places where they have resided to return to preach and exercise other functions of the ministery in the paroch churches where they formerly served (provyded they be vacant) and to allow patrones to present to other vacant churches such others of them as yow shall approve of, and that such of these ministers as shall take collation from the bishop of the diocie and keip presbyteries and synods may be warranted to lift their stipends as other ministers of the kingdome, bot for such as are not or shall not be collated by the bishopes that they have no warrand to medle with the locall stipend, bot only to possesse the manse and glebe, and that yow appoynt a collectour for those and all other vacant stipends, who shall issue the same and pay a yearly mantinence to the saids not collated ministers as yow shall sie fitt to appoynt.

That all who are restored or allowed to exercise the ministry be . . . enjoyned to . . . keep presbyteries and synods . . . and that such of them as shall not obey our commands in keeping presbyteries be confyned within the bounds of the parishes where they preach ay and while they give assurance to keep presbyteries for the future.

That all who shall be allowed to preach be strictly enjoyned not to admitt any of their neighbour or other paroches into their communiones, nor baptise their childrein, nor mary any of them without the allowance of the minister of the paroch to which they belong, unless it be vacant. . . .

That such of the outed ministers who live peaceablie and orderly and are not re-entered or presented as aforsaid have allowed to them 400 merks Scotts yearlie out of the vacant church for their mantinence till they be provyded of churches, and that even such who shall give assurance to live so for the future be allowed the same yearly mantinence.

And seing wee have by these orders taken away all pretences for conventicles and provyded for the wants of such as are and will be peaceable, if any shall be found hereafter to preach without authority or keep conventicles, our expresse pleasur is that yow proceid with all severity against the preachers and hearers as seditious persons and contemners of our authority.

R.P.C., 3rd ser., iii, 38-40.

1672   ACT ANENT TRADE OF BURGHS

One of the many indications of the effort being made to develop the Scottish economy in this period was the creation of a large number of non-royal burghs, no less than 110 of which received charters between 1660 and 1707. It was only logical correspondingly to reduce the special trading privileges of the royal burghs, and this act opened up a wide commercial scope for burghs of barony and regality. Protests by the royal burghs led to a partial restoration of their old privileges in 1690, but it proved impossible to maintain their monopoly of foreign trade.

It shall be leisome to any of his Majesties good subjects, or any persone that shall buy from them, to export furth of this kingdome, by sea or land all maner of cornes that are of the grouth of the kingdome, all maner of cattell, nolt, sheip and horse, coall, salt and wooll, skins, hydes and all uther native commodities of the kingdome; And that it shall be leisom to the burghs of regalitie and barronie, by any of their burgessis or members of society to export all their owne proper manufacture, or such goods as shall be bought by them in faires or markets. And that it shall be leisom to the saids burghs of regalitie or barrony or societies erected or to be erected for manufactours and all uthers exporting the native grouth of the kingdome as afoirsaid, to import in returne of the saids goods exported, or of the frawght & hire of the shipes, the goods & commodities following: viz. timber, iron, tar, soap, lint, lintseed, hemp, onions or uther necessars for tillage or building, or for the use of their forsaid manu-factours; and als to tope & retail all commodities whatso-evir. . . .

A.P.S., viii, 63, c. 5.

1679 GOVERNMENT ACTION IN THE HIGHLANDS

The administration of Charles II, which was much occupied with the disturbances caused by the conventiclers in the south-west, had its troubles in the Highlands as well. The following documents are dated 27 May 1679, and they must be read in the light of contemporary events elsewhere — the murder of Archbishop Sharp on 3 May, the outbreak of what was to prove a serious rebellion on 29 May and the defeat of the rebels at Bothwell Brig on 22 June.

(i)

Charles [etc.]. Forasmuch as diverse persons of the name of McDonald and McClain, rebells, and their associats, having convocat themselves in armes in the Highlands, and by armed force having dispossest severall of our good and peace-able subjects furth of their just rights and possessions, and wee with advice of our Privy Councill having, for preventing the beginnings of a rebellion and for restoring and maintain-ing of our peaceable subjects in the possession of their just rights, by a commission of the twelt of Aprile last, given full power and authority to . . . Archibald, Earle of Argyle, to reduce these rebells to the obedience of our laws, by which commission the said Earle of Argyle was impowered to call to his assistance such heretors of the shire of Inverness and uther shires therein specified for themselves, their tennents and servants, with such of the fourty dayes provision allowed by law as the said Earle should find necessar, and did give and grant to the said Earle severall powers and instructions in manner at length contained in his commission; and, whereas it is informed that some of the heretours of the said shire of Inverness or their vassals, men, tennants and servants or dependars upon them, have upon inadvertence or some uther pretext joined in armes with the saids rebells in opposition to our authority, wee doe hereby require and command the saids heretours and uthers foresaids to relinquish and leave that rebellious party and joyne in concurrence with the said Earle of Argyle. . . .

R.P.C., 3rd. ser., vi, 203-4.

(ii)

[To the Earl of Argyll, from the Privy Council.] Upon receipt of your Lordships letter of the 20 instant, advertisement was given to the Lords of Privy Councill to meet this day, and accordingly, they being mett, your Lordships letter of the 24th instant was communicate to them and, upon perusall thereof and serious consideration of the affaire, order was immediatly given for dispatching the powder and ball which was formerly ordered to be sent to yow by the commissioners of the Thesaury. A letter is writen to the Earle of Cathnes requiring him with all that hee can command to concurr with and assist yow. Missive letters are also written to the sheriffs of Invernes, Dumbarton and their deputs, and a proclamation issued as to those of the shire of Invernes, whereof coppies are here inclosed; but, considering the insolencies committed by these frequenting field conventicles, wee conceaved it not safe to send any of the standing forces at this time.

Ibid., 205.

1680-85 CAMERONIAN DECLARATIONS

The alternating policies of conciliation and repression wore down the opposition, until militant nonconformity was confined to the small body of Cameronians, under Donald Cargill and Richard Cameron. In the various papers which expounded

*their standpoint we see the logical conclusions of some of the
arguments of Andrew Melville and their issue in repudiation
of the civil government.*

(i) The Queensferry Paper, 1680.

We confess with our mouth and believe with our hearts that
the doctrine of the reformed churches, especially that of
Scotland, contained in the Scriptures, summed up in our
confessions of faith, and engaged to by us in our covenants,
is the only true doctrine of God, and that we purpose to
persevere in it to the end; and that the pure worship required
and prescribed in the scriptures, without the inventions,
additions, adornings or corruptions of men is the only true
worship of God; and the presbyterian government exercised
by lawful ministers and elders in kirk-sessions, presbyteries,
synods, and general assemblies is the only right government
of the Church, and that this government is a distinct government from the civil, and ought distinctly to be exercised not
after a carnal manner by the plurality of votes, or authority
of a single person, but according to the word of God; so that
the word makes and carries the sentence and not plurality
of votes.

We shall endeavour to our utmost, the overthrow of the
kingdom of darkness, and whatever is contrary to the kingdom
of Christ, especially idolatry and popery in all the articles of
it, as we are bound in our national covenants; superstition,
will-worship and prelacy, with its hierarchy, as we are bound
in our solemn league and covenant: and that we shall with the
same sincerity endeavour the overthrow of that power (it
being no more authority) that hath established and upholds
that kingdom of darkness, that prelacy to wit and erastianism
over the church, and hath exercised such a lustful and arbitrary
tyranny over the subjects, taking all power in their hand, that
they may at their pleasure introduce popery in the church,
as they have done arbitrary government in the state. . . .

Considering that the line and succession of our king and
rulers hath been against the power and purity of Religion
and godliness, and Christ's reigning over his church, and its
freedom, and so against God, and hath degenerate from that
virtue, moderation, sobriety and good government which
was the tenor and right by which their ancestors kept their

crowns (for when they left that, they themselves were laid aside, as our chronicles and registers do record) into an idle and sinful magnificence where the all and only government is to keep up their own absoluteness and tyranny, and to keep on a yoke of thraldom upon the subjects, and to squeeze from them their substance to uphold their lustful and pompous superfluities; . . . we do declare that we shall set up over ourselves and over what God shall give us power of, government and governors according to the word of God . . . ; That we shall no more commit the government of ourselves and the making of laws for us, to any one single person or lineal successor . . ., this kind of government by a single person being most liable to inconveniencies, and aptest to degenerate into tyranny as sad and long experience has taught us. . . .

Robert Wodrow, Sufferings of the Church of Scotland (1721), ii, app. xlvi.

(ii) The Sanquhar Declaration, 22 June 1680.

Although we be for government and governors such as the word of God and our covenant allows, yet we for ourselves and all that will adhere to us, as the representative of the true presbyterian kirk and covenanted nation of Scotland, considering the great hazard of lying under such a sin any longer, do by thir presents disown Charles Stuart, that has been reigning (or rather tyrannizing as we may say) on the throne of Britain these years bygone, as having any right, title to, or interest in the said crown of Scotland for government, as forfeited several years since by his perjury and breach of covenant both to God and his Kirk, and usurpation of his crown and royal prerogatives therein, and many other breaches in matters ecclesiastic, and by his tyranny and breach of the very *leges regnandi* in matters civil. . . . As also, we being under the standard of our Lord Jesus Christ, Captain of salvation, do declare a war with such a tyrant and usurper and the men of his practices, as enemies to our Lord Jesus Christ, and his cause and covenants. . . . As also we disown, and by this resent the reception of the Duke of York, that professed papist, as repugnant to our principles and vows to the most high God, and as that which is the great, though not alone, just reproach of our kirk and nation. We also by this protest against his succeeding to the crown; and whatever has been done, or any are essaying to do in this land (given to the Lord) in prejudice to our work of reformation.

Wodrow, ii, app. xlvii.

(iii) The Apologetical Declaration, 1684.

For preventing further mistakes anent our purposes, we do hereby jointly and unanimously testify and declare that as we utterly detest and abhor that hellish principle of killing all who differ in judgment and persuasion from us, it having no bottom upon the Word of God, or right reason, so we look upon it as a duty binding upon us to publish openly unto the world that forasmuch as we are firmly and really purposed not to injure or offend any whomsoever, but to pursue the ends of our covenants, in standing to the defence of our glorious work of reformation and of our own lives: yet (we say) we do hereby declare unto all, that whosoever stretcheth forth their hands against us, while we are maintaining the cause and interest of Christ against his enemies in the defence of our covenanted reformation, by shedding our blood actually, either by authoritative commanding, such as bloody counsellors (bloody we say) insinuating clearly by this and the other adjective epithets an open distinction betwixt the cruel and blood-thirsty and the more sober and moderate, especially that (so called) Justiciary, Generals of Forces, Adjutants, Captains, Lieutenants and all in civil and military power who make it their work to embrue their hands in our blood, or by obeying such commands, such as bloody Militia Men, malicious Troopers, Soldiers and Dragoons . . . We say all and every one of such shall be reputed by us enemies to God and the covenanted work of reformation, and punished as such, according to our power and the degree of their offence. . . .

Wodrow, ii, app. xcix.

(iv) The Sanquhar Protestation, 28 May 1685.

A few wicked and unprincipled men of this kingdom having by open proclamation proclaimed James, duke of York, though a professed papist and excommunicate person and not yet received into the church, to be king of Scotland, England, France and Ireland: we the contending and suffering remnant of the true presbyterians of the Church . . . do here deliberately, jointly and unanimously protest against the foresaid proclamation of James, duke of York, to be king, as said is, in regard that it is the choosing a murderer to be a governor, who hath shed the blood of the saints of God; in regard that it is the height of confederacy with an idolater, which is forbidden by the law of God. . . .

Moreover, taking to our serious consideration the low, deplorable and obscured state of the churches of England and Ireland, and that we are all bound in one covenant and solemn league together, we . . . do in like manner hereby admonish you our brethren in these our neighbouring and covenanted lands that ye remember how far ye have sadly failed in pursuing the ends of our covenants. . . . Stretch your hands to the helping, strengthening, encouraging and comforting a poor wasted, wronged, wounded, reproached, despised and bleeding remnant (with whom you are in covenant) setting ourselves against all the injuries and affronts done to our blessed Lord Jesus Christ, against the man of sin, the kingdom of Antichrist and all the limbs and parts thereof. . . .

An Informatory Vindication (Edinburgh, 1744), 102-6.

1681   TEST OATH

The oath imposed by the Test Act, to be taken by all who held office in either central or local government, all members of parliament, all bishops and ministers and all teachers in universities and schools, was designed to exclude from public trust both Roman Catholics on the one hand and covenanters on the other. It was much criticised for the sweeping terms in which it asserted the royal supremacy over the church and for its reliance on the outdated and little known Confession of Faith of 1560, and it therefore proved unacceptable to many episcopalians as well.

I A:B: Solemnlie swear in presence of the Eternal God, whom I invocat as judge and witness of my sincere intention of this my oath, That I own and sincerely profess the true protestant religion contained in the Confession of Faith recorded in the first Parliament of King James the Sixth, And that I beleive the same to be founded on and agreeable to the written word of God. And I promise and swear that I shall adhere therto during all the days of my lifetime, And shall endeavour to educat my children therin: And shall never consent to any change nor alteration contrary therto: And that I dissown and renunce all such principles, doctrines, or practises, whether Popish or Phanaticall, which are contrary unto and inconsistent with the said Protestant Religion and Confession of Faith. And for testification of my obedience to my Most Gracious Soveraigne Charles the Second, I doe affirm and swear by this my solemn oath that the Kings Majesty is the only Supream Governour of this Realme, over all persons and in all causes as weill Ecclesiastical as Civill; And that no forraigne Prince, Person, Pope, Prelate, State, or Potentat, hath or ought to have any jurisdiction, power, superiority, preheminency, or authority ecclesiastical or civil within this Realme; And therfore I doe utterly renunce and forsake all forraigne jurisdictions, powers, superiorities, and authorities, And doe promise that from henceforth I shall bear faith and true allegiance to the Kings Majestie his heirs and laufull successors. And to my power shall assist and defend all rights, jurisdictions, prerogatives, privileges, preheminencies and authorities belonging to the Kings Majestie his heirs and laufull successors. And I farder affirm and swear by this my solemn oath that I judge it unlauful for subjects upon pretence of reformation or any other pretence whatsoever, to enter into Covenants or Leagues, or to convocat, conveen or assemble in any Councills, Conventions or Assemblies, to treat, consult or determine in any mater of State, civil or ecclesiastick without his Majesties special command or express licence had thereto, Or to take up arms against the king or those commissionated by him: And that I shall never so rise in arms or enter into such Covenant or Assemblies: And that ther lyes no obligation on me from the National Covenant or the Solemn League and Covenant (so commonlie called) or any other manner of way whatsoever, to endeavour any change or alteration in the Government, either in Church or State, as it is now established by the Laws of this kingdom. And I promise and swear that I shall with my utmost power defend, assist and mantein His Majesties jurisdiction foresaid against all deadly: And I shall never decline his Majesties power and jurisdiction, As I shall answer to God. And finally I affirm and swear that this my solemn oath is given in the plain genuine sense and meaning of the words without any equivocation, mental reservation, or any manner of evasion whatsoever; And that I shall not accept or use any dispensation from any creature whatsoever. So help me God.

A.P.S., viii, 244-5.

1681 COUNTY FRANCHISE ACT

An act of 1661 had defined the county franchise as pertaining to those holding a forty-shilling land immediately of the crown, and certain others holding of the crown with a yearly rent of 10 chalders of victual or £1000. The more specific act of 1681, like much of the legislation of this period, remained in force until the nineteenth century, for it determined the county franchise until 1832.

His majesty with advice and consent of his estates of parliament statuts and ordains that none shall have vote in the elections of commissioners for shires or stewartries which have been in use to be represented in parliament and conventions, but those who at that time shall be publicklie infeft in property or superiority and in possession of a fourty shilling land of old extent holden off the king or prince distinct from the few duties in fewlands, or wher the said old extent appears not shall be infeft in lands lyable in publick burden for his majesties supplies for four hundred punds of valued rent, whether kirk-lands now holden of the king or other lands holding few, waird or blensh, off his majestie as king or prince of Scotland, . . . and likewise proper wodsetters having lands of the holding, extent or valuation foresaid . . ., appeirand heirs being in possession by vertue of their predicessors infeftment of the holding, extent and valuation foresaid, and lykways liferenters and husbands for the freeholds of their wyves. . . .

Likeas his majesty ordains the whole freeholders of each shire and stewartry having election of commissioners to meet and conveen at the head burghs thereof, and to make up a roll of all the freeholds within the same . . . according as the same shall be instructed to be of the holding, extent or valuation foresaid, containing the names and designations of the fiars, liferenters and husbands having right to vote . . . and expressing the extent or valuations of the saids freeholds. . . . Likeas the saids freeholders shall meet and conveen at the head burghs of the saids shires and stewartries respective at the Michaelmes head court yearly thereafter and shall revise the said roll of election. . . .

A.P.S., viii, 353, c. 87.

1681 MEMORIAL ON SCOTTISH TRADE

Some of the thought which lay behind the economic legislation of this period is succinctly expressed in this Memorial, which was to be 'exhibite to the honourable Committee of Trade in Scotland'.

In all trade and commerce I lay it as a sure principle and ground that the true and just proportione betwixt the export of native comodities from aney countreys and the import or return from forreigne countreys ought to be als duly observed as can be and so the trade ballanced, money keeped in the cuntrey, navigatione and home bred manufactors encuraged, which is the lyfe and substance of all well ordered commonwealthes, so that, on the contraire, wher this proportion is not observed it is evident token of the poverty and decay of that cuntrey so practising; and, if the distemper in trade continue for a tract of years, remedies may be easily found but not so easily applyed for curing therof, as wee have seen by experience in this kingdome oftener than once: . . . as to give one example, from November 1667 to November 1668, customes of all goods outwards amounted to £63,345, 16s. 4d. Scots and custom and excyse inward £317,930, 6s. 8d. Scots.

[The memorialist goes on to review trade with the Low
Countries, France, England, Spain, Norway and the Baltic
and finds that they are all declining except that with England,
which, however, is hampered by restrictions. The document
also contains one of several proposals made about this time
for a Scottish colony, this one to be in Cape Florida; one
advantage of it would be the removing of 'very maney both
idle and dissenting persones'.]

R.P.C., 3rd. ser., vii, 665-71.

1685   PREAMBLE TO THE EXCISE ACT

*On the accession of James VII, the parliament, in an excess
of loyalty, annexed the excise to the crown in perpetuity.
The preamble to the act is perhaps the most fulsome and
extravagant enunciation of the principles of the divine right
of kings which appeared in the whole century.*

The estates of parliament . . . taking into their consideration
how this nation hath continued now upwards of two thousand
years in the unaltered form of our monarchical government,
under the uninterrupted line of one hundered and eleven
kings, whose sacred authority and power hath been upon all
signall occasions so owned and assisted by Almighty God that
our kingdom hath been protected from conquest, our possessions defended from strangers, our civil commotions
brought into wished events, our laws vigorously executed,
our propertys legally fixed and our lives securely preserved,
so that we and our ancestors have enjoyed those securitys
and tranquillities which the greater and more flourishing
kingdoms have frequently wanted, those great blessings we
owe in the first place to divine mercy, and, in dependance on
that, to the sacred race of our glorious kings and to the solid,
absolute authority wherwith they were invested by the first
and fundamentall law of our monarchy, nor can either our
records or our experience instance our being deprived of
those happy effects but when a rebellious party did by commotions and seditions invade the kings soveraign authority,

which was the cause of our prosperity, . . . Therfor the estates of parliament . . . declare . . . that they abhor and detest not only the authors and actors of all preceeding rebellions against the soveraign, but likways all principles and positions which are contrary or derogatory to the kings sacred, supream, absolute power . . . and as their dutie formerly did bind them to owne and assert the just and legall succession of the sacred line as unalterable by any human jurisdiction, so now they hold themselves on this occasion obliged for themselves and the whole nation represented by them in most humble and dutifull maner to renew the hearty and sincere offer of their lives and fortunes to assist, support, defend and mentain King James the Seventh, their present glorious monarch, and his heirs and lawfull successors, in the possession of their crowns, soveraignty, prerogatives, authority, dignity, rights and possessions against all mortalls, and withall to assure all his enemies who shall adventure on the disloyalty of disobeying his laws or on the impiety of invading his rights, that such shall sooner weary of their wickedness then they of their dutie, and that they firmly resolve to give their entire obedience to his majestie without reserve, and to concurr against all his enemies, forraign or intestine, and they solemnly declare that as they are bound by law so they are voluntarly and firmly resolved that all of this nation, betuixt sixty and sixteen, armed and provyded according to their abilities, shall be in readiness for his majesties service where and as oft as it shall be his royal pleasure to require them.

A.P.S., viii, 459-60.

1686 JAMES VII'S PROPOSAL FOR TOLERATION

In the parliament of 1686, James VII in effect offered the prospect of free trade with England in return for the toleration of Roman catholics, but was rebuffed.

A letter from his Majesty to the Parliament being presented
was twice read and ordained to be recorded: . . .

James R

My Lords and Gentlemen:

Wee have considered your interest as much as our distance
from you could bring into our prospect, and those things
which wee found proper for it whether in relation to trade
and commerce or easing some things uneasie to you amongst
your selves. Wee have fully instructed our Commissioner
(with your advice and consent) to conclude soe as may be
most for the general good of that our ancient Kingdom. We
have made the opening of a free trade with England our
particular care and are proceeding in it with all imaginable
application, and are hopefull in a short tyme to have considerable advances made in it.

Wee have considered the truble that many ar putt to
dayly by prosecutions befor our judges or the hazard that
they lye under for their accession to the late rebellions: And
to show the world (even our greatest enemies themselves)
that mercy is our inclination, and severity what is by their
wickednes extorted from us, Wee have sent doun to be past in
your presence our full and ample Indemnity for all crymes
committed against our royal persone or authority. And whilst
wee show these Acts of mercy to the enemies of our person,
Croun and royal dignity, Wee can not be unmindfull of others
our innocent subjects, those of the Roman Catholick religion,
who have with the hazard of their lives and fortunes been
alwayes assistant to the Crown in the worst of rebellions and
usurpations, though they lay under discouradgements hardly
to be named. Them wee doe heartily recommend to your care
to the end that as they have given good experience of their
true loyalty and peaceable behaviour, soe by your assistance
they may have the protectione of our lawes and that security
under our government which others of our subjects have,
not suffering them to lye under obligations which their
religion can not admitt of. By doeing whereof you will give
a demonstration of the duety and affection you have for us
and doe us most acceptable service. . . .

Soe not only expecting your complyance with us but that
by the manner of it you will show the world your readiness

to meet our inclinations, Wee bid you most heartily farewell. Given at our Court at Whitehall the 12th day of April 1686 and of our Reigne the 2nd year.

The draught of a letter from the Parliament to the King in answer to his Majesties Letter being brought in by the Lords of the Articles and several tymes read, sundry members of Parliament did object against these words of the Letter 'subjects of the Roman Catholick religion' as ane designation not fitt to be given by the Parliament to these of the Romish persuasione, and after debate it being putt to the vote if the letter as it was brought in by the Lords of the articles containing the forsaid words, should be approven or amended, the letter was approven, this not being ane publict act of Parliament but a letter written in answer to his Majesties letter containing the forsaid expression and this letter only resuming the same, which was ordained to be marked in the Minuts and it was ordered that the letter should be signed by the Lord Chancellar in name of the Parliament, wherof the tenor followes:
. . . Your Majesties care of the trade of this kingdome (which is at present exceedingly decayed) and particularly your royal endeavors to procure us a free trade with your kingdome of England will very much enable us to make these supplies effectual which wee have soe heartily and willingly undertaken for the security of the Croun and safety of the kingdom. . . .
As to that pairt of your Majesties letter relateing to your subjects of the Roman Catholick religion, wee shall in obedience to your Majesties commands and with tendernes to their persones take the same into our serious and duetifull consideration and goe as great lengths therin as our conscience will allow, not doubting that your Majesty will be carefull to secure the Protestant religion established by law.

A.P.S., viii, 579-81.

James proceeded to grant toleration by royal proclamation.
His first indulgence, in February 1687, imposed considerable
restrictions on presbyterians, but these were removed in a
second indulgence, in June.

(i)

In the first place, we allow and tolerate the moderate presbyterians to meet in their private houses and there to hear all
such ministers as either have or are willing to accept of our
indulgence allanerly, and none other, and that there be not
anything said or done contrary to the weal and peace of our
reign, seditious or treasonable, under the highest pains these
crimes will import; nor are they to presume to build meeting-
houses, or to use out-houses or barns, but only to exercise
in their private houses, as said is. In the mean time it is our
royal will and pleasure that field-conventicles and such as
preach or exercise at them, or who shall any wise assist or con-
nive at them, shall be prosecuted according to the utmost
severity of our laws made against them. . . . In like manner
we do hereby tolerate Quakers, to meet and exercise in their
form, in any place or places appointed for their worship. And
considering the severe and cruel laws made against Roman catholics (therein called Papists) . . . we, of our certain knowledge
and long experience knowing that the Catholics, as it is their
principle to be good Christians so it is to be dutiful subjects,
and that they have likewise on all occasions shewn themselves
good and faithful subjects to us and our royal predecessors . . .
do therefore . . . suspend, stop and disable all laws or acts of
parliament, customs or constitutions made or executed against
any of our Roman Catholic subjects in any time past, to all
intents and purposes, making void all prohibitions therein
mentioned, pains or penalties therein ordained to be in-
flicted, so that they shall, in all things, be as free, in all
respects, as any of our protestant subjects whatsoever, not
only to exercise their religion but to enjoy all offices, benefices and others which we shall think fit to bestow upon them
in all time coming: nevertheless it is our will and pleasure and
we do hereby command all catholics, at their highest pains,
only to exercise their religious worship in houses or chapels,

and that they presume not to preach in the open fields or to invade the protestant churches by force . . . nor shall they presume to make public processions in the high streets of any of our royal burghs. . . .

Wodrow, ii, Appendix cxxix; cf. *R.P.C.*, 3rd. ser., xiii, 123-4.

(ii)

We do likewise . . . suspend, stop and disable all penal and sanguinary laws made against any for nonconformity to the religion established by law in that our ancient kingdom, or for exercising their respective worships, religions, rites and ceremonies, all which laws are hereby stopt, suspended and disabled to all intents and purposes. . . . As we do give them leave to meet and serve God after their own way and manner, be it in private houses, chapels or places purposely hired or built for that use, so that they take care that nothing be preached or taught among them which may any ways tend to alienate the hearts of our people from us or our government, and that their meetings be peaceable, openly and publicly held, and all persons freely admitted to them, and that they do signify and make known to some one or more of the next privy councillors, sheriffs, stewarts, bailies, justices of the peace or magistrates of burghs royal, what place or places they set apart for these uses, with the names of the preachers. . . . Provided always that their meetings be in houses, or places provided for the purpose, and not in the open fields, for which now after this our royal grace and favour shewn . . . there is not the least shadow of excuse left; which meetings in fields we do hereby strictly prohibit and forbid, against all which we do leave our laws and acts of parliament in full force and vigour, notwithstanding the premisses. . . .

Ibid., Appendix cxxxiv (*R.P.C.*, 3rd ser., xiii, 156-8).

1689 CLAIM OF RIGHT

The revolution of 1688-9 began in England, with the landing of William of Orange on 5 November. James fled on

22 December, and on 13 February the crown of England was offered to, and accepted by, William and Mary. A convention met in Edinburgh on 14 March, and on 11 April it adopted the Claim of Right.

Declaration of the Estates of the Kingdom of Scotland, containing the Claim of Right, and the offer of the Crown to their Majesties King William and Queen Mary.

Whereas King James the Seventh, being a profest Papist, did assume the regal power, and acted as King, without ever taking the oath required by law, whereby the King at his access to the Government, is obliged to swear, to maintain the Protestant religion, and to rule the people according to the laudable laws; And did, by the advice of wicked and evil counsellors, invade the fundamental constitution of this Kingdom, and altered it from a legal limited monarchy, to an arbitrary despotic power; And in a public proclamation, asserted an absolute power, to cass, annul and disable all the laws, particularly arraigning all the laws establishing the Protestant religion, and did exercise that power, to the subversion of the Protestant religion, and to the violation of the laws and liberties of the Kingdom.

By erecting public schools and societies of the Jesuits; and not only allowing the Mass to be publicly said, but also inverting Protestant chappels and churches to public Masshouses, contrary to the express laws against saying and hearing of Mass.

By allowing Popish books to be printed and dispersed by a gift to a Popish printer; Designing him printer to His Majesty's Household, College and Chappel, contrary to the laws.

By taking the children of Protestant Noblemen and Gentlemen, sending and keeping them abroad, to be bred Papists, making great fonds and dotations to Popish schools and colleges abroad; bestowing pensions upon priests; and perverting Protestants from their religion, by offers of places, preferments, and pensions.

By disarming Protestants, while at the same time he imployed Papists, in the places of greatest trust, civil and military, such as Chancellor, Secretaries, Privy Counsellors, and Lords of Session, thrusting out Protestants, to make room for Papists, and entrusting the forts and magazines of the Kingdom in their hands.

By imposing oaths contrary to law.

By giving gifts and grants for exacting money, without consent of Parliament, or convention of Estates.

By levying or keeping on foot a standing army in time of peace, without consent of Parliament, which army did exact locality, free and dry quarters.

By imploying the officers of the army, as Judges through the Kingdom, and imposing them where there were Heretable offices and jurisdictions, by whom many of the Leidges were put to death summarly, without legal tryal, jury or record.

By imposing exorbitant fines, to the value of the parties' estates, exacting extravagant bale; and disposing fines and forfaultures before any process or conviction.

By imprisoning persons without expressing the reason, and delaying to put them to tryal.

By causing persue and forefault several persons upon stretches of old and obsolete laws, upon frivolous and weak pretences, upon lame and defective probations: As particularly the late Earl of Argyle, to the scandal and reproach of the justice of the Nation.

By subverting the right of the Royal Burghs, the third Estate of Parliament, imposing upon them not only Magistrats, but also the whole Town-council, and Clerks, contrary to their liberties, and express Charters, without the pretence either of sentence, Surrender or Consent, so that the Commissioners to Parliaments being chosen by the Magistrats and Council, the King might in effect als well nominat that entire Estate of Parliament; and many of the saids Magistrats put in by him, were avowed Papists, and the Burghs were forced to pay money for the Letters imposing these illegal Magistrats and Councils upon them.

By sending letters to the chief Courts of Justice, not only ordaining the Judges to stop and desist *sine die* to determine causes; but also ordering and commanding them how to proceed, in cases depending before them, contrary to the express laws; and by changing the nature of the Judges' Gifts *ad vitam aut culpam,* and giving them Commissions *ad bene placitum,* to dispose them to complyance with arbitrary courses, and turning them out of their Offices, when they did not comply.

By granting personal Protections for civil debts, contrary to law.

All which are utterly and directly contrary to the known laws, statutes and freedoms of this Realm.

Therefore the Estates of the Kingdom of Scotland, Find and Declare that King James the Seventh being a professed Papist, did assume the Regal power, and acted as King, without ever taking the oath required by law, and hath by the advice of evil and wicked counsellors, invaded the fundamental constitution of the Kingdom, and altered it from a legal limited Monarchy, to an arbitrary despotick Power, and hath exercised the same, to the subversion of the Protestant religion, and the violation of the laws and liberties of the Kingdom, inverting all the ends of Government, whereby he hath forefaulted the right to the Crown, and the Throne is become vacant.

And Whereas His Royal Highness, William then Prince of Orange, now King of England, whom it hath pleased Almighty God to make the Glorious Instrument of delivering these Kingdoms from Popery and arbitrary power, did, by the advice of several Lords and Gentlemen of this Nation, at London for the time, call the Estates of this Kingdom to meet the Fourteenth of March last, in order to such an Establishment as that their Religion, Laws and Liberties might not be again in danger of being subverted; And the saids Estates being now assembled in a full and free Representative of this Nation, taking to their most serious consideration the best means for attaining the ends aforesaid, Do, in the first place, as their Ancestors in the like cases have usually done, for the vindicating and asserting their ancient rights and liberties, Declare,

That by the law of this Kingdom, no Papist can be King or Queen of this Realm, nor bear any office whatsoever therein; nor can any Protestant Successor exercise the Regal Power, until He or She swear the Coronation Oath.

That all Proclamations asserting an absolute power, to cass, annull, and disable laws, the erecting schools and colledges for Jesuits, the inverting Protestant Chappels & churches to public Mass-houses, and the allowing Mass to be said, are contrary to law.

[At this point a dozen more of James's misdeeds, from the allowing of popish books to be printed to 'the granting of personal protections for civil debts' are recited afresh and each declared to be 'contrary to law'.]

That the forcing the Leiges to depone against themselves in capital crimes, however the punishment be restricted, is contrary to law.

That the using Torture without evidence, or in ordinary crimes is contrary to law.

That the sending of an army in an hostile manner, upon any pairt of the Kingdom in a peaceable time, and exacting of Locality, and any manner of free quarters, is contrary to law.

That the charging of the Leiges with Law-borrows at the King's instance, and the imposing of Bonds without the authority of Parliament, and the suspending Advocats from their imployment, for not compearing when such Bonds were offered, were contrary to law.

That the putting of garisons in privat men's houses in time of peace, without their consent, or the authority of Parliament, is contrary to law.

That the opinions of the Lords of Session in the two cases following, were contrary to law, viz. 1. That the concealing the demand of a supply for a forefaulted person, although not given, is treason. 2. That persons refusing to discover what are their private thoughts and judgements in relation to points of treason, or other men's actions, are guilty of treason.

That the fyning husbands for their wives withdrawing from the Church was contrary to law.

That Prelacy and the superiority of any office in the Church above Presbyters, is, and hath been a great and insupportable grievance and trouble to this Nation, and contrary to the inclinations of the generality of the people, ever since the Reformation (they having reformed from Popery by Presbyters), and therefore ought to be abolished.

That it is the right and privilege of the Subjects to protest for Remeed of law to the King and Parliament, against sentences pronounced by the Lords of Session, providing the same do not stop execution of these sentences.

That it is the right of the subjects to petition the King, and that all imprisonments and prosecutions for such petitioning, are contrary to law.

That for redress of all grievances, and for the amending, strengthening and preserving of the laws, Parliaments ought to be frequently called, and allowed to sit, and the freedom of speech and debate secured to the members.

And they do claim, demand and insist upon all and sundry the premisses as their undoubted rights and liberties, and that no declarations, doings, or proceedings, to the prejudice of the people, in any of the said premisses, ought in any ways to be drawn hereafter, in consequence or example, but that all forefaultures, fines, loss of offices, imprisonments, banishments, pursuits, persecutions, tortures and rigorous executions be considered, and the parties lesed be redressed.

To which demand of their rights, and redressing of their grievances, they are particularly encouraged by His Majesty the King of England his declaration for the Kingdom of Scotland, of the [10th] day of October last, as being the only means for obtaining a full redress and remedy therein.

Having therefore an entire confidence, that His said Majesty the King of England, will perfect the deliverance so far advanced by Him, and will still preserve them from the violation of their rights which they have here asserted, and from all other attempts upon their Religion, Laws, and Liberties.

The said Estates of the Kingdom of Scotland, Do resolve that WILLIAM and MARY, King and Queen of England, France and Ireland, Be, and Be Declared King and Queen of Scotland, to hold the Crown and Royal Dignity of the said Kingdom of Scotland, to them the said King and Queen, during their lives, and the longest liver of them, and that the sole and full exercise of the Regal power be only in, and exercised by Him the said King, in the names of the said King and Queen during their joynt lives; and after their decease, the said Crown and Royal Dignity of the said Kingdom, to be to the Heirs of the body of the said Queen; which failing to the Princess Anne of Denmark, and the Heirs of her body; which also failing, to the Heirs of the body of the said William King of England.

And they do pray the said King and Queen of England to accept the same accordingly.

And that the oath hereafter mentioned, be taken by all Protestants, of whom the oath of allegiance, and any other oaths and declarations might be required by law, instead of them, and that the said oath of allegiance, and other oaths and declarations may be abrogated:

'I, A.B. Do sincerely promise and swear, That I will be faithfull, and bear true allegiance to their Majesties King William and Queen Mary. So help me God.'

A.P.S., ix, 37; D.O. Dykes, *Source Book of Constitutional History*, 122-7.

1689   ACT ABOLISHING PRELACY

Our soveraigne lord and lady the king and queens majesties with advyce and consent of the estates of parliament doe hereby abolish prelacie and all superioritie of any office in the church in this kingdome above presbyters, and hereby rescinds, casses and annulls the first act of the second session of the first parliament of King Charles II, and the second act of the third session of the first parliament of King Charles II, and the fourth act of the third parliament of King Charles II, and all other acts, statutes and constitutiones in so farr allennerly as they are inconsistent with this act and doe establish prelacie or the superioritie of church officers above presbiters, and the king and queens majesties doe declaire that they, with advyce and consent of the estates of this parliament, will settle by law that church government in this kingdome which is most agreeable to the inclinationes of the people.

A.P.S., ix, 104.

1690   ABOLITION OF COMMITTEE OF ARTICLES

Two days after adopting the Claim of Right, the Convention had adopted certain Articles of Grievances, one of which declared that 'the committee of parliament called the

Articles is a great grievance to the nation, and that there ought to be no committees of parliament but such as are freely chosen by the estates to prepare motions and overtures that are first made in the house' (A.P.S., ix, 45).

Our soverayne lord and lady the king and queens majesties, with advyce and consent of the estates of parliament, doe heirby discharge and abrogate in all tyme comeing the forsaid committie of parliament called the Articles, . . . lykeas their majesties, with advyce and consent forsaid, doe heirby enact and declare that this present and all succeiding parliaments and three estates thereof may choise and appoint committies of what numbers they please, there being alwayes ane equall number of each estate to be chosen, viz. the noblemen by the estate of noblemen, the barrons by the estate of barrons, and the burrowes by the estate of burrowes, for prepareing all motions and overtures first made in the house, and they may alter and change the saids committies at their pleasure, without prejudice alwayes to the estates of parliament to treate, vote and conclude upon matters proponed or brought before them in plaine parliament without committies as they shall think fitt, and alsoe provydeing that in all committies to be hereafter appointed some of the officers of state may be present by their majesties or their commissioners appointment as to them shall seeme necessary, and that to the effect and with power to the saids officers of state present in the saids committies freely to propose and debate allennarly but not to vote, declareing lykeas it is hereby declared that no officers of state shall be other wayes admitted in any committie of parliament but as it is here allowed, but prejudice alwayes to the estate of the noblemen to choise such of their owne bench as are officers of state to be members of the committies if they thinke fit.

A.P.S., ix, 113.

1690 ACTS ESTABLISHING PRESBYTERIAN GOVERNMENT AND TRANSFERRING PATRONAGE

(i)

Their majesties, with advyce and consent of the saidis three estates, . . . doe establish, ratifie and confirme the presbyterian church government and discipline, that is to say the government of the church by kirke sessions, presbyteries, provinciall synods and generall assemblies, ratified and established by the 114 Act Ja. 6 parl. 12 anno 1592, entituled Ratification of the liberty of the true kirke etc., and thereafter received by the generall consent of this nation, to be the only government of Christs Church within this kingdome; reviveing, renewing and confirmeing the forsaid act of parliament in the haill heids thereof, except that part of it relateing to patronages, which is hereafter to be taken into consideration; [and annulling several acts in favour of episcopal government and prejudicial to presbyterianism].

Their majesties doe hereby appoint the first meeting of the generall assembly of this church as above established to be at Edinburgh the third Thursday of October nexttocome in this instant yeare [1690].

A.P.S., ix, 133-4.

(ii)

And to the effect the calling and entering ministers in all tymes comeing may be orderly and regularly performed, their majesties with consent of the estates of parliament doe statute and declare that in case of the vacancie of any particular church and for supplyeing the same with a minister the heretors of the said parish (being protestants) and the elders are to name and propose the persone to the whole congregatione to be either approven or disapproven by them, and, if they disapprove, that the disapprovers give in their reasons to the effect the affair may be cognosced upon by the presbytery of the bounds; [and in the event of failure to present within six months the right to appoint devolves to the presbytery]. It is always hereby declared that this act shall be bot[1] prejudice of the calling of ministers to royall burghs by the magistrats, toune counsell and kirke sessione of the burgh where there is no landward parish, as they have been in use before the yeare 1660, and where there is a considerable part of the parish in landward, that the call shall be by the magistrats, toune counsell, kirke sessione and the heretors of the landward paroch. . . .

A.P.S., ix, 196-7.

1 without.

1695   ACT ESTABLISHING
COMPANY OF SCOTLAND

His majesty, understanding that several persons as well forreigners as natives of this kingdom are willing to engage themselves with great soumes of money in an American, Affrican and Indian trade, to be exercised in and from this kingdom, . . . therefore . . . doth . . . constitut John, Lord Belhaven [and twenty other named persons] . . . and all others whom the forsaids persons and these joyned with them, or major part of them being assembled, shall admitt and joyn into their joynt stock and trade . . . to be one body incorporat, and a free incorporation, with perpetual succession, by the name of the Company of Scotland tradeing to Affrica and the Indies, providing allwayes, likeas it is hereby in the first place provided, that of the fond or capital stock that shall be agreed to be advanced and imployed by the forsaid undertakers, and their copartners, the halfe at least shall be appoynted and allotted for Scottish men within this kingdom [failing subscription by whom by 1 August 1696, Scotsmen residing abroad or foreigners may subscribe] ; lik as the quota of every mans part of the said stock . . . shall be for the least one hundred pound sterlin, and for the highest or greatest, thre thousand pound sterlin. . . .

With power to the said company to have a common seal . . . as also to plead and sue, and be sued, and to purchase, acquire, possess and enjoy lordships, lands, tenements with other estate real or personal . . . and to dispose upon and alienat the same . . .

With power likewise to the forsaid company, by subscription or otherwise, . . . to raise a joynt stock or capital fond of such a sum or sums of money and under and subject unto such rules, conditions and qualifications as by the forsaid company, or major part of them when assembled, shall be limited and appoynted to begin, carry on and support their intended trade of navigation and whatever may contribut to the advancement therof. . . .

And the said company is hereby impowered to equip, fitt, sett out, fraught and navigat their own or hired ships in such manner as they shall think fitt . . . from any of the ports or places of this kingdom, or from any other ports or places in amity, or not in hostility with his majesty, in warlike or other manner to any lands, islands, countreyes or places in Asia, Affrica, or America, and there to plant collonies, build cityes, touns or forts, in or upon the places not inhabited, or in or upon any other place, by consent of the natives or inhabitants therof and not possest by any European soveraign, potentate, prince or state . . . and by force of arms to defend their trade and navigation, colonies, cityes, tounes, forts and plantations . . . and to make and conclude treaties of peace and commerce with the soveraigns, princes, estates, rulers, governours or proprietors of the forsaids lands, islands, countries or places. . . .

None of the liedges of this kingdom shall or may trade or navigat to any lands, islands, countreyes or places in Asia, or Affrica in any time hereafter, or in America for and during the space of thirty one years . . . without license and permission in writing from the said company. . . .

And it is further hereby enacted that the said company shall have the free and absolut right and property (only relieving and holding of his majesty . . . for the only acknowledgement of their alleagiance, and paying yearly a hogshead of tobacco, in the name of blensh duty, if required allennarly) in and to all such lands . . . that they shall come to . . . possess . . . as also to all manner of treasures, wealth, riches, profits, mines, minerals, fishings, with the whole product and benefit therof. . . .

And farder it is hereby statute that all ships, vessels, merchandise, goods, and other effects whatsoever belonging to

262

the said company shall be free of all manner of restraints or prohibitions, and of all customs, taxes, cesses, supplies or other duties imposed, or to be imposed, by act of parliament or otherwise, for and during the space of twenty one years. . . .

A.P.S., ix, 377-80.

1696   EDUCATION ACT

After episcopal government had ceased to operate in 1638, eight years had passed before statutory provision was made for educational administration under presbyteries (p. 213 above), and six years elapsed between the establishment of presbyterian government in 1690 and the next statute anent schools. The act of 1696 was substantially a re-enactment of the act of 1646, with the addition of a clause empowering the presbyteries to call on the commissioners of supply should the heritors fail to act.

Our Soveraign Lord considering how prejudiciall the want of schools in many places have been and how beneficiall the establishing and setleing therof in every paroch will be to this Church and Kingdom: Therfor His Majestie with the advice and consent of the Estates of Parliament statutes and ordains that there be a school settled and established & a school-master appointed in every paroch, not already provided, by advice of the heritors and minister of the paroch; And for that effect that the heritors in every paroch meet and provide a commodious house for a school and settle and modifie a sallary to a schoolmaster which shall not be under one hundred merks nor above two hundred merks, to be payed yearly at two terms, Whitsunday and Martinmass, by equall portions, and that they stent.and lay on the said sallary conform to every heritors valued rent within the paroch, allowing each heritor relieff from his tennents of the half of his proportion for settling and maintaining of a school and payment of the schoolmasters sallary, which sallary is declared to be by and attour the casualities which formerly belonged to the readers and clerks of the kirk session. And if the heritors or major part of them shall not conveen, or being conveened shall not agree among themselves, then and in that case the presbitrie shall apply to the Commissioners of the Supply of the shire who, or any five of them, shall have power to establish a school and settle and modifie a sallary for a schoolmaster not being under one hundred merks nor above two hundred merks yearly as said is, and to stent and lay on the samen upon the heritors conform to their valued rent which shall be alse valid and effectuall as if it had been done by the heritors themselves. . . . And lastly his Majestie with advice and consent forsaid ratifies and approves all former lawes customs and constitutions made for establishing and maintaining of schools within the Kingdom in so far as the same are not altered nor innovat by this present Act.

A.P.S., x, 63, c. 26.

c. 1700 'THE SEVEN ILL YEARS'

There is ample evidence of a series of bad harvests in the 1690s, especially from 1695 to 1699, and of their effect in producing poverty and even starvation. It is not, however, clear that conditions were uniformly bad in all parts of the country during a period of seven years.

These unheard-of manifold Judgments continued seven Years, not always alike, but the Seasons, *Summer* and *Winter,* so cold and barren, and the wonted Heat of the Sun so much withholden, that it was discernible upon the Cattle, flying Fowls and Insects decaying, that seldom a Fly or Gleg was to be seen: Our Harvests not in the ordinary Months; many shearing in *November* and *December,* yea, some in *January* and *February;* The Names of the Places I can instruct: Many contracting their Deaths, and losing the Use of their Feet and Hands sharing[1] and working amongst it in Frost and Snow; and after all some of it standing still, and rotting upon the Ground, and much of it for little Use either to Man or Beast, and which had no Taste or Colour of Meal.

1 shearing.

Meal became so scarce, that it was at Two Shillings a Peck, and many could not get it. It was not then with many, *Where will we get Silver? but, Where will we get Meal for Silver?* I have seen, when Meal was all sold in Markets, Women clapping their Hands, and tearing the Clothes off their Heads, crying, *How shall we go home and see our Children die in Hunger? They have got no Meat these two Days, and we have nothing to give them.*

Through the long Continuance of these manifold Judgments, Deaths and Burials were so many and common, that the Living were wearied in the Burying of the Dead. I have seen Corpses drawn in Sleds, many got neither Coffin nor Winding-sheet. . . .

Patrick Walker, Biographia Presbyteriana (1727-32), ii, 25-6.

1703-5   ANTECEDENTS OF
THE TREATY OF UNION

A number of incidents in William's reign had shown that the personal union between England and Scotland was likely to be subjected to intolerable strain in a situation where the parliaments of the two countries could pursue divergent and perhaps conflicting policies. Friction came to a climax in the Darien episode, when the Scots believed that the English parliament and the English king had thwarted their efforts to found a colony. A further, and graver, difficulty could be foreseen in the question of the royal succession. By the time Anne became queen, in 1702, the last of her children was dead and the succession undefined. England, in 1701, had settled the succession on the Hanoverian line, but no such provision had been made in Scotland. This meant that on Anne's death, either the personal union might be dissolved or the relations between the two countries could be revised. The Scottish parliament which met in 1703 could not be controlled by the court, and it passed acts which contained threats that Scotland would pursue an independent foreign policy and might appoint a different successor from the successor to the English throne. England retaliated in 1705 with the Alien Act, which declared that, until Scotland accepted the Hanoverian succession, all Scots would be treated as aliens in England and the import of cattle, sheep, coal and linen from Scotland into England would not be allowed; this measure stimulated the Scots into appointing commissioners to treat for union.

(i) Act anent peace and war (1703).

Our Sovereign Lady, with advice and consent of the Estates of Parliament, statutes, enacts, and declares, That after her Majesty's decease, and failyieing heirs of her body, no person being King or Queen of Scotland and England, shall have the sole power of makeing War with any Prince, Potentate or State whatsoever without consent of Parliament; and that no Declaration of War without consent foresaid, shall be binding on the subjects of this Kingdom, Declaring alwayes, that this shall no ways be understood to impede the Soveraign of this Kingdom to call furth, command, and imploy the subjects thereof to suppress any insurrection within the Kingdom, or repell any invasion from abroad, according to former Laws; and also Declaring, that everything which relates to Treaties of Peace, Alliance and Commerce, is left to the wisdom of the Sovereign, with consent of the Estates of Parliament who shall declare the War: And her Majesty with consent foresaid, repells, casses, and annulls all former Acts of Parliament, in so far as they are contrair hereunto or inconsistent herewith.

A.P.S., xi, 107, c. 6.

(ii) The Wine Act (1703).

Our Sovereign Lady with advice and consent of the Estates of Parliament Statutes and Declares that it shall be lawfull from and after the date hereof to import into this Kingdom all sorts of Wines and other Forreign Liquors, any former Act or Statute in the contrary notwithstanding, which her Majestie with advice and consent foresaid Rescinds and Declares void and null in so far as they are inconsistent with or contrare to this present Act. The said Wines or other liquors which shall be imported paying allwayes the former customes, excise and other duties, reserveing to the Peers and Barons of the Kingdom the same immunities and freedoms from customes for wines which they had by the two hundreth fifty first Act fifteenth Parliament King James the Sixth.

A.P.S., xi, 112, c. 13.

(iii) The Act of Security (1704).

Our Sovereign Lady, the Queen's Majesty, with advice and consent of the Estates of Parliament, doth hereby statute and ordain, That in the event of her Majesties death, or of the death of any of her Majesties heirs or successors, Kings or Queens of this Realm, this present Parliament or any other parliament that shall be then in being, shall not be dissolved by the said death. . . . And if the said Parliament be under adjournment the time of the said death, it shall notwithstanding meet precisely at Edinburgh the twentieth day after the said death, excluding the day thereof, whether the day of the said adjournment be sooner or later. And it is further statute and ordained, that in case there shall be no Parliament in being at the time of the death foresaid, then the Estates or members of the last preceding Parliament, without regard to any Parliament that may be indicted but never met nor constituted, shall meet at Edinburgh on the twentieth day after the said death, the day thereof excluded. . . . And the said Estates of Parliament, appointed in case of the death foresaid, to continue or meet as above, are hereby authorised and impowered to act and administrate the government in manner after-mentioned; that is, that upon the death of her Majesty, leaving heirs of her own body, or failyieing thereof lawful successors designed or appointed by her Majesty and the Estates of Parliament, or upon the death of any succeeding King or Queen, leaving lawful heirs and successors, as said is, the said Estates of Parliament are authorised and impowered, after having read to the said heir or successor the Claim of Right, and desired them to accept the government in the terms thereof, to require of, and administrate to the said heir or lawful successors, by themselves, or such as they shall commissionat, the Coronation Oath, and that with all convenient speed, . . . in order to their exercising the regal power, conform to the Declaration of the Estates containing the Claim of Right. . . . And further, upon the said death of her Majesty, without heirs of her body, or a successor lawfully designed and appointed as above, or in the case of any other King or Queen thereafter succeeding and deceasing without lawful heir or successor, the foresaid Estates of Parliament conveened or meeting are hereby authorised and impowered to nominat and declare the successor to the Imperial Crown of this Realm, and to settle the succession thereof upon the heirs of the said successors body, the said successor, and the heirs of the successors body, being always of the Royal Line of Scotland and of the true Protestant Religion. Providing always, That the same be not successor to the Crown of England, unless that in this present session of Parliament, or any other session of this or any ensuing Parliament during her Majesties reign there be such condicions of government settled and enacted, as may secure the honour and soveraignty of this Crown and Kingdom, the freedom, frequency and power of Parliaments, the religion, liberty and trade of the nation from English, or any foreign, influence, with power to the said meeting of Estates to add such further conditions of government as they shall think necessary, the same being consistent with, and no ways derogatory from those which shall be enacted in this and any other session of Parliament during her Majesties reign. . . .

[It is further enacted] that the whole protestant heretors and all the burghs within the same [kingdom] shall furthwith provide themselves with fire arms for all the fencible men who are Protestants within their respective bounds . . . and the said heretors and burghs are hereby impowered and ordained to discipline and exercise their said fencible men once in the moneth at least. . . .

A.P.S., xi, 136, c. 3.

1706-7 THE ARTICLES OF UNION

Commissioners representing Scotland and England sat from 16 April 1706 to 22 July, when the Articles of Union were signed. The Articles were debated in the Scottish parliament from 3 October 1706 to 16 January 1707, when they were ratified with only minor changes. The English parliament then likewise adopted them, and they received the royal assent on 6 March.

I. That the Two Kingdoms of England and Scotland shall upon the First day of May which shall be in the year One thousand seven hundred and seven, and for ever after, be united into one Kingdom by the name of Great Britain; and that the Ensigns Armorial of the said United Kingdom be such as Her Majesty shall appoint, and the Crosses of St. George and St. Andrew be conjoined in such manner as Her Majesty shall think fit, and used in all Flags, Banners, Standards and Ensigns, both at Sea and Land.

II. That the Succession to the Monarchy of the United Kingdom of Great Britain, and of the Dominions thereunto belonging, after Her most Sacred Majesty, and in default of Issue of her Majesty, be, remain, and continue to the most excellent Princess Sophia, Electoress and Duchess Dowager of Hanover, and the Heirs of her Body being Protestants, upon whom the Crown of England is settled by an Act of Parliament made in England in the Twelfth year of the Reign of his late Majesty King William the Third, intituled, An Act for the further Limitation of the Crown, and better securing the Rights and Liberties of the Subject:[1] And that all Papists, and persons marrying Papists, shall be excluded from, and for ever incapable to inherit, possess, or enjoy the Imperial Crown of Great Britain, and the Dominions thereunto belonging, or any part thereof. . . .

III. That the United Kingdom of Great Britain be represented by One and the same Parliament, to be stiled, the Parliament of Great Britain.

IV. That all the Subjects of the United Kingdom of Great Britain shall, from and after the Union, have full Freedom and Intercourse of Trade and Navigation to and from any Port or Place within the said United Kingdom, and the Dominions and Plantations thereunto belonging; and that there be a communication of all other Rights, Privileges, and Advantages, which do or may belong to the Subjects of either Kingdom; except where it is otherwise expressly agreed in these Articles.

V. That all ships or vessels belonging to Her Majesty's

1 Act of Settlement.

Subjects of Scotland, at the time of ratifying the Treaty of Union of the two Kingdoms in the Parliament of Scotland, though foreign built, be deemed, and pass as ships of the build of Great Britain. . . .

VI. That all parts of the United Kingdom for ever from and after the Union shall have the same allowances, encouragements and drawbacks, and be under the same prohibitions, restrictions and regulations of trade, and lyable to the same customs and duties on import and export . . . ; and that from and after the Union no Scots cattle carried into England shall be lyable to any other duties . . . than these duties to which the cattle of England are or shall be lyable. . . .

VII. That all parts of the United Kingdom be for ever from and after the Union lyable to the same excises upon all exciseable liquors. . . .

VIII. . . . Scotland shall for the space of seven years from the said Union be exempted from paying in Scotland for salt made there the dutie or excise now payable for salt made in England. . . .

IX. That whenever the sum of [£1,997,763, 8s. 4½d.] shall be enacted . . . to be raised in that part of the United Kingdom now called England, on land and other things usually charged in Acts of Parliament there for granting an aid to the Crown by a land tax, that part of the United Kingdom now called Scotland shall be charged by the same Act with a further sum of [£48,000] free of all charges, as the quota of Scotland to such tax, and so proportionably. . . .

X-XIII. [Scotland exempted from existing English duties on stamped paper, vellum and parchment, windows and lights, coal, culm and cinders, and malt.]

XIV. . . . That any malt to be made and consumed in that part of the United Kingdom now called Scotland shall not be charged with any imposition upon malt during this present war. . . .

XV. [Whereas Scotland will become liable to customs and excise duties which will be applicable to the payment of England's existing National Debt, and whereas the yield of these duties will increase and a portion of the increase will be applied to the same end, Scotland is to receive as an 'Equivalent': (1) a lump sum of £398,085, 10s. and (2) the increase in Scotland's customs and excise revenue for the first seven years after the Union, and thereafter such part of the increase as would be required for the debt. This 'Equivalent' is to be devoted to (a) recompensing those who lost through the standardising of the coinage, (b) payment of the capital (with interest) advanced for the Company of Scotland (which is to be dissolved), (c) the payment of the public debts of the Scottish Crown, and (d) payment of £2000 yearly for seven years to encourage the wool manufacture and thereafter to promote fisheries and other 'manufactures and improvements'.]

XVI. That from and after the Union, the Coin shall be of the same standard and value throughout the United Kingdom, as now in England, and a Mint shall be continued in Scotland, under the same Rules as the Mint in England, and the present Officers of the Mint continued, subject to such Regulations and Alterations as Her Majesty, Her Heirs or Successors, or the Parliament of Great Britain shall think fit.

XVII. That from and after the Union, the same Weights and Measures shall be used throughout the United Kingdom, as are established in England. . . .

XVIII. That the Laws concerning Regulation of Trade, Customs, and such Excises to which Scotland is, by virtue of this Treaty, to be liable, be the same in Scotland from and after the Union as in England; and that all other Laws in use within the Kingdom of Scotland, do after the Union, and notwithstanding thereof, remain in the same force as before, (except such as are contrary to, or inconsistent with this Treaty) but alterable by the Parliament of Great Britain: with this difference betwixt the Laws concerning Public Right, Policy and Civil Government, and those which concern Private Right, that the Laws which concern Public Right, Policy, and Civil Government, may be made the same throughout the whole United Kingdom; But that no alteration be made in Laws which concern private Right, except for evident utility of the Subjects within Scotland.

XIX. That the Court of Session, or College of Justice, do after the Union, and notwithstanding thereof, remain in all time coming within Scotland, as it is now constituted by the Laws of that Kingdom, and with the same Authority and

Privileges as before the Union, subject nevertheless to such
Regulations for the better Administration of Justice as shall
be made by the Parliament of Great Britain. . . . And that
the Court of Justiciary do also after the Union, and notwithstanding thereof, remain in all time coming within Scotland,
as it is now constituted by the Laws of that Kingdom, and
with the same Authority and Privileges as before the Union,
subject nevertheless to such Regulations as shall be made by
the Parliament of Great Britain, and without prejudice of
other Rights of Justiciary. And that all Admiralty Jurisdictions
be under the Lord High Admiral or Commissioners for the
Admiralty of Great Britain for the time being; and that the
Court of Admiralty now established in Scotland be continued,
and all Reviews, Reductions, or Suspensions of the Sentences
in maritime Cases competent to the Jurisdiction of that
Court remain in the same manner after the Union as now in
Scotland, until the Parliament of Great Britain shall make
such Regulations and Alterations as shall be judged expedient
for the whole United Kingdom, so as there be always continued in Scotland a Court of Admiralty, . . . subject nevertheless to such Regulations and Alterations as shall be thought
proper to be made by the Parliament of Great Britain; And
that the Heretable Rights of Admiralty and Vice-Admiralties
in Scotland be reserved to the respective Proprietors as Rights
of Property, subject nevertheless, as to the manner of exercising
such Heretable Rights, to such Regulations and Alterations
as shall be thought proper to be made by the Parliament of
Great Britain. And that all other Courts now in being within the
Kingdom of Scotland do remain, but subject to alterations by
the Parliament of Great Britain; And that all Inferior Courts
within the said limits do remain subordinate, as they now
are, to the Supreme Courts of Justice within the same in all
time coming; And that no Causes in Scotland be Cognisable
by the Courts of Chancery, Queen's Bench, Common Pleas,
or any other Court in Westminster Hall; and that the said
Courts, or any other of the like nature, after the Union, shall
have no power to cognosce, review, or alter the Acts or
Sentences of the Judicatures within Scotland or to stop the
execution of the same; And that there be a Court of Exchequer
in Scotland after the Union, for deciding questions concerning
the Revenues of Customs and Excises there, having the same

power and authority in such cases, as the Court of Exchequer has in England; and that the said Court of Exchequer in Scotland have power of passing Signatures, Gifts, Tutories, and in other things as the Court of Exchequer at present in Scotland hath; and that the Court of Exchequer that now is in Scotland do remain, until a new Court of Exchequer be settled by the Parliament of Great Britain in Scotland after the Union; and that after the Union, the Queen's Majesty, and her Royal Successors, may continue a Privy Council in Scotland, for preserving of public Peace and Order, until the Parliament of Great Britain shall think fit to alter it, or establish any other effectual method for that end.

XX. That all Heretable Offices, Superiorities, Heretable Jurisdictions, Offices for Life, and Jurisdictions for Life, be reserved to the Owners thereof, as Rights of Property in the same manner as they are now enjoyed by the Laws of Scotland, notwithstanding of this Treaty.

XXI. That the Rights and Privileges of the Royal Burghs in Scotland, as they now are, do remain entire after the Union, and notwithstanding thereof.

XXII. That by virtue of this Treaty, of the Peers of Scotland at the time of the Union, Sixteen shall be the number to sit and vote in the House of Lords, and Forty-five the Number of the Representatives of Scotland in the House of Commons of the Parliament of Great Britain; . . . And that if her Majesty, on or before the First day of May next, on which day the Union is to take place, shall declare under the Great Seal of England, that it is expedient that the Lords of Parliament of England, and Commons of the present Parliament of England, should be the Members of the respective Houses of the First Parliament of Great Britain, for and on the part of England, then the said Lords of Parliament of England, and Commons of the present Parliament of England shall be the Members of the respective Houses of the First Parliament of Great Britain for and on the part of England; . . . and the Lords of Parliament of England and the Sixteen Peers of Scotland . . . and the Members of the House of Commons of the said Parliament of England and the Forty-five Members for Scotland . . . shall be the two Houses of the First Parliament of Great Britain; and that Parliament may continue for such time only, as the present Parliament of England might have continued if the Union of the Two Kingdoms had not been made, unless sooner dissolved by Her Majesty. . . .

XXIII. That the aforesaid Sixteen Peers mentioned in the last preceding Article, to sit in the House of Lords of the Parliament of Great Britain, shall have all Privileges of Parliament which the Peers of England now have, and which they or any Peers of Great Britain shall have after the Union, and particularly the Right of Sitting upon the Trials of Peers: . . . and that all Peers of Scotland, and their Successors in their Honours and Dignities, shall from and after the Union be Peers of Great Britain, and have Rank and Precedency next and immediately after the Peers of the like Orders and Degrees in England at the time of the Union, and before all Peers of Great Britain of the like Orders and Degrees who may be created after the Union, and shall be tried as Peers of Great Britain, and shall enjoy all privileges of Peers as fully as the Peers of England do now, or as they, or any other Peers of Great Britain may hereafter enjoy the same, except the Right and Privilege of sitting in the House of Lords, and the Privileges depending thereon, and particularly the right of sitting upon the Trials of Peers.

XXIV. That from and after the Union there be one Great Seal for the United Kingdom of Great Britain, which shall be different from the Great Seal now used in either Kingdom; And that the Quartering the Arms, and the Rank and Precedency of the Lyon King of Arms of the Kingdom of Scotland, as may best suit the Union, be left to Her Majesty; and that in the meantime the Great Seal of England be used as the Great Seal of the United Kingdom, and that the Great Seal of the United Kingdom be used for sealing Writs to elect and summon the Parliament of Great Britain, and for sealing all Treaties with Foreign Princes and States, and all public Acts, Instruments, and Orders of State which concern the whole United Kingdom, and in all other matters relating to England as the Great Seal of England is now used. And that a Seal in Scotland after the Union be always kept and made use of in all things relating to private Rights or Grants, which have usually passed the Great Seal of Scotland, and which only concern Offices, Grants, Commissions and private Rights within that Kingdom; and that until such Seal shall be appointed by her Majesty, the present Great Seal of Scotland shall be used for such purposes: And that the privy Seal, Signet, Casset, Signet of the Justiciary Court, Quarter Seal, and Seals of Court now used in Scotland be continued; but that the said Seals be altered and adapted to the State of the Union, as her Majesty shall think fit; and the said Seals, and all of them, and the Keepers of them, shall be subject to such Regulations as the Parliament of Great Britain shall hereafter make. And that the Crown, Sceptre, and Sword of State, the Records of Parliament, and all other Records, Rolls, and Registers whatsoever, both Public and Private, General and Particular, and Warrants thereof, continue to be kept as they are within that part of the United Kingdom now called Scotland; and that they shall so remain in all time coming notwithstanding the Union.

XXV. That all Laws and Statutes in either Kingdom, so far as they are contrary to, or inconsistent with, the Terms of these Articles, or any of them, shall from and after the Union, cease and become void, and shall be so declared to be, by the respective Parliaments of the said Kingdoms.

Original in Reg. Ho.; *A.P.S.*, xi, 406-13, George 3. Pryde, *The Treaty of Union.*

1707 ACT FOR SECURITY OF CHURCH OF SCOTLAND

The commissioners who negotiated the Articles of Union had been forbidden to treat of ecclesiastical matters. In separate acts, the parliaments of Scotland and England provided for the security of the two established churches, and these acts were integral parts of the Union.

Our Sovereign Lady and the Estates of Parliament considering That by the late Act of Parliament for a Treaty with England for an Union of both Kingdoms It is provided That the Commissioners for that Treaty should not Treat of or concerning any alteration of the Worship Discipline and Government of the Church of this Kingdom as now by Law established, Which Treaty being now reported to the Parliament, and it being reasonable and necessary that the True Protestant Religion, as presently professed within this Kingdom with the Worship Discipline and Government of this Church should be effectually and unalterably secured; Therefore Her Majesty with advice and consent of the said Estates of Parliament Doth hereby Establish and Confirm the said True Protestant Religion and the Worship Discipline and Government of this Church to continue without any alteration to the people of this Land in all succeeding generations. . . . And Her Majesty with advice and consent foresaid expressly Provides and Declares That the foresaid True Protestant Religion contained in the abovementioned Confession of Faith with the form and purity of Worship presently in use within this Church and its Presbyterian Church Government and Discipline, that is to say, the Government of the Church by Kirk Sessions, Presbytries, Provincial Synods and Generall Assemblies, all established by the forsaid Acts of Parliament pursuant to the Claim of Right shall Remain and Continue unalterable, and that the said Presbyterian Government shall be the only Government of the Church within the Kingdom of Scotland.

And further for the greater security of the foresaid Protestant Religion and of the Worship Discipline and Government of this Church as above established Her Majesty with advice and consent foresaid Statutes and Ordains That the Universities and Colledges of Saint Andrews Glasgow Aberdeen and Edinburgh as now Established by Law shall Continue within this Kingdom for ever. And that in all time comeing no Professors, Principalls, Regents, Masters or others bearing office in any University Colledge or School within this Kingdom be capable or be admitted or allowed to continue in the Exercise of their said functions but such as shall own and acknowledge the Civill Government in manner prescribed or to be prescribed by the Acts of Parliament. As also that before or at their Admissions they do and shall acknowledge and profess and shall subscribe to the foresaid Confession of Faith as the Confession of their faith, and that they will practise and conform themselves to the Worship presently in use in this Church and submit themselves to the Government and Discipline thereof and never endeavour directly or indirectly the prejudice or subversion of the same, and that

before the respective Presbytries of their bounds by whatsoever gift presentation or provision they may be thereto provided. . . .

And Lastly that after the Decease of Her present Majesty
(whom God long preserve) the Sovereign succeeding to her
in the Royal Government of the Kingdom of Great Britain
shall in all time comeing at his or her accession to the Crown
Swear and Subscribe That they shall inviolably maintain and
preserve the foresaid settlement of the True Protestant
Religion with the Government Worship Discipline Right and
Priviledges of this Church as above established by the Laws
of this Kingdom in prosecution of the Claim of Right.

And it is hereby Statute and Ordained That this Act of
Parliament with the Establishment therein contained shall
be held and observed in all time coming as a fundamentall
and essentiall Condition of any Treaty or Union to be Concluded betwixt the Two Kingdoms without any Alteration
thereof or Derogation thereto in any sort for ever. As also
that this Act of Parliament and Settlement therein contained
shall be Insert and Repeated in any Act of Parliament that
shall pass for agreeing and concluding the foresaid Treaty or
Union betwixt the Two Kingdoms. And that the same shall
be therein expressly Declared to be a fundamentall and
essentiall Condition of the said Treaty or Union in all time
coming.

A.P.S., xi, 402, c. 6.

APPENDIX

The English Succession

As a result of the marriage of James IV to Margaret Tudor, successive Scottish sovereigns — James V, Mary and James VI — were, by right of blood, heirs presumptive to the English crown for almost a century and stood nearer to it than any other person except between 1516 (when Mary Tudor was born) and 1558 (when she died). Henry VIII provided that the descendants of his younger sister, Mary, should be preferred to those of Margaret, and this threw a certain dubiety over the Scottish claim. On the other hand, it was hard to believe that, if Queen Mary Tudor was Henry's lawful daughter, Elizabeth could also be his lawful daughter, for it was only by the annulment of his marriage to Catherine of Aragon, Mary's mother, that he had become the husband of Elizabeth's mother, Anne Boleyn. It was argued from the Roman Catholic side that Henry had been married lawfully to Catherine but not to Anne and that therefore, on the death of Mary Tudor, the English crown ought to go to Mary, Queen of Scots. Mary did in fact assume the style and arms of sovereign of England, and this threat was one reason for Elizabeth's readiness to assist the Scottish reformers against the French in 1560. By the Treaty of Edinburgh (p. 120 above), it was agreed that Mary should abstain from using the English title and arms 'henceforth.' Mary refused to ratify the treaty, because its phraseology might be taken to imply that she would have no claim to England even on Elizabeth's death. After her return to Scotland in August 1561 little time was lost in making an approach to Elizabeth for an acknowledgment of Mary's rights as her heir presumptive. Elizabeth's answer, as reported by William Maitland of Lethington after he interviewed her in September or October 1561, represented a standpoint from which she was never to deviate. The language of this extract has been modernised.

[Elizabeth:] I looked for another message from the queen

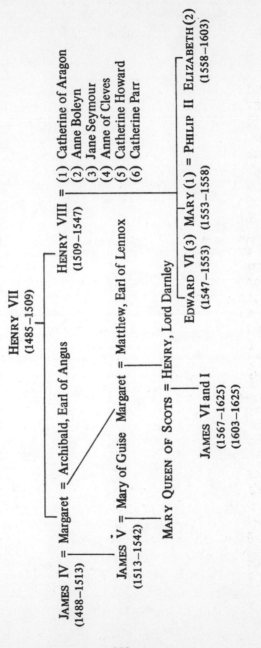

SUCCESSION TO THE ENGLISH THRONE

HENRY VII
(1485–1509)

JAMES IV = Margaret = Archibald, Earl of Angus
(1488–1513)

JAMES V = Mary of Guise   Margaret = Matthew, Earl of Lennox
(1513–1542)

MARY QUEEN OF SCOTS = HENRY, Lord Darnley

JAMES VI and I
(1567–1625)
(1603–1625)

HENRY VIII = (1) Catherine of Aragon
(1509–1547)   (2) Anne Boleyn
               (3) Jane Seymour
               (4) Anne of Cleves
               (5) Catherine Howard
               (6) Catherine Parr

EDWARD VI (3) MARY (1) = PHILIP II   ELIZABETH (2)
(1547–1553)   (1553–1558)   (1558–1603)

279

your sovereign, and marvel that she remembers not better her promise made to me before her departing from France, after many delays of that thing which she in honour is bound to do, to wit the ratification of the treaty wherein she promised to answer me directly at her homecoming. I have long enough been fed with fair words. It had been time I should before now have seen the effect of so many good words.

[Maitland:] Madame, her majesty was not fully fifteen days at home when I was despatched towards your highness. . . . I doubt not but your majesty will perceive that her highness could not have the consultation and means requisite in a matter of such importance.

[Elizabeth:] What consultation needs the queen to fulfil the thing whereunto she is obliged by her seal and handwriting? . . . You put me in remembrance that she is of the blood of England, my cousin and next kinswoman, so that nature must bind me to love her duly, all which I must confess to be true. . . . In time of most offence and when she, by bearing my arms and claiming the title of my crown, had given me just cause to be most angry with her, yet could I never find in my heart to hate her, imputing rather the fault to others than to herself. And as for the title of my crown, for my time I think she will not attain it, nor make impediment to my issue if any shall come of my body: for so long as I live there shall be no other queen in England but I. . . . If her right be good she may be sure I will never hurt her, and I here protest to you in the presence of God I for my part know none better that myself would prefer to her, or yet, to be plain with you, that case occurring that might debar her from it. . . . I marvel what the nobility of Scotland should mean to send me such a message even at the first of their sovereign's homecoming, knowing that the principal offence between us is not as yet taken away. They wish, being injured and offended without any reparation, that I shall gratify her with so high a benefit. It seems to me to import some menacing. . . .

[Maitland:] The desire they have that her majesty may be in tender friendship with your highness, with whom they dare be bolder for the experience they have had of your good will towards them, than they would be with any other prince, and partly their own security, whose lives (for duty's sake) must be hazarded in prosecution of this quarrel, if hereof any impediment be made by whatsoever party to her right, or a breach happen therefor between the realms, and whereupon they have just occasion to desire earnestly that in the mean time the matter may be made amicable in good security.

[Elizabeth:] Yes, if I meant to do anything to hurt her right they have occasion to desire me to reform it, but this desire is without an example, to require me in my own life to set my winding-sheet before my eye, the like was never required of any prince.

J.H. Pollen, *Queen Mary's Letter to the Duke of Guise* (Scot. Hist. Soc.)., 38-40.

INDEX

Inchaffray, charter to, 26
Indulgences, (1669, 1672, 1679)
 235-7; (1687) 251-2
Innocent VIII, Indult of, 89
Inventories of movables, 162
Iona, 1-2, 8-9
 Statutes of, 171

James I, 73-81, 90
James II, 81-2
James III, 82-90
James IV, 92-6
James V, 98-109
James VI, 137-85, 192
James VII, 247-55
Jedburgh, 27, 66
John, King of Scots, *see* Balliol
John, King of England, 33
John XXII, Pope, letter to, 55
Justice, administration of, 22, 65,
 77, 79, 93, 271-2; *see also*
 Court of Session
Justices of the Peace, 169

Kelso, rental of, 46
Kenneth, son of Alpin, 9
Kintyre, 12, 22
Kirk sessions, 132-3, 146, 147,
 212

Land Tenure, 46-8, 72-3, 95, 100,
 108-9, 163-5; *see also* Feu-
 ferm, Military service and
 Naval service
Leith, convention of, 157-8
Lennox, Esmé Stewart, Duke of,
 150, 153
Lesley, George, charter to, 71
Lochleven, culdees of, 15-6, 23
Lochmaben, castle of, 66
Lollards of Kyle, Articles of, 90
London, Treaty of, 73
Lord of the Isles, 64, 82-3

Macbeth, King of Scots, 15

Magnus Barelegs, King of Norway,
 12
Maintenance, Bond of, 97
Major, John, extracts from, 100
Malcolm II, 12, 14
Malcolm III, 13, 16
Malcolm IV, 24-5, 29-30
Malise, Earl of Strathearn, 26
Man, Isle of, 10, 12, 34-5, 62, 64
Manrent, Bonds of, 97, 161
Margaret, Maid of Norway, 37-43,
 49
Mary of Guise, 116, 119, 120
Mary, Queen of Scots, 109-36,
 278
Mass forbidden, 125
Melrose, abbey of, 25-6
Melville, Andrew, 143
Methven, lordship of, 95
Military service, 24, 54
Mills, 21-2
Ministers of reformed church,
 127, 145, 172, 211
Moreville, Richard de, 25

National Covenant, 194
Naval service, 7-8, 51
Nechtan, King of Picts, 4-5
Nechtansmere, 3-4
Negative Confession, 150, 194
Newbattle, abbey of, 25, 26
Ninian, 1
Norse Law in Orkney and
 Shetland, 177
Northampton, Treaty of, *see*
 Edinburgh
Norway, 'Annual' of, 36, 85-6

Officers of State, appointment of,
 122-3, 207
Orkney, 10-12, 35, 42, 85-7, 177

Parliament, burgesses in, 59; shire
 commissioners in, 80, 158; *see*
 also County Franchise Act